Cuba Theme Issue

The Journal of Decorative and Propaganda Arts is published annually by The Wolfson Foundation of Decorative and Propaganda Arts, Inc. Subscription rates per issue including shipping and handling: US, individuals $24, institutions $30; foreign (payable in US dollars), individuals $29, institutions $35. Back issues available at $30 US, $35 foreign (payable in US dollars).

Send address changes to *The Journal of Decorative and Propaganda Arts*, 2399 N.E. Second Avenue, Miami, Florida 33137 USA or fax 305/573-0409.

For advertising rates and schedules, write to *The Journal of Decorative and Propaganda Arts* or call 305/573-9170.

Printed in Japan by Nissha Printing Co., Ltd.

Cover: The *centellador* on top of the Capitolio, Havana. From *Album fotográfico de los actos celebrados con motivo de la toma de posesión de la presidencia de la República por el General Gerardo Machado y Morales* (Havana: Secretaría de Obras Públicas, 1929). The Mitchell Wolfson Jr. Collection, The Wolfsonian, Miami Beach, Florida, and Genoa, Italy. (See page 185.)

22

The Journal of Decorative and Propaganda Arts   1875–1945

Publisher and Executive Editor
Cathy Leff

Guest Editor
Narciso G. Menocal

Assistant Editor
Susan Campbell

Advertising and Sales
Natascha Otero-Santiago

Design Director
Jacques Auger

Designer
Frank Begrowicz,
Jacques Auger Design
Associates, Inc.

Spanish Supplement

Editor
Narciso G. Menocal

Assistant Editor
José Monleón

Editorial Assistant
Natascha Otero-Santiago

Acknowledgments

By Cathy Leff

The articles that have been written for this special Cuba issue of *The Journal* would be important in any serious discourse regarding Cuban art and architecture. However, because The Wolfson Foundation of Decorative and Propaganda Arts is based in Miami, a city strongly influenced and enriched by Cuban culture, this project took on an even greater dimension. The culmination of more than three years of research and preparation, the Cuba edition happily coincides with *The Journal*'s ten-year anniversary.

Most of us only have a vision of Cuba gleaned from photographs, film, literature, music, and reminiscences of friends. But, for Mitchell Wolfson Jr., founder of *The Journal of Decorative and Propaganda Arts*, the images are real and have worked on his mind and memories, particularly since he knew Cuba, and especially Havana, from early travels. This edition is a result of his desire to investigate and record Cuba's contributions to the history of art and architecture, exploring its international and cross-cultural influences, specifically of the period 1875 to 1945.

The Cuba volume provided a remarkable occasion for academic and cultural interchange among scholars who ordinarily have little opportunity for mutual collaboration. Foremost, we are indebted to our guest editor Narciso Menocal, an eminent scholar, whose intellectual and emotional commitment to this project over the last two years has made this publication possible.

Narciso was born in Havana and began his undergraduate studies there; his post-graduate and doctoral degrees were granted in the United States. Further highlights of his distinguished career are noted in the margin of the articles he contributed to this issue. It was at his wife Marta's urging that he agreed to collaborate on our project in spite of an already busy academic career and two other books in progress. Narciso is a tireless man of remarkable intellect, with a probing mind leaving no question unanswered. Concurrent with his work on this issue, he researched and wrote an exhibition catalogue on the lithography and architecture of the tobacco industry for the Cuban National Heritage and developed a new course of study on Cuban art and architecture for the University of Wisconsin.

The complicated but most worthy effort of producing the Cuba edition was made possible by the generous support of The Rockefeller Foundation, the Samuel H. Kress Foundation, the Graham Foundation for Advanced Studies in the Fine Arts, and The Reed Foundation. We also thank InterAmericas for underwriting distribution of this journal to libraries of Latin American and Caribbean studies.

It would be impossible to acknowledge the generosity of the many people we met in the course of preparing this issue, all of whom in some way helped shape our work. We do however wish to mention those colleagues and friends whose assistance, expertise, and wise counsel we frequently called upon.

In Charlottesville, Virginia, we express gratitude to Richard Guy Wilson.

In Genoa, Italy, our sincere thanks to Ina and Nicola Costa.

In Havana, we are grateful for the support provided by the staff of the United States Interests Section, particularly Gene Bigler, former public affairs officer, USIS; Merrie Blocker, public affairs officer, USIS; Eduardo Moras, cultural assistant, USIS; Margaret Moses, assistant public affairs officer, USIS; and Richard Weston, former budget and fiscal officer, who magnanimously volunteered to photograph a large number of buildings to illustrate our articles.

We also would like to recognize Alejandro Alonso, Llilian Llanes, Carmen Peláez, and in particular, Eduardo Luis Rodríguez, who acted as our liaison.

In Miami, we extend our appreciation to Raúl Rodríguez, whose commitment and interest in promoting the study of Cuban architecture can be seen in the many photographs he provided for this issue. Raúl has been enthusiastic about this project since we first sought his advice and has been helpful in innumerable ways.

Others in Miami to whom we owe profound thanks are: José Ayala, Conchita and Lodovico Blanc, Cathy Booth, Margarita Cano, Magdalena Casero, Graciella Cruz-Taura, the Cuban National Heritage, Andrés Duany, Beth Dunlop, James Findlay, Josefina Hernández, Patricia Lee, Peggy Loar, María Luisa Lobo, Finlay Matheson, Penelope McPhee, Salvatore Mottola, Marta Peláez, Nicolás Quintana, César Trasobares, Lesbia Varona, Susan Vodicka, and Elizabeth Plater-Zyberk.

In New York City, our appreciation goes to Holly Block, Michele Oka Doner, Angela Giral, Manuel Gonzalez, Jane Gregory Rubin, and Raul Suarez.

We salute Alberto Bustamante in Orlando, Florida, founder of the Cuban National Heritage, for sharing with us his knowledge of and enthusiasm for Cuban history and culture.

In Princeton, New Jersey, Pamela Johnson, *The Journal*'s founding editor, was always available to guide and assist us. It is because of her creative leadership that *The Journal* has gained its worldwide following and has become the substantial and often groundbreaking scholarly publication it is today.

In Washington, D.C., Miguel Bretos, Emilio Cueto, Carlos Gles, and Wayne Smith were valuable advisers.

In Mexico City, we welcomed the friendship and help of Félix Beltrán.

Shima and Tetsuo Fukaya of Tokyo traveled to Havana and took photographs for our articles, for which we are most appreciative.

Our commendations to José Alonso, John Beusterien, Carmen Pereira-Muro, Ana Pineda Jimeno, Renato Perez, and Edward Shaw for their fine translations, and most especially to José Monleón for his editorial assistance with the Spanish supplement.

Without the enthusiasm, understanding, and beyond-the-call-of-duty commitment to this project of my colleagues at *The Journal*, Susan Campbell and Natascha Otero-Santiago, this undertaking would not have been possible. The result of their efforts is evidenced in the pages of this publication.

As we celebrate our tenth year, we acknowledge the brillaint contribution of Jacques Auger Design Associates, Inc., which since the beginning, has been responsible for creating *The Journal*'s award-winning aesthetic.

Finally, it is our sad duty to recall the passing of Giulio Blanc, a friend and colleague, who died while this issue was in preparation. Love of scholarship never reached such heroic proportions as with Giulio. Faithful to his exacting standards to the very end, he sent us his article the day before he passed away. His many contributions shall always remain a testimony to his devotion to Cuban culture as much as to his exceptional qualities as an art historian. □

On Cuban Culture and the Contents of this Issue

By Narciso G. Menocal

The period *The Journal* traditionally studies —from 1875 to 1945—was exceptionally rich for the arts and architecture of Cuba. Two events were central to that growth: the widening of entrepreneurial circles in the nineteenth century and the ensuing strengthening of the middle class. One early economic reason for such a relationship of art, commerce, and social change emerged in the 1850s when the former colonial plantational organization became a modern industrialized system demanding quick decisions concerning production, mechanization, trade, and financing. A result of that transformation was that by the late 1860s the patriciate —as the old colonial aristocracy was known — had lost much of its power; most of its members chose not to pay heed to new conditions in a sugar industry that was fast turning to modern corporate financial structures. The ravages of the Ten Years' War (1868–1878) and the fall of the American market in 1873 brought to near bottom the downward turn the patriciate had begun taking some thirty years earlier.

The middle class grew significantly while those changes were taking place. By the 1850s the United States was Cuba's major import and export market; lured by excellent business opportunities, Spanish immigrants came in waves through the mid-1920s, independence from Spain on 1 January 1899 notwithstanding. As a result of the new economic and demographic conditions most of the large twentieth-century fortunes were made by new people, both immigrants and Cuban-born, generally during the first quarter of the century. This new entrepreneurial class developed a brilliant social life and absorbed into its ranks what was left of the old patriciate, mostly through marriage. These were also the peak years of American influence on the island. Under the aegis of American and Cuban corporations, the sugar industry created unparalleled wealth, the country was teeming with business opportunities, and notions of "American comfort" became commonplaces of everyday life.

The constant flow of exchanges, opportunities, and ideas generated by a flourishing free-enterprise system was the all-important factor that established the climate for a vibrant cultural life. The haute bourgeoisie was not an aristocracy living off the land, but a class of merchants, businessmen, and industrialists who found it to their advantage to strengthen a middle class that provided them with the engineers, accountants, lawyers, administrators, architects, doctors, technicians, and clerks upon whom financial success ultimately hinged. These professional and white-collar workers also required the services of similar people, and they, in turn, those of others. And thus the economic cycle came full turn, fostering the right conditions for a cultural development that naturally depended on intellectuals and artists.

Cultural patronage also changed in time. During the first half of the nineteenth century patricians with a cultural bent had surrounded themselves with poets, novelists, essayists, and painters. By the twentieth century, writers, intellectuals, artists, and architects were mostly of middle- and working-class origins and depended professionally on the needs of an industrialized society and the opportunities it offered. Together, these men and women created the extraordinarily rich production we have recorded, one in which tall commercial structures, imposing public buildings, palatial residences, and grand boulevards became the flip side of an image that also featured Afro-Cuban themes.

These and other aspects of the arts and architecture of Cuba are the subject matter of the thirteen articles that follow. Some readers may wish to approach them separately and others may prefer to become acquainted with them in sequence. The latter will profit from the realization that the material may be grouped into four broad categories, together telling an overarching story.

The first three articles comprise the first group; they cover mostly the last quarter of the nineteenth century and the first decade of the twentieth. The opening collaboration, by Carlos Venegas, studies the significance of the architectural and urban expansion of Havana at the time. Those were years in which, although still very much a Spanish colony politically and militarily, Cuba, and most especially Havana, had already established a flourishing economy of its own. New building types appeared, styles proliferated, often in novel combinations, and Havana obtained its characteristic *fin-de-siècle* flair, one that by extension it passed down to other cities as well. Lohania Aruca, through her article on the Cristóbal Colón Cemetery, creates a sharp image of the architectural development of one of the most important collections of funerary monuments in the Americas. My note on Hallet should be seen as an adjunct to Aruca's article, rounding out the information, as it were.

The next five articles constitute the second section. They cover the years from approximately 1899 to 1930. The American occupation of Cuba from 1 January 1899 to 20 May 1902 — an aftermath to the 1898 Spanish-American War — becomes the focus of Felipe Préstamo's and Miguel Bretos's contributions. The rich links in Cuban-American trade and commerce that existed since the mid-nineteenth century increased exponentially during those years, and new American and Cuban corporations developed the sugar industry to levels that would have been short of incredible a few years earlier. Préstamo explains how the United Fruit Company established an urban design of high efficiency for its sugar mills, as well as an architectural style proper to its needs. Bretos tells another story. He shows how the decay — and even horror — caused by the War of Independence (1895–1898) was recorded photographically by the American occupation authorities and, for obvious political reasons, contrasted against measures that had almost immediately been taken to improve the overall situation.

María Luisa Lobo and Zoila Lapique's article shows that in a few short years, when *Social* published its first issue in 1916, Cuba had grown to the point that its economy was capable of sustaining a brilliant, cosmopolitan society. Moreover, Lobo and Lapique place in evidence the importance of the graphic arts of the period by focusing on the extraordinary talents of Conrado W. Massaguer, editor of the magazine, and his collaborators.

The next article, by José Gelabert-Navia, picks up on the importance of American influence by looking at the work of American architects in Havana roughly between 1900 and 1930. Gelabert's contribution would allow a reader to conclude that a fully defined sense of style had evolved in Cuba by that time, a fact other sources also make clear, the monthly architectural section of *Social* among them. Préstamo also makes this point in connection with the "Americanness" of the architecture of the United Fruit Company sugar mills.

Jean-François Lejeune's article closes the second section. It begins with a sweeping panorama of the architectural growth of Havana during the first quarter of the century. Against that background Lejeune unfolds his vision of the vast architectural and urban program conducted by the administration of President Machado (1925–1933) and directed by Jean Claude Nicolas Forestier, a measure that brought Havana up to the ranks of the great cities of the world.

The third section deals with painting. In my article I argue that from approximately 1865 to 1945 nationalism was a major concern of Cuban art, that it developed in three stages, and that the nationalist themes painters explored resonated first in literature. Juan Antonio Molina has written what amounts to an acutely perceptive poem in prose about his first visit to the house of Amelia Peláez, arguibly the most Cuban of painters, as Helen Kohen calls her in the introduction she wrote to Molina's piece. Through his sensitivity, Molina invites the reader to experience the importance of Peláez's house, a cultural monument that explains much of her art and illustrates as well a way of life that has vanished into history. Finally, the late Giulio Blanc gives us insights into the 95-year-old artist Enrique Riverón, one of the last remaining members of the early *vanguardia*.

The fourth and last section covers the 1930s and 1940s. Eduardo Luis Rodríguez provides a very thorough account of the development of Art Deco architecture in Havana, ending with examples of buildings from the 1950s and 1960s. Paula Harper's contribution, on the other hand, covers Cuban influences in the graphic arts and architecture of Florida from the 1870s to mid-1940s.

Our issue, then, shows the culture of Cuba, a new nation that had just come into its own and was searching for its characteristic imagery but paradoxically tracing most of its forms, rhythms, and textures to a distant colonial past. Its preeminent quality was therefore given by a rich dynamic of the old turning into the new and also, as well, of Europe and Africa—or better still, the ideas that Cubans had of them—coexisting side by side. While ignoring each other in some instances, these two concepts nevertheless often fused themselves into magnificently energetic syntheses, as the art of Lam makes evident. There is also a surprising element of time to be taken into account. The events we have covered took place in an astonishingly short period of time. Looking at a random selection signaling economic and social growth, we realize that only fourteen years elapsed between the misery recorded in Charles Edward Doty's photographs Bretos studied and the cultural explosion that the first issue of *Social* represented, in 1916. Only nine years later Forestier began to transform Havana into the magnificent city that it later became. □

Note

We wish to point out that we have kept local idiosyncracies for giving addresses. Cubans will give the name of the street first, followed by the building's number and the names of the two cross streets. For instance, the well-known White House address of 1600 Pennsylvania Avenue would be rendered as Avenida Pennsylvania 1600 between 15 and 17. To keep a "Cuban flavor," the "th" that would make a number ordinal, as well as the word "Street", should be omitted in translation. In the case of a corner building, the phrase "corner to" is included in the address with the name of the cross street. Thus, the address of Tiffany's in New York would not be given as 727 Fifth Avenue but as Quinta Avenida 727 corner to 57 (never 57th). The name of a suburb, such as Vedado, Miramar, or Marianao, is added at the end, if appropriate. Concerning the two latter, for historical puposes, the convention that Miramar is part of Marianao has been retained. As of the late 1970s, Miramar was made part of the Playa municipality.

Fig. 1. Zulueta Street, seen from Neptuno Street at the turn of the century.

Havana between Two Centuries

By Carlos Venegas Fornias

Translated by Narciso G. Menocal and Edward Shaw

Carlos Venegas Fornias is an architectural historian, restorer, and conservationist at the CENCREM (Centro de Restauración, Conservación y Museología), Havana. He is the author of *La urbanización de las murallas: dependencia y modernidad* (Havana: Editorial Letras Cubanas, 1990) and of many articles on the architecture of Havana.

At the end of the nineteenth century Havana was the last bastion of the Spanish Empire in America. For some the city's name still evoked an exotic and dazzling image of riches and pleasure, a setting of formidable fortresses that guarded the palaces of a colonial aristocracy who, made wealthy by supplying the world with sugar, required the services of scores of black servants and enjoyed every European luxury (fig. 1). But this tropical fantasy was no more than a beautiful stereotype on the verge of being substituted by the realities of a city struggling to adapt to modernization, for Havana had become an important urban conglomerate. In no other period in its history had it developed such a sharp appetite for models of universal urban culture. But in spite of such impulses, Havana, nevertheless, managed to maintain its own urban identity, its original personality.

Cuba's transition from a dependent colonial regime to a republican one brought a period of social change that ended in 1902 after the nation had absorbed the abolition of slavery (1886), a second war of independence (1895–1898), and almost four years of occupation by the United States (1899–1902). In spite of these unsettling events, life in the island's capital remained relatively calm, with no violent internal upheavals nor any degree of physical destruction.

The city grew at a steady pace. In 1887 the population was approximately 250,000. Two decades later it had grown to 300,000, but its composition had changed. Recently arrived white Spanish immigrants constituted a quarter of the total population, matching the number of blacks and *mestizos*. Internal migration from the country and a small colony of Chinese complete the picture. Groups of diverse origins coexisted in a spirit of tolerance and cordiality.

Culture began to reach broader spectrums of the population by 1880, touching even the poorest. With the opening of new institutions and the granting of greater liberties regarding the right of association, larger numbers of people participated in civil activities. Concurrently, the weakening of the power of the former slave-holding aristocracy facilitated social mobility and integration. Associations dedicated to charitable activities and recreational pastimes proliferated. The first sporting clubs appeared, as did popular illustrated publications; theatrical and musical performances catered to a broader public. Stimulated by the new republican political structure, urban life developed with a more dynamic rhythm than heretofore.

The artisan working class found new forms of organization, both in terms of work methods and the training of apprentices. Architecture improved with the increase in the number of qualified builders, and the Escuela Profesional de Maestros de Obras, Agrimensores y Aparejadores, the professional school that

Fig. 2. Eugenio Rayneri, Vapor food market as reconstructed in 1874–1879.

trained construction foremen, revised its programs. Modifications incorporated in the curriculum in 1902 led to a course in architecture, opening the possibilities for natives of Havana to attain a technical education that included access to a formal academic repertory. Newly graduated architects and civil engineers educated abroad (the former mostly in Spain and the latter in the United States), together with an immigration of excellent construction foremen from Spain, also had a decisive influence on the architectural development of the city; they made many styles popular at the turn of the century.[1]

The growth of Havana had been basically determined by strategic needs since the sixteenth century because of the activities of the military engineers. Participation of the military in architecture never disappeared during the Spanish domination or the brief intervention by the United States, but it gradually became replaced by graduates from civilian schools. Urban renewal within the old fortified city found its first significant opportunity with the demolition

1. On the transition from colonial to republican architecture, see Ramón Meza, "Las Casas Habaneras," *La Habana Literaria,* no. 8 (December 1891): 176. This essay was the first study on the architecture of Havana and also witnesses the renovation that had already begun there. Other publications are: Leonardo Morales "La arquitectura en Cuba de 1898 a 1929," *El Arquitecto* (May 1928); Pedro Martínez Inclán, *La Habana actual: estudio de la capital de Cuba desde el punto de vista de la arquitectura de ciudades* (Havana: Imprenta de P. Fernández y Cía., 1925); and Joaquín E. Weiss, *Medio siglo de arquitectura cubana* (Havana: Imprenta Universitaria, 1950); Emilia Cobos Mancebo, "Arquitectura cubana del siglo XX," *Estudios Americanos* 28 (January 1954); and José María Bens Arrarte, "La evolución de La Habana desde mediados del siglo XIX hasta las primeras décadas del siglo XX," *Arquitectura-Cuba,* no. 327–329 (October–December 1960). For more recent studies, see Vivien Acosta, "De Europa a Cuba: Art Nouveau," *Universidad de La Habana* 193 (January–March 1969): 45; Roberto Segre's "Continuidad y renovación en la arquitectura Cubana del siglo XX" from *Lectura crítica del entorno cubano* (Havana, 1990); and Enma Álvarez-Tabío, *Vida, mansión y muerte de la burguesía cubana* (Havana: Editorial Letras Cubanas: 1989); Carlos Venegas Fornias, *La urbanización de las murallas: dependencia y modernidad* (Havana: Editorial Letras Cubanas, 1990); and Llilian Llanes, *1898–1921: La transformación de La Habana a través de su arquitectura* (Havana: Editorial Letras Cubanas, 1993).

Fig. 3. Combination permanent and transient housing-warehouse building, 1880. (Address: Prado corner to Dragones, Havana.)

of the city walls in 1863 and the development of the coastal area located to the west. These areas, formally under strict military control, suddenly became a resource for urban expansion.

The thrust of the new was not aimed at wiping out all traces of past urban development but rather at assimilating it and conserving its essence for the future. The area freed by the tearing down of the city walls was prime real estate surrounded by a tightly woven network of densely built city blocks. From there the city was crisscrossed by a system of avenues and wide streets lined with galleries or arcades. Creating a new city plan within a limited area where already every imaginable kind of activity was contained — theaters, markets (fig. 2), homes, recreational facilities, and hotels — was carried out in harmony with existing patterns. Yet the plan had a systematic monumental uniformity previously unknown to Havana. Buildings were beveled at the corners of intersections, metal structures were used where required, pedestrians were provided with covered passageways, and a homogeneous whole that enhanced the beauty of the urban landscape was achieved while doing no violence to the characteristics of compact city blocks (fig. 3). A similar style extended to the nearby Paseo del Prado and to a lesser degree spilled out as well to the recently opened Avenida del Golfo (1902), known as the Malecón — a long thoroughfare running along the coast with a magnificent perspective of the sea.

Outside the city limits, the development of El Vedado, the name given to the coastal area where building formerly had been forbidden to fight attacks in case of foreign landings, became a model for the extension of the city. Contrasting against the tendency for tall buildings erected in compact blocks that predominated in the city, houses in El Vedado were systematically surrounded by private gardens as well as by green public spaces laid out along avenues. This

Fig. 5. Joaquín Ruiz,

engineer, Havana

waterworks, entrance, 1893.

approach emphasized the freestanding residence as a building type, allowing for modern urban hygiene for perhaps the first time in Spanish America (fig. 4). While the freestanding single-family house surrounded by a garden had its origins in the Anglo-Saxon world, suburban summer houses surrounded by gardens appeared quite early in areas beyond the Havana city limits. Such a tradition began in Cuba with the grand houses and gardens of coffee and sugar plantations, where landowners sought to reproduce a neat and orderly natural landscape inspired by Versailles and redefined by French colonial architecture in the plantations of the Antilles.

Architecture in Havana at the turn of the century was based, therefore, on two new urban models of the industrialized world: the multistory urban building and the suburban residence set on its own plot in an uncontaminated landscape. Thus, the transformation of the city was achieved by adapting solutions developed in Europe and the United States to local traditions but never by reproducing them exactly.

The development of the city was not based on a specific regulatory plan. Growth was subject to the impulses of private initiative albeit formalized by the Ordenanzas de Construcción (Ordinances of Construction), of 1861. Many problems had to be confronted. One was that the area of the city was considered to be too large because most of the buildings were single-story. Expansion had to be accompanied by a gradual improvement of the infrastructure and other technical networks (fig. 5). Concurrently, the urban railroad extended lines to new neighborhoods and a slow but foresighted construction of an aqueduct designed for a population of 450,000 was undertaken. At the beginning of the twentieth century, tram service, expansion of the electric and telephone systems, paving of streets, and the modernization of the sewage system contributed to improve the city.

Architecture became an important manifestation of radical transformation as well, but changes in taste gradually took place during the last two decades of the nineteenth century. Important among the new characteristics was the fact that houses lost in spaciousness and solidity what they gained in refinement and lightness (fig. 6). Also an increased use of brick and cement and the

Fig. 7. *Mamparas* (half-doors) in a house in El Vedado, 1896. Photograph by Richard Weston, 1995. (Address: 11 № 761 between Paseo and 2, Vedado.)

Fig. 6. Main door of a house in El Vedado, 1886. Photograph by Richard Weston, 1995.

substitution of cast iron for wood in columns gave buildings a new look. Natural lighting improved as thick iron grillework gave way to thinner iron rails used in lace-like designs, stained-glass windows added a new chromatism, and plaster ceilings became decorated with reliefs and moldings (fig. 7). Both cast iron and glass were produced locally as a result of a growing industrialization, but took on a handmade, highly creative character in buildings, with little reference to a mass-produced look. Instead of having interior walls separating reception rooms from each other, one or more archways determined a new fluidity of space

Fig. 9. Francisco López García, former Club Americano, ca. 1887–1902. Example of a building designed by a master builder graduated from the Escuela Profesional de La Habana. (Address: Prado 309 corner to Virtudes, Havana.)

Fig. 8. Drawing room in a residence at the turn of the century.

and provided unusual decorative effects. Also, lighter Vienna bentwood furniture sets replaced the earlier Louis XVI and Victorian Queen Anne styles. Curtains, rugs, and wallpaper appeared and were adapted to the local climate (fig. 8).

On exteriors classical pilasters, cornices, and moldings were favored along with Gothic and Baroque decorations, all spread uniformly across facades (fig. 9). Arcades required by the building code on major avenues were designed with more refined solutions than before. Formerly, arcades were at times too tall to accommodate traditional mezzanines above the ground floor; elimination of the mezzanine allowed for better proportioned designs that came close to ancient Roman elegance in the best examples.

Builders also faced new problems of distribution of spaces and the furnishing of houses with modern services and adequate accesses. Modern installations for running water and sanitary equipment made the bathroom a priority in turn-of-the-century planning. No longer tucked in a corner at the back of the building, the "connecting" bathroom, a symbol of republican comfort, became an integral part of the home, finding a new location between two bedrooms. The traditional entryway and its old Spanish door, wide and thick, came to be seen as inefficient as middle-class housing became multistoried. Vestibules were no longer expressions of seignorial ancestry and were made to adapt to the times, allowing for a more utilitarian function of providing access to both ground and upper floors. These new conditions led to the appearance of the shared entrance hall, an original solution widely accepted in the early decades of the twentieth century. Main doorways were designed with divided, decorated panels, providing a single door for each floor, each leading into a different entryway separated from each other with a thin partition wall (fig. 10). Each floor, therefore, had direct access to the street. Another solution consisted of a small, shared vestibule, with handsome wrought-iron grillework isolating the stairway from the ground floor. When the ground floor was taken up by a business, the second-floor living quarters seemed suspended above cast-iron columns on the first floor, and rolling metallic curtains shut tight the wide bays every night.

Fig. 10. Example of a *puerta compartida* (two-family door), ca. 1900–1910. Photograph by Richard Weston, 1995. (Address: Virtudes 165, Havana.)

The development of subdivisions brought about radical transformations in the plans of suburban houses. Interior courtyards were eliminated in El Vedado, and in their place a central hall or passageway offered access to the different rooms and also served as a dining room on occasions (figs. 11 and 12). The idea of the central hall was imported from England and probably reached Cuba through the United States. This alteration of such a vital component of the architecture of Havana as the courtyard took place only because new houses were built freestanding on lots. Lighting and ventilation suddenly depended on windows in exterior walls instead of courtyards.

Fig. 12. *Lucernario* (monitor window) in the central hallway of the Domingo Méndez Capote residence, ca. 1900–1905. Photograph by Richard Weston, 1995.

Fig. 11. Central hallway of the Domingo Méndez Capote residence, ca. 1900–1905. Photograph by Richard Weston, 1995. (Address: 15 corner to B, Vedado.)

Fig. 13. View of Obispo Street

at the beginning of the century.

From a postcard.

The industrial architecture of Havana presented singular characteristics. It was mostly identified by tobacco manufacturing—Havana was home of *habanos* (cigars) of worldwide fame such as Henry Clay or Romeo y Julieta. The industry was highly concentrated, hiring thousands of immigrant workers and an ever growing number of natives. Cigar making is basically a manual activity, not one dependent on machinery. It is also a clean industry, producing no waste, obnoxious odors, noise, or smoke. Cigar factories were therefore allowed in the center of the city, next to theaters, recreational facilities, and residences. Large-scale tobacco manufacturing dates from the 1870s and 1880s. These new factories were housed in large buildings following the general lines of traditional residential types, yet adapted to factory conditions, with large open spaces where cast-iron columns were the predominant structural elements. The buildings were perfectly integrated into the urban landscape and were in no way formally separated from it. Facades were treated in the same academic style as in any other building of similar importance. This refinement, one not common to industrial architecture elsewhere, was also applied to offices and reception rooms. Several of the larger factories occupied three of the most important former palaces in the city.

Commerce was mostly dominated by Spaniards, who owned a majority of the cigar factories and adapted new architectural forms to traditional schemes. The best shops were located on narrow streets, such as Obispo (fig. 13) and O'Reilly. Shop fronts were covered with awnings, a custom inherited from the Near East and frequently found in parts of Spain, but in Havana, underneath the awnings, businesses had updated their appearance with modern shop windows supported on cast-iron pillars. The nineteenth-century European idea of a bazaar within a covered passageway was introduced with the design of the Hotel Pasaje, built in 1876 (fig. 14). Nearly twenty years later an ambitious attempt was made in a more complex project of two interior streets crossing within a building that took up an entire city block. The Manzana de Gómez took two decades to complete, finally including two theaters supported on a metallic structure on the second floor—the Politeama Grande and the Politeama Chico (fig. 15). The hotel industry also grew as increasing numbers of American tourists visited Havana in the winter. New hotels, such as the Inglaterra and the Pasaje, installed the city's first elevators and refurbished their interiors to satisfy their new clientele.

With the growth of the city came demand for low-cost housing. The *ciudadela*, or *solar* (tenement), as it was called in Havana, was a prevailing model dating from the eighteenth century and similar to rental-property types that developed in other cities in Latin America under different names. This was a multi-family residential building with one main entrance and rooms giving onto a central courtyard or a main hallway, with common areas for cooking, bathing, and washing clothes. These structures offered transitory housing to immigrants and their families, providing them with a place to live until they were able to find their own single-family house. Yet in 1902 there were more than two thousand tenements of this kind, housing over a third of the city's total population in conditions that at times were more than precarious and that created serious social problems. The Havana *solar* was the pillar of a culture centered on the *barrio* (neighborhood). Popular in the sense that everyone participated in a communal life, the *barrios* developed identities and created the stereotypes of Havana's urban culture, such as the *gallego* (a Spanish immigrant), the *mulata*, and the *negrito*, all of whom were used as characters in Havana's burlesque and comical theaters.

The rise of the tenements was not a result of a programmed urban policy. Their growth responded to private speculation, which, although it did not provide a solution to the housing problem, it did enrich the local tradition. In many of the tenements, the courtyard eventually turned into a public passageway, or *pasaje*, and the large rooms were traded for what was to become a basic unit for urban living, a dwelling composed of two rooms, a kitchen, and a small courtyard — a model that gradually alleviated the effects of over-population.

Spanish immigration brought with it the tradition of regional mutual benefit societies and centers. These organizations participated in Havana's architectural renewal with club buildings in the city's center and hospitals on the outskirts. The plans of the latter were based on independent pavilions, a trend that appeared in 1886 with the remodeling of Havana's municipal hospital using American and English ideas. Buildings organized around large open spaces, like the clinics, the cemetery, and the water reservoirs, made use of impressive entrances highlighted by a triumphal arch that stood in place of the missing facade. Archways were also used for provisional or ephemeral settings, as those erected for civic ceremonies of the young Republic (fig. 16).

By the early decades of the twentieth century all of these architectural trends were assimilated within the exuberant development of Eclecticism and Historicism. An ongoing process of transformation had begun during the colonial period and continued without interruption through the first republican administrations, leaving its imprint on Cuban architecture. That process gained speed at the beginning of the century due to an unprecedented building boom. Also, new technical resources and novel forms of expression insured that this growth would continue on.

The advent of the Republic in 1902 was an incentive for investment, both local and foreign, and businesses in the city multiplied, stimulated by the economic climate. The number of banks and trading companies also increased tremendously. Export-import companies and financial firms spread their networks all over the country, as did railways and construction companies. Havana proudly

Fig. 15. Manzana de Gómez,

original design of 1895.

(Address: City block bound by

Zulueta, Neptuno, San Rafael,

and Monserrate, Havana.)

Fig. 16. Triumphal Arch, 1902.

reaffirmed its role as the capital. At the same time, it rejected the old colonial order and its architectural past (fig. 17). In the opinion of most, Havana should have abandoned its look of an old-fashioned Spanish city built according to outdated models of urban planning and become a completely modern metropolis, showing what were considered to be the refinements of good taste and the correct historic styles of the times (fig. 18). The architectural renovation of the nineteenth century had taken place without forfeiting traditional models, but now, at the birth of the Republic, tradition was becoming a distant memory. An ideology of progress led builders to turn their backs on history and look for new directions in the international repertory and to the introduction of new techniques of construction, such as reinforced concrete. Building itself became more organized with the appearance of American contractors and better professionally managed local construction firms. Cement consumption skyrocketed to sixty thousand tons a year. Architects found that these novel materials and building techniques allowed them possibilities for satisfying their clients' increasingly demanding decorative and functional expectations.

The first multistory office building was constructed on a corner in the old city for a British company in 1896. It was immediately referred to as the *casa nueva* (the new building) because it was such an innovation. In just a few years most companies housed their offices in similar buildings. Reinforced concrete allowed for taller structures and open floor plans brought flexibility to the distribution of rooms. The Banco Nacional de Cuba (National Bank of Cuba) and the Lonja del Comercio (Stock Exchange), built in 1907 and 1908, respectively, were the landmarks of this style of construction (fig. 19). The city's largest stores also participated in the modernization of Havana. Spurred by an explosion in consumer buying, store owners needed more space for displaying and storing merchandise, more facilities for customers and employees, larger workshops for production, and more ample office space (fig. 20). One of these, built on the corner of the old streets of Amargura and Teniente Rey, in addition to housing its own operations, leased space to the Chamber of Commerce. This building had a metallic structure and walls of exquisitely worked masonry. The post office, located nearby, occupied a small skyscraper, diagonally across from the old plaza of the colonial market, originally built with private capital.

Government investment in building was hardly perceptible during these boom years. The House of Representatives (1911), by Emilio Heredia, and the Aula Magna at the new site of the University of Havana (1911), by Francisco Ramírez Ovando, the first Cuban architect to graduate from the École des Beaux-Arts in Paris, were the only important official buildings constructed at the time. Commemorative public monuments were also few, all important sculpture being commissioned for the Cristóbal Colón Cemetery. Exceptions were the monuments to the engineer Francisco Albear and José Martí, both made in an academic Italian style by José Vilalta Saavedra, one of the first Cuban sculptors to be awarded a grant to work in Rome. Neither did religious architecture prosper during this period. The Catholic Church already had a wide network of important buildings, dating back to earlier periods. Church building was limited to Protestant churches, which had had no earlier presence in Cuba. In 1905 the Santísima Trinidad Episcopal Cathedral was designed, and in 1907 the Presbyterian Church inaugurated its first building (cf. Gelabert, fig. 1, this issue).

During the early years of the century private enterprise supplied architecture with the patronage it lacked from church and government. Within the confines of Old Havana, financial companies and large department stores built according to new plans, beveling street corners to ease traffic circulation and taking advantage of the large spaces and best perspectives of broad avenues and parks in the ring, while at the same time introducing new structural technologies.

Recreational associations also added buildings of major importance to the city's landscape. The Centro de Dependientes del Comercio (Center for Shop Clerks), the Casino Español (Spanish Casino), and the Centro Gallego (Galician Center) constructed important landmarks never surpassed in size or quality (figs. 21 and 22). These were in fact monuments to the prosperity of the commercial classes, since most members of these associations were merchants. The monumentality of these middle-class clubs, made evident by their grand staircases and regal reception rooms, outshone by far similar facilities of the aristocracy (fig. 23).

In point of fact, the social activity of the upper classes had been considerably reduced since the turn of the century. Changes from a plantation system

left,

Fig. 21. Arturo Amigó, Centro

de Dependientes del Comercio,

1902–1907. Photograph by

Richard Weston, 1995.

Address: Prado 207 corner to

Trocadero, Havana.)

right,

Fig. 22. Luis Dediot, Casino

Español, 1912–1914. Photograph

by Richard Weston, 1995.

Address: Prado 302

corner to Ánimas, Havana.)

Fig. 23. Luis Dediot, Casino Español, staircase, 1912–1914. Photograph by Richard Weston, 1995.

Fig. 24. Hilario del Castillo,

José Miguel Gómez

residence, 1912. Photograph

by Richard Weston, 1995.

(Address: Prado 212 corner

to Trocadero, Havana.)

to one of corporate structures in the sugar industry and the two wars of independence had taken their toll. The founding of the Republic attracted many families of the old aristocracy into government, a measure that improved the standards of social conduct among many politicians. Architecture did not remain at the margin of these objectives (figs. 24 and 25). A cultural ideal inspired by Old-World refinement dominated most drawing rooms. The press applauded social events and helped to create a positive image for changing social patterns. The Abreu family put themselves forward and provided examples of dwellings for the Havana elite with Las Delicias, their suburban estate, and their palace on the Paseo del Prado. One was a late Gothic-style castle and the other featured a Renaissance interior design with eclectic overtones (fig. 26). Several years later a president of the Republic built a similar palace on the Paseo del Prado, the city's most elegant avenue at the time. Its large mansions were reproduced on picture postcards and published in journals as models of a new Cuban architecture.

Eclecticism allowed for even greater experimentation in the suburbs. In 1903 El Vedado had tripled in size in less than three years, and both there and in the higher areas of La Víbora mansions were built. Set in the midst of beautiful gardens, albeit on lots that were not particularly large, these homes took full advantage of an intimate style that featured terraces, porches, and small watch towers with roofs of French tile. With complete stylistic freedom numerous chalets echoed the appearance of American cottages and of models from the *faubourgs* of European cities (figs. 27, 28, and 29).

Concurrently, housing found a different kind of setting in the center of the city. The combination of dwellings and ground-floor businesses in multistory buildings gave way to the apartment house, adapted directly into Spanish as *apartamentos* (fig. 30). The type had a foreign origin, and the notion that a building with an entrance serving several different dwellings expressed a way of life related to poverty and to the tenements of yore had to be overcome. Apartment-house designers had to take such a factor into account when

Fig. 28. Martínez-Piloto residence, ca. 1900–1910. Photograph by Richard Weston, 1995. (Address: O corner to 19, Vedado.)

Fig. 27. Arts and Crafts cottage, ca. 1910. Photograph by Richard Weston, 1995. (Address: Heredia 109 between Estrada Palma and Luis Estévez, La Víbora.)

Fig. 26. Pedro Estévez Abreu residence, ca. 1902–1905. Example of drawing-room furniture purchased in Paris. (Address: Prado corner to Refugio, Havana.)

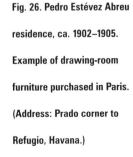

planning staircases for joint use, at times up to three floors, and had to vary the designs of facades. Architectural innovation did not go much further than these considerations. Builders followed standard distributions of space for apartments. However, they adapted the typology to the new structural methods and buildings were designed for a social class able to pay the high rents owners demanded.

Traditionally, houses in Havana had large reception areas. That custom was not only maintained but became even more complex, especially in houses for the upper classes (fig. 31). Bedrooms were placed on different floors from reception rooms; studies, dining rooms, and living rooms were distributed in ways

that gave them more privacy and each one of these rooms was given a special treatment within the stylistic range of Eclecticism. Windows, grilles, and ceiling stuccoes were granted a new importance in the definition and expression of style. Furniture echoed the stylistic plurality of the architecture. The ruling taste was European, predominantly French, at times imported directly by the richest families. English and Art Nouveau furniture also found followers in cosmopolitan Havana. Increase in trade with the United States brought a variety of household objects and popularized inexpensive furniture, such as sets of rattan for galleries and porches; a version of the typical American furniture of light structure came to be called "Republican."

Of all the signs of change in architecture at the beginning of the century, none conveyed a clearer message of modernity than the use of historical styles, which were brought up to a level of sophistication similar to that of most major cities abroad. In a few short years the city underwent what one chronicler defined as a craze for building and decorating with different kinds of stone that produced a new formal language master masons, engineers, architects, and contractors elaborated with great zest. Just about every conceivable version of French, Spanish, and Italian neostyles flourished alongside the monumental classicism of banks, the Neo-Gothic and the Neo-Moorish, and even mixtures of several of these expressions on the same building (figs. 32 and 33).

Such a renaissance cannot be conceived without taking into account the academic training of designers. Long years of study and programs geared to local needs helped to make the building boom a reality. Most architects with professional degrees from the first decade of the twentieth century were former master builders granted professional credentials on merit. As their training was based more on experience than theory, they were unable to follow too closely the rules of composition in academic styles (fig. 34).

Immigration of Spanish master builders, especially from Catalonia, was not a new thing; Catalans had played an important role in the city's growth during the nineteenth century. There is evidence, however, that these artisans were responsible for the rapid acceptance of Art Nouveau in Havana during the

Fig. 30. Art Nouveau apartment building, ca. 1900–1910. Photograph by Richard Weston, 1995.

(Address: Ánimas 320 between Blanco and Águila, Havana.)

Fig. 31. José Crusellas resi-

dence, 1908. Photograph by

Richard Weston, 1995.

Address: Reina 352 corner to

Campanario, Havana.)

Fig. 33. José F. Mata, Hotel
Plaza, Neoclassical vestibule,
1910. Photograph by
Richard Weston, 1995.
(Address: Neptuno corner
to Zulueta, Havana.)

early years of the new century. This style became an important variation among the alternatives of Eclecticism since it conveyed an idea of architectural renovation without being dependent on the prestige of the past (fig. 35). A large number of Art Nouveau buildings were constructed by Cuban master builders who became familiar with the style in such sources as European journals. The participation of master masons from Barcelona seems — in terms of numbers — to have been grossly exaggerated; no documentation confirms popularly perceived notions. Although the Catalonian business community was large, immigration from that region was less than from other areas in Spain in the twentieth century. Only three Catalan master builders appear in consular records from 1900 to 1926.

Fig. 34. Francisco Pujol, master builder, Ramón Larrea residence, ca. 1900. Photograph by Richard Weston, 1995. (Address: Salud 253 between Lealtad and Escobar, Havana.)

Fig. 35. Alberto de Castro, Cayetano Tarruell residence, 1908. Photograph by Richard Weston, 1995. (Address: Cárdenas 101–103 corner to Apodaca, Havana.)

Nevertheless, a number of Spanish businessmen, especially Catalans, had established construction companies or sold building materials and were, in fact, responsible for introducing new techniques and services to the building industry. The so-called workshops for decorative detail in Havana were small and made "artificial stone" prepared from cement and sand. They mass-produced columns, friezes, staircases, cornices, banisters, and corbels — even funerary monuments and water tanks — made in every style imaginable, and these found ready markets. Art Nouveau, known as *modernismo* in Havana as in Catalonia, appeared at this time, sometimes accompanied by eclectic decoration. A number of singular and extremely popular buildings, such as the pavilions in the public gardens of La Tropical beer factory, inspired by the parks of Barcelona, contributed to establish a presence of Art Nouveau in its original peninsular version. It has been thought that a Modernism of clearly Catalan origin was accepted in Havana so recently after independence from Spain because Cubans felt a rapport with the separatist spirit of that region. In any case it was just one more style among many and was no more important than others popular at the time, all of which combined with each other and shared their decorative characteristics in local interpretations of Eclecticism (figs. 36 and 37).

The manufacturers of ornamentation were as responsible for the transformation of the city as the large construction companies and industries that produced cast-iron structures. Not only could they furnish individual pieces but even their production reached such levels of sophistication that they were able to supply builders and architects with complete designs for entire facades in the Modernist style or any other popular at the period. At the same time less qualified artisans could make use of these new elements to decorate interiors and exteriors of buildings to suit their clients' wishes, as ornamentation could now be supplied and installed independently of the construction of the building itself.

This freedom of choice in decoration led to a situation where no particular style prevailed. There was no aesthetic codification, just a highly imaginative use of Eclecticism, the results of which mixed or clashed, sometimes in exaggerated ways, providing a wide variety of solutions in the search for an attractive effect to insure the building's impact on the cityscape. A dialectical expression mixing anthropomorphically sculptural figuration derived from

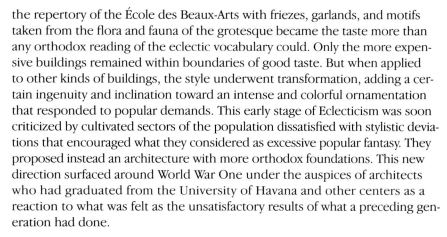

Fig. 36. Mario Rotllant, Dámaso

Gutiérrez residence, 1913.

Photograph by Richard Weston,

1995. (Address: Patrocinio 103

between O'Farrill and Heredia,

La Víbora.)

◄

the repertory of the École des Beaux-Arts with friezes, garlands, and motifs taken from the flora and fauna of the grotesque became the taste more than any orthodox reading of the eclectic vocabulary could. Only the more expensive buildings remained within boundaries of good taste. But when applied to other kinds of buildings, the style underwent transformation, adding a certain ingenuity and inclination toward an intense and colorful ornamentation that responded to popular demands. This early stage of Eclecticism was soon criticized by cultivated sectors of the population dissatisfied with stylistic deviations that encouraged what they considered as excessive popular fantasy. They proposed instead an architecture with more orthodox foundations. This new direction surfaced around World War One under the auspices of architects who had graduated from the University of Havana and other centers as a reaction to what was felt as the unsatisfactory results of what a preceding generation had done.

Between 1875 and 1914, then, the wave of modernization that swept over Cuban architecture appeared first on the exterior of buildings, moved on to interior decoration, and finally spread to spatial transformations and further experiments in ornamentation. Builders and contractors were far more responsible for these changes than professional architects. The spontaneity, pragmatism, and even, at times, naiveté of these men produced a fresh and vibrant expression of paradoxical originality.

As a result, the old city was radically and intensely renovated, almost building by building. Earlier regulations that prohibited heights beyond 2.4 times the width of streets were ignored to allow for construction of four- or five-story buildings that spread their overlapping cornices above narrow streets below. Novelist Alejo Carpentier, who studied the process, turned it into a literary metaphor in his novel *El recurso del método:*

Fig. 37. Mario Rotllant, Dámaso

Gutiérrez residence, door

detail, 1913. Photograph by

Richard Weston, 1995.

> And the old city, with its two-story houses, quickly became an invisible city. Invisible because on passing from horizontal to vertical there were no longer any eyes that knew it and recognized it. Every architect, bent on making his buildings taller than those that came before, thought only about the kind of aesthetic he should employ on its facade, as if there were any possibility for contemplating it in perspective a hundred yards away, when the streets, which only offered passage to a single oncoming coach — or a pack of animals, a mule train, or a small cart — were only six or seven yards wide. Standing with his back to this endless column of traffic, the pedestrian tried in vain to contemplate the exquisiteness of ornamental details lost in clouds of buzzards and vultures. It was known that, way up there, there were garlands, cornucopias, caducei, even a Greek temple perched above the fifth floor with Phidias's horses and the whole works, but it was only known, because these castles, these cupolas, these entablatures reigned — a city on top of a city—in a kingdom forbidden to the eye of the passing viewer.[2]

A system of arcaded avenues spread out beyond the old city. These were large boulevards where columns took the place of trees and where sidewalks were wide, like in Europe (fig. 38). Havana had been transformed into the city of columns. The variety of republican styles allowed for all other styles of supports, and a pedestrian could advance through this forest of columns for several miles. Then, just a few minutes by tram from this downtown network

2. Alejo Carpentier, *El recurso del método* (Barcelona: Bruguera, 1974), 164.

of arcades, a city of gardens emerged, taking advantage of higher grounds with panoramic views opening to the sea. There, villas of different styles were built, even small castles reminiscent of European cities at the time the Renaissance appeared here and there in the midst of Havana's tropical vegetation. In the end a new urban reality had been implanted without anyone consciously realizing it: the architectural personality and individuality of the city seemed to consist in not having any definite style. It would be Carpentier himself, converted into a chronicler of the republican city, who would best define the phenomenon years later in his essay *La ciudad de las columnas* (The City of Columns).

> The superpositioning of styles, the innovation of styles, good and bad, more often bad than good, went into creating this "style without style" in Havana, which, in the long run, through symbiosis, through amalgamation, has imposed a strange baroquism that replaces any style, filling a new page in the history of urban behavior. Because, little by little, from these ill-assorted combinations, from the melanges, from the flinging together of different realities, sprout the lasting features of the overall idiosyncracy that distinguishes Havana from other cities in the continent.[3] □

3. Alejo Carpentier, *La ciudad de las columnas* (Barcelona: Editorial Lumen, 1970), n.p.

Note

The author wishes to thank the Biblioteca Nacional, the Museo de la Cuidad, and the Centro Nacional de Conservación, Restauración y Museología for generously loaning archival photographs to illustrate this article.

Fig. 38. Calzada del Monte at the turn of the century.

Fig. 1. Calixto de Loira and Eugenio Rayneri, Puerta de la Paz, 1871. Photograph by Raúl L. Rodríguez, 1993.

The Cristóbal Colón Cemetery in Havana

By Lohania Aruca

Translated by Narciso G. Menocal and Edward Shaw

Lohania Aruca is an architectural historian who has published extensively and is the foremost expert on the history of the Cristóbal Colón Cemetery in Havana.

The Puerta de la Paz (Gate of Peace), the imposing main entrance of the Cristóbal Colón Cemetery, is its most representative monument (fig. 1).[1] A striking Romanesque-Byzantine triumphal arch rendered in grey stone, the massive structure is divided into three sections corresponding with three entrance arches. A colossal sculpture representing *The Theological Virtues* caps the composition. Carved from a single block of Carrara marble by Cuban sculptor José Vilalta Saavedra (1865–ca.1912) and placed on site in 1902, the group consists of four figures: three matrons symbolizing Faith, Hope, and Charity and a child representing a newly arrived soul in Heaven who still looks westward toward the setting sun, a standard image of death. An inscription at the foot of the sculpture reads, JANUA SUM PACIS (I Am the Doorway to Peace). Extending the iconography, carvings representing inverted torches (symbols of death) appear left and right of the main arch and branches of myrtle tied with a ribbon (symbols of resurrection) are located next to the side arches. Finally, the two main funerary themes of the gospels, *The Crucifixion* and *The Resurrection of Lazarus*, also by Vilalta, are carved in high relief on semicircular tablets of white marble placed above the main arch to the front and rear of the gate, respectively.[2]

1. For references on the Cristóbal Colón Cemetery, see: Luis Bay Sevilla, "El panteón de los veteranos de la independencia," *Arquitectura* 146 (September 1945); Fernando J. Díaz Castañeda, "Escultura tumbal de la vanguardia cubana en la Necrópolis Cristóbal Colón" (undergraduate thesis, Department of Art History, University of Havana, 1992); Domitila García de Coronado, *Cementerio de La Habana: apuntes de su fundación* (Havana: La Propaganda Literaria, 1888); Ignacio González Ibáñez, "Arquitectura funeraria y organización institucional de la emigración: capillas y panteones de sociedades españolas de beneficencia en la Necrópolis Cristóbal Colón de la Ciudad de La Habana," (master's thesis, Department of Art History, University of Havana, 1993); Antonio de Gordon y de Acosta, *Datos históricos acerca de los cementerios de la ciudad de La Habana* (Havana: Imprenta de J. Huguet, 1901); Pedro Martínez Inclán, *La Habana actual: estudio de la capital de Cuba desde el punto de vista de la arquitectura de ciudades* (Havana: Imprenta de P. Fernández y Cía., 1925); Enrique Martínez y Martínez, *Sucinta descripción de los cementerios de la antigüedad, primitivos de La Habana y el de Cristóbal Colón* (Havana: Úcar García Impresores, 1928); Enrique Martínez y Martínez, "El Cementerio Cristóbal Colón," *Arquitectura* 23 (July 1955): 341–347, reproduced in Felipe J. Préstamo, ed., *Cuba: arquitectura y urbanismo* (Miami: Ediciones Universal, 1995), 407–415; Domingo Rosaín Lubián, *Necrópolis de La Habana* (Havana: Imprenta El Trabajo, 1870); Eugenio Sánchez de Fuente y Peláez, *Cuba monumental, estuaria y epigráfica* (Havana: Imprenta Solana y Cía., 1916); Martín Socarrás Matos, *La Necrópolis Cristóbal Colón* (Havana: Editorial Arte y Literatura, 1975); Joaquín E. Weiss, *La arquitectura cubana del siglo XIX* (Havana: Publicaciones de la Junta Nacional de Arqueología y Etnología, 1960).

2. José Vilalta Saavedra was born in Havana in 1865 and died in Italy ca. 1912. "Owing to the generosity of Mr. Miguel Valls, the sculptor from Cienfuegos who paid for his studies in Italy, and in whose marble workshop on the Perla del Sur Vilalta worked for two years, the artist could enter the Reale Accademia delle Belle Arti in Carrara, where he was an outstanding student, according to a certificate issued by the director of the academy, Ferdinando S. Micia." See Eugenio Sánchez de Fuentes, *Cuba monumental, estatuaria y epigráfica,* quoted in Luis de Soto y Sagarra, *La escultura en Cuba,* (Havana: El Fígaro, 1927), 10. Vilalta's works in the Cristóbal Colón Cemetery are the mausoleum to the students executed by the Spanish government in 1871 (1890), the sculptures on the Puerta de la Paz (1900), and the statue of Amelia Goyri Adot (1909).

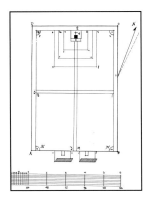

Fig. 2. Allet, Cementerio General de La Habana (Espada Cemetery), 1806. Copy of a plan dated 1840 by Oscar Pérez Prada.

Although the site had been used for burials since 1868, construction of the new Cristóbal Colón Cemetery began on Monday, 30 October 1871, when the first stone was placed marking the Puerta de la Paz, almost twenty years after the first initiatives to find a location for a new cemetery. The rapid growth of the population and the consequent expansion of the city limits required these measures.[3] In addition to the need for a new cemetery, there was also a wish to pay homage to Christopher Columbus, whose remains had been brought from Santo Domingo in 1796 and were considered as the most important historic relic in the country. Inasmuch as Isabella II had ordered that the remains were to stay in Cuba forever, dedicating the new cemetery to the memory of Columbus seemed appropriate. (In spite of Isabella's royal order, Columbus's remains were transferred to the Cathedral of Seville when Cuba won its independence from Spain.)

The inauguration of Havana's first general cemetery, known to everyone as the Espada Cemetery in recognition of the decisive role that Bishop Juan José Díaz de Espada y Landa (1756–1832) had played in its construction, had taken place in 1806. Its design, in a Neoclassical style, was the work of an architect named Allet, who had been responsible for the main facade (to the south), chapel, surrounding walls, and service buildings (fig. 2).[4] The Espada Cemetery was a major accomplishment in public health, a concern of many people at the time; Bishop Espada was a leading figure in progressive circles in Havana.[5]

Owing to a rapid growth in population, the Espada Cemetery was enlarged in 1840 by erecting high walls with niches covered with marble tablets in its western sector. Part of that marble came from quarries discovered in 1834 on the Isle of Pines. In 1847, under the administration of Captain General Leopoldo O'Donnell, "a contract for five years was granted to the Sociedad Anónima de las Canteras O'Donnell" (O'Donnell Quarries, Inc.).[6] Since the increase in the burial capacity of the cemetery was insufficient to meet fully the needs of the community and the resulting environmental contamination was a health hazard, the government decided to close it in 1878.

The competition for the new Cristóbal Colón Cemetery had taken place nine years earlier, in November 1869. The winning design, labeled *Pallida Mors aequo pulsat pede Tabernas Pauperum Regnum que Turres* (Wan Death Arrives Without Distinction at Hovels and at the Palaces of Kings), had been submitted by a Galician architect, Calixto de Loira (1840–1872).[7] The land chosen by the

3. "Including the suburbs, the total population of the capital reached 129,944 in the decade of [18]50." Socarrás, *La Necrópolis Cristóbal Colón*, 14. The dimensions of the Cristóbal Colón Cemetery were established by Dr. Ambrosio González del Valle for a population five times that of the city in 1860, that is to say, for approximately five hundred thousand inhabitants.

4. See Gordon, *Datos históricos*. About Allet, or Hallet, see Narciso G. Menocal, "Étienne-Sulpice Hallet and the Espada Cemetery: A Note" in this publication.

5. Another important figure in this group was Dr. Tomás Romay Chacón (1764–1849), author of a magnificent defense of suburban cemeteries and of the most complete description of the Espada Cemetery I could find. See Tomás Romay, "Discurso sobre las sepulturas fuera de los pueblos" (1806), in Tomás Romay Chacón, *Obras completas*, ed. José López Sánchez (Havana: Academia de Ciencias de Cuba, 1965), I:127–141.

6. This was one of the most lucrative businesses undertaken at that cemetery. See Juan de las Cuevas Toraya, *La industria cubana de materiales de construcción* (Havana: Ministerio de la Industria de Materiales de Construcción, 1993), 115.

7. His full name was Calixto Aureliano de Loira y Cardoso, born in 1840 in El Ferrol (Galicia) and died in 1872 in Havana. The architect graduated from the Academia de San Fernando, Madrid, and became one of the close colleagues of the engineer D. Francisco Albear y Fernández de Lara. The building of the Asilo de Mendigos de San José on Belascoaín Street, now destroyed, is attributed to him. "The most interesting of these enlargements...[was that] of the Real Casa de Beneficencia, probably in 1861 and in the Neoclassic style," according to Weiss, *La arquitectura cubana del siglo XIX*, xxi.

Committee for Cemeteries of the City of Havana consisted of a rectangle covering four *caballerías* (132.74 acres or 53.72 hectares) formed by the purchase or donation of six farms: La Baeza, La Currita, La Noria, La Campana, Las Torres, and La Portuguesa. The Royal Corps of Military Engineers approved the choice of the site as part of the general plan for the development of the city. The cemetery covered an area measuring 810 meters from east to west and 620.20 meters from north to south, for a total area of 504,458.22 square meters, just over 50 hectares. Construction began a month after the inauguration of the site. Building was to start in the four quadrants into which the plot had been divided. Loira oversaw the clearing of the land and the construction of the first quadrant, next to the walls and roads on the northern side of the cemetery.

Concurrently Loira planned and directed the works at the Galería de Tobías, the first funerary structure of any importance built at the cemetery. An underground barrel vault with two accesses covered by cloister vaults, it is ninety meters long and contains 526 niches. Surprisingly, the Galería de Tobías became Loira's tomb, who died suddenly at age thirty-two, on 29 September 1872.

Loira's successor, the architect Eugenio Rayneri y Sorrentino, a graduate, as was his predecessor, of the Academia de San Fernando in Madrid and a former professor of the Escuela Profesional de la Isla de Cuba, modified some details of Loira's original project, as required by the competition jury.[8] Thus, Rayneri added his contribution to the design of the Puerta de la Paz. The contractor with the successful bid for the first, second, and third quadrants of the cemetery was a builder named José Vega Flores.

The first stage of construction was delayed due to conflicts between the bishop and Vega Flores. Also, a hurricane interrupted the work in 1876. (One remarkable event related to this hurricane was the funeral of the Count of Barreto. The wake was held during the hurricane and a flash flood swept the coffin into the Almendares River. A painting by P. Toretti, *El funeral del Conde de Barreto*, shows the moment in which the coffin was recovered at the mouth of the river, near the fort of La Chorrera. On the far bank the undertakers and the funeral carriage await to carry the body to the Colón Cemetery [fig. 3].)

Fig. 3. P. Toretti, *El funeral del Conde de Barreto*, oil on canvas, 37 x 68 cm, ca. 1880. Colón Cemetery collection.

The urgent need to close the Espada Cemetery in 1878 convinced public officials to accelerate construction of the Colón Cemetery, which had been progressing slowly since 1871. The new gate, walls, pavement and landscaping of the principal avenues, and construction of the administration buildings and public ossuary were for the most part finished that year. The fourth quadrant remained unbuilt for several years, as did the main chapel, inaugurated in 1886 when the cemetery was essentially completed.

The plan of the cemetery is laid out on a pattern of five crosses, following a tradition established by Pope St. Gregory (590–604) (fig. 4). Two avenues, one

8. The jury of selection was presided by Rafael Clavijo, head of the military engineers of the Real Cuerpo de Ingenieros. Other members of the jury were Francisco Albear y Fernández de Lara, Antonio Molina, both military engineers; Ricardo Brusqueta, civil engineer; Antonio Pereira, a priest representing the bishopric of Havana, Julián de Zulueta, for the city government of Havana; and Antonio Ecay, of the city's cemetery commission. They awarded the prize of two thousand *escudos* on 19 September 1870 to Calixto de Loira. The jury made several recommendations: eliminate the crypt in the central chapel; move the administration buildings from the north and south doors to the east and the west, enlarge the interior plazas next to these gates, add arcades or porticoes to the northern gates; diminish the height of the north door, and simplify the decoration on the facade. (The columns now embedded in the wall were originally designed as freestanding.) See Gordon, *Datos históricos*, 28; Martínez, "Cementerio Cristóbal Colón," 342, and Plano 1.553L, Archivo Nacional de Cuba, "Estudio geotopográfico para la construcción del Cementerio Cristóbal Colón y de sus principales obras."

Fig. 4. Cristóbal Colón

Cemetery, plan, 1915.

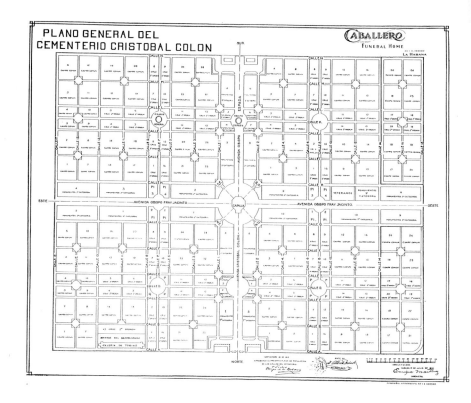

running north to south (front to back) and the other east to west (side to side), determine the main cross. A ninety-meter-wide circular plaza marks the intersection, where the main chapel stands. Each of the avenues is twenty-one meters wide with sidewalks two meters wide. The one starting at the entrance carries the names of Cristóbal Colón up to the chapel and Obispo Espada from the main chapel to the rear gate. The east-west avenue is named after Fray Jacinto, the bishop of Havana who worked hard to establish the new cemetery.

The main cross divides the cemetery into four areas: the northeast, southeast, northwest, and southwest quadrants. Each quadrant, in turn, is also subdivided into four sections by two avenues that cross each other at a small circular plaza. These secondary avenues are seven meters wide with sidewalks fifty centimeters wide. The areas beyond them constitute the common grounds, where streets are five meters wide and sidewalks fifty centimeters wide.[9] Loira, therefore, incorporated the papal tradition of the five crosses into a plan of a standard ancient Roman city, thus turning the cemetery into a veritable "city of the dead."[10]

Besides the main central plaza and the secondary ones in the four quadrants, Loira added circular rotundas at crossings of streets in the common grounds, for a total of twenty-four, thus increasing the formal richness of the plan and providing an orderly regimentation to the landscape.

9. The streets were named in alphabetical order from A to N (north to south) and with uneven numbers, 1 to 17, from Cristóbal Colón and Bishop Espada Avenues to the east and with even numbers, 2 to 18, to the west.

10. The notions of hygiene, beauty, and urbanistic functionality that characterized Calixto de Loira's project were framed in accordance with the ordinances of construction of 1861. The project took into account the most modern ideas of Spanish and French urbanism, represented by Idelfons Cerdà in Barcelona and Baron Haussmann in Paris. See Lohania Aruca, *Estudio de las ordenanzas de construcción para la ciudad de La Habana y pueblos de su término municipal, de 1861* (Havana: Simposio de Cultura de la Ciudad de la Habana, 1989).

Fig. 5. Cristóbal Colón
Avenue, from the Puerta
de la Paz. Photograph by
Raúl L. Rodríguez, 1990.

A hierarchical order was imposed on the division of the land (fig. 5). A zone for monuments of the first order was established along the main avenue of Cristóbal Colón. Zones for monuments of the second and third order were laid out along Obispo Espada and Fray Jacinto Avenues. The former were next to the central chapel and the latter near the east, south, and west gates. The sixteen rectangles comprising the rest of the cemetery were labeled as *campos comunes* (common fields), a term to be interpreted here in the sense of area rather than of an expanse of grass, which they were not. It should also be understood that these divisions were only characterizations of the land. In no way were they meant to determine the grandeur or modesty of any tomb.

The walls surrounding the cemetery were designed — as was the rest of the work — according to the Ordenanzas de Construcción (Ordinances of Construction), of 1861. The design alternates stretches of solid high walls and wrought-iron grilles. Each wall section is decorated with three large crosses in high relief and a black cinerary metal urn standing on the masonry at each end; the rails of the grilles have finials shaped like lance tips.

Following a pattern set for the Puerta de la Paz, the south gate, and the public ossuary, the main chapel was designed in a Romanesque-Byzantine style (figs. 6 and 7). It was built by Francisco Marcótegui, an engineer working for the bishopric, who modified the original plans.[11] The contractor, Ciriaco Rodríguez, was apparently a builder with no professional degree.

The main chapel is an octagonal structure. Its central space is shaped by eight pillars sustaining an octagonal vault 22.5 meters high, reinforced with interior stone ribs and ends with a cross. This space is surrounded by an ambulatory. The chapel is of ample dimensions, it has a total of 263 square meters; 22 are taken by the sacristy and the remaining space of 241 square meters is large enough to accommodate seven hundred people standing.

11. Francisco Marcótegui, engineer of the bishopric of Havana, was the acting director of the works at the cemetery from 1875 to 1914. See Martínez, "El Cementerio de Colón" and *Boletín del Obispado de La Habana* (1886).

Fig. 7. Main chapel, north side. Photograph by Raúl L. Rodríguez, 1990.

Fig. 6. J. Lluch, *Osario, Cementerio de Colón*, oil on canvas, 35 x 33 cm, 1887. Colón Cemetery collection.

Stained-glass windows in the cupula, the drum, and a lower clerestory suffuse the light and tone down the weightiness of the masonry. In addition, on the north wall, a rose window of German stained glass carries an image of the face of Jesus crowned with thorns. To complete the interior space, Miguel Melero (1836–1907), director of Havana's Academia de Pintura y Escultura de San Alejandro, was entrusted with its decoration. Following an example that Giuseppe Perovani (ca. 1765–1835) had set in the chapel of the Espada Cemetery, Melero, who worked in a style highly influenced by El Greco, painted a *Final Judgment* on the retable and *The Ascension of the Lord* on the cupola. The latter is now totally covered by layers of paint. At the front of the building a projecting mass capped with a tower faces the Puerta de la Paz. It houses the vestibule and two smaller spaces, one of which encloses the staircase leading to the choir loft. The vestibule features a barrel vault and leads to the chapel through an archway. The main door, decorated with funerary imagery, is made of fine Cuban woods, as is all of the building's carpentry. Completing the building, a gallery with three arches on each side circles the rest of the octagonal structure except at the rear, where the space is taken up by the sacristy. The building was originally painted grey, but is now a light cream. The cross above the dome, at 28 meters from the ground, is the highest point in the cemetery.

Numerous marble tombs decorated with simple inscriptions or with encrusted lead letters were built during the nineteenth century. Some false vaults providing a base for gravestones were decorated with sculptural forms carved in marble.

Fig. 8. Tomb of Julián Alvarez, 1886. Photograph by Raúl L. Rodríguez, 1990.

Since the mid-nineteenth century, many of these works were created by the owners of the oldest marble workshops in Old Havana. A number of artisans in those workshops were Italian immigrants who imported marble from Carrara; among them appears the names of Serrichi, at 65 O'Reilly Street, and Triscornia, at 104 Habana Street, whose name is found on a large number of tombs, among them the mausoleum of Bishop Espada, whose remains were transferred from the Espada Cemetery to the Colón Cemetery in 1878. However, in the nineteenth century builders of tombs were mostly master masons with no university degree, and therefore did not sign their work.

Some small chapels appear among the many graves surrounded by iron grilles or railings. The chapel of Julián Alvarez, a tobacco magnate, has an inscription referring to its builders: "Ingeniero (engineer) F. de P. Rodríguez and J. P. Sirgado, 1886." This structure is one of the most beautiful examples of an early Havana Eclectic style (fig. 8). The walls were decorated inside with large white porcelain floral wreaths and there is a bust of the deceased on a pedestal, all made of white Italian marble and signed by D. Poernio, Genoa.

Another type of chapel was the hypogeum, usually covered with a vault embellished with statues or with elaborate Neo-Gothic "towers of triumph." An example of this style is the chapel of Francisco Rossel Saurí and family, later acquired by Gaston Azcárate, its second owner. The Modernist poet Julián del Casal was buried there.

left,

Fig. 9. José Vilalta Saavedra, tomb of the eight medical students executed on 27 November 1871, dedicated 1890. Photograph by Raúl L. Rodríguez, 1990.

right,

Fig. 10. Agustín Querol, sculptor, and Julio Martínez Zapata, architect, tomb of the volunteer firemen of Havana who perished in the fire of 17 May 1890, dedicated 1897. From a postcard. Narciso Menocal collection

The first of the two most important mausoleums of the final decade of the nineteenth century is dedicated "To the Eight Innocent Medical Students, Executed By Havana Volunteers on November 27, 1871" (fig. 9), designed by José Vilalta Saavedra and dedicated in March 1890. The second most outstanding monument was erected to honor the memory of the victims of the fire that took place on 17 May 1890. The inscription on this mausoleum reads: "To Havana's Volunteer Firemen." This monument is the work of the Spanish sculptor Agustín Querol y Subirats and the architect Julio Martínez Zapata, also a Spaniard (fig. 10). It was dedicated on 24 July 1897 in a ceremony attended by Captain General Valeriano Weyler.

One senses antagonism between these two works, albeit both are of irregular artistic value. Querol's is the better of the two and is considered one of his finest sculptures. The students' mausoleum, nevertheless, was the first national expression of funerary sculpture in large format created by a Cuban artist.

After the Republic was established in 1902 the economy flourished and stimulated construction, particularly favoring a development of funerary art at the Colón Cemetery. New artistic developments in architecture were taken into account by designers as much as influences from the national and international avant-gardes. The fact that many of the new master builders were graduates of the Escuela de Artes y Oficios de La Habana (School of Arts and Crafts of Havana) undoubtedly also improved the quality of the work. Also to be taken into consideration is the remarkable skills of many construction workers, acquired through generations.

Concrete, known in Cuba since 1870, was used exposed in several of the tombs or on their roofs. The tomb of the Franchi Alfaro family is an example, and in addition it is a very late representative of the Eclecticism of the early twentieth century. The tomb is built on a small artificial hill, which sets it off, and its access is limited to a stairway built in grey stone masonry; there is a small temple reminiscent of the Mausoleum of Halicarnassus on its concrete roof (fig. 11).

Fig. 11. Tomb of the Franchi Alfaro family, ca. 1915. Photograph by Raúl L. Rodríguez, 1990.

Eclectic tendencies may be seen in tombs shaped like Egyptian pyramids, which appear sometimes as small elements of decoration. This is the case of a tomb, with royal palms at two of its angles, dedicated to the architect José F. Mata by the Colegio de Arquitectos (College of Architects) in 1920 (fig. 12). The Neo-Gothic was also used in the twentieth century, as in the mausoleum of the Sociedad de Beneficencia Montañesa, enlarged and remodeled by architect Francisco Salaya in 1953 (fig. 13). This period of the early twentieth century, nevertheless, did not produce works to surpass, or even equal, those of the nineteenth century.

Fig. 12. Tomb of José F. Mata,

1920. Photograph by

Raúl L. Rodríguez, 1990.

Fig. 13. Mausoleum of the

Sociedad de Beneficencia

Montañesa, altered

by Francisco Salaya in

1953. Photograph by

Raúl L. Rodríguez, 1990.

A 1925 opinion of the architect Pedro Martínez Inclán concerning the buildings in the Colón Cemetery is critical:

> Most of the tombs in our cemetery are rectangular in shape, just over a meter high, lined with white Carrara marble, covering the entire plot of land. Toward the center of this hollow structure, two, three, or four plaques in three-inch-thick marble may be seen. They are the normal size for a grave, with bronze decorations at the corners…surrounded by more-or-less artistic wrought-iron or bronze grillework with pillars of marble, balustrades, etc…. When the monument becomes more pretentious toward the rear, in the axis of the large base, a pillar crowned by a sculpture arises.[12]

This almost commercial architectural style allowed for quick construction, providing the cemetery with a large number of tombs.

Toward the end of the 1920s, the use of rock-based materials, offering new textures and a variety of colors, became standard. Blocks of black, brown, grey, beige, or red granite were imported, in addition to green marble from Santa Clara and several tones of pink from the eastern provinces. Since the nineteenth century the Isle of Pines traditionally supplied white, pearl, or striped grey marbles, highly appreciated for their sculptural qualities and their resistance to the outdoors. A touch of color was added to the cemetery's landscape with the use of these materials. It also reinforced a tendency to emphasize the individuality of owners, and gave the artist a greater freedom to interpret funeral themes.

The tomb of Generalissimo Máximo Gómez, one of the heroes of the wars of independence, paid for by public appeal, like those of many other patriots,

---

12. Pedro Martínez Inclán was an architect, civil engineer, and professor at the University of Havana School of Architecture. He founded the chair of Architecture of Cities, and was responsible for stimulating the modernization of city planning in the twentieth century, following Rationalist and Functionalist styles. He was the author of *Carta de La Habana* (Havana Charter) (1949), inspired by the *Carta de Atenas* (Athens Charter) (1941). In this work he makes reference to his work *La Habana actual: estudio de la capital de Cuba desde el punto de vista de la arquitectura de ciudades* (1925). The *Carta de La Habana* is reproduced in Préstamo, *Cuba*, 437–449.

was placed in the zone of Monuments of the First Order. It stands out from many of the monuments that surround it because of its color — chestnut, grey, and different shades of beige — and the solidity and elegance of its simple composition, which follows the model described by Martínez Inclán. The design put to good use the possibilities of color and texture of marble, whether polished, rough, or just dressed. One particular decoration identifies this tomb at first sight: the magnificent bronze medallion in medium relief with the profile of the generalissimo. It is signed and dated Aurelio Melero, 1906, brother of Miguel Melero, previously mentioned. The medallion was also signed by Isidoro Casals, at whose foundry it was cast, in recognition of the importance and quality of the work. Casals cast many of the sculptural works in metal found in the cemetery.

The cemetery has 420 small chapels belonging to families, immigrants' charitable associations, professional associations, and trade unions. Inside these chapels, besides several tombs, there is usually an altar. The different ways in which the altar and the tombs were related to each other within the overall architectural composition allowed for variations that individualized design within the limits of a building type. There were other possibilities as well for making each monument different from the rest. The space where the chapel was located could be at ground level or below it, following the tradition of the crypt or the hypogeum, and might have different types of roofs — flat or vaulted — or could be roofless, open to the sky, as was the case of many built in the 1950s.

Most of the authors of these funerary works are rarely identifiable and remain anonymous even for the twentieth century, except in cases of designs by first-class architects. For instance, the firms of Govantes y Cabarrocas, Eugenio Batista, or Max Borges Jr. usually worked in conjunction with well-known Cuban artists, such as Juan José Sicre, Florencio Gelabert, Rita Longa, and René Portocarrero. They also worked with foreign artists, such as the Italians Rafaello Romanelli, Angelo Vanetti, Giovanni Niccolini, and F. Bossi; the Frenchmen Auguste Maillard and René Lalique; the Spaniards Moisés de la Huerta and Mariano Benlliure; and the Serb Alexander Sambougnack.

The artistic quality of the monuments in the Cristóbal Colón Cemetery is, then, indeed remarkable. For instance, just a few steps from the Puerta de la Paz is the chapel of Andrés Gómez Mena (ca. 1920). An octagonal prism built in smooth, clear beige stone, it stands out in a small garden planted with grass. Three tall square steps serve as a pedestal (fig. 14). The bronze door is decorated with a lion's head cast in low relief to allow for hieratic female figures on the inside of the jambs. The chapel is covered with a cupola that rises in steps harmonizing with those of the base. A frieze at the top carries an inscription with the name of the owner and a phrase in Latin. The ends are protected by stylized angels, floating horizontally, their volumetric presence increasing the elegance of this monument. The work announces the approach of Art Deco, a style that prevailed in the 1930s and 1940s.

On Cristóbal Colón Avenue is one of the most beautiful and monumental chapels. It was built in honor of Catalina Lasa by her widower, Juan Pedro Baró, and designed by René Lalique (1936). The materials are white marble, black granite, and purple crystal. What is most impressive about this chapel is the perfect balance of its two volumes, that of the main facade with the black granite door, in bas-relief, and that of the apse, vaulted and decorated with blocks of Murano crystal in which Lalique carved Catalina Lasa roses (figs. 15, 16, and 17).

Fig. 14. Tomb of Andrés Gómez
Mena, ca. 1920. Photograph
by Raúl L. Rodríguez, 1990.

▲

Fig. 15. René Lalique,
tomb of Catalina Lasa,
front, 1936. Photograph by
Raúl L. Rodríguez, 1990.

▼

Fig. 16. René Lalique, tomb of
Catalina Lasa, detail of door,
1936. Photograph by
Cathy Leff, 1992.

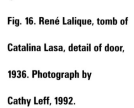

At the end of the opposite sidewalk, the Falla Bonet family built a chapel in the form of a grey granite pyramid, decorated with large sculptures of bronze and white marble. The front door is decorated entirely with a bronze bas-relief depicting two male figures with their backs to the viewers lifting a sarcophagus onto their shoulders and climbing a staircase that continues beyond the shadow of the door's threshold. Open curtains appear at the edges on the sides of the door. They emphasize the perspective of the staircase and frame the central scene. The position of the coffin, moving upward, guides the eyes in the direction of the inscription on the door, FAMILIA FALLA BONET. Above these two lines, over the truncated apex, is a freestanding sculpture, cast in bronze, of the *Ascension of the Lord*, a work by the Spanish sculptor Mariano Benlliure (fig. 18).

Fig. 17. René Lalique, tomb of Catalina Lasa, rear, 1936. Photograph by Raúl L. Rodríguez, 1990.

Fig. 19. Tomb of Frank

Steinhart, ca. 1937. Stained-

glass window representing

St. Theresa of the Infant

Jesus. Photograph by

Richard Weston, 1995.

The chapel of Frank Steinhart, owner of Havana's electric trams, is near the east door of the principal chapel. It is a tall rectangular structure with front and rear covered with stained-glass windows. Furthermore, Cuban sculptor Juan José Sicre created *La Ascensión* (1937) for the upper part of the main facade. The enormous window on the rear is especially noteworthy. It is almost three meters high and represents *Santa Teresa del Niño Jesús* (St. Theresa of the Infant Jesus) (fig. 19).

Across, and to the west, stands another tall and cubical building, one with a Neo-Romanesque air. It is preceded by a spacious plaza with tombs, and it is surrounded by a metal railing. On the front of this monument, facing north, the initials S. A. B. stand for Sociedad Asturiana de Beneficencia (Asturian Charitable Society) (fig. 20). A monumental image of Nuestra Señora de Covadonga, patronness of Asturias, presides over the chapel, protected by a gilt mantle.

Fig. 21. Mausoleum of the

Sociedad de Beneficencia de

Naturales de Galicia, 1936.

Photograph by Raúl L.

Rodríguez, 1990.

Fig. 20. Mausoleum of

the Sociedad Asturiana

de Beneficencia,

ca. 1934. Photograph by

Raúl L. Rodríguez, 1990.

This is one of the most important monuments among the ninety-seven tombs, ossuaries, and chapels belonging to charitable associations of immigrants from different parts of Spain and built in the cemetery from the end of the nineteenth century through the first half of the twentieth. Other mausoleums of this type are those of the Sociedad Vasco-Navarra de Beneficencia (Basque-Navarre Charitable Society), built in 1888 and acquired by the Society in 1898; the Sociedad de Beneficencia Montañesa, referred to previously; the Sociedad de Beneficencia de Naturales de Galicia (Galician Charitable Society) (fig. 21); and the Sociedad de Beneficencia de Naturales de Ortigueira (Charitable Society for Naturals of Ortigueira), in which, on the northeastern angle of its facade, a replica of the tower of the church of Santa Marta de Ortigueira (Galicia) may be seen.

On Fray Jacinto Avenue there are a number of monuments in the Art Deco style. Among them is the mausoleum of the Veterans of the Wars of Independence of Cuba, built in the mid-1940s (fig. 22). It covers an entire block and was built under the direction of the architect Luis Dauval, although the original design was by the architect Enrique Luis Varela. Its most outstanding characteristic is its horizontality, emphasized by large bronze panels in relief that elegantly decorate the altar, the upper part of the monument, and the wide frieze at the head of the stairway that leads to two underground levels of burial niches. Two sculptors worked on these reliefs. Florencio Gelabert did the central mural, *El ara de la patria* (The Altar of the Fatherland), and two lateral ones; Juan José Sicre did the panels narrating the deaths of Carlos Manuel de Céspedes, Ignacio Agramonte, Antonio Maceo, and José Martí. This is an important body of work in the development of Cuban avant-garde sculpture (fig. 23).

The 1950s produced important pieces of funerary architecture that point to an interest of designers to express new ideas through architectural elements.

Among these architects is Eugenio Batista, who did the Raúl de Zárraga chapel, a cube of raw concrete left in its natural state that features interesting effects of lateral natural lighting coming from the rear facade to illuminate the interior in a tenuous way (fig. 24). A mural in enameled stoneware representing the Virgin, by René Portocarrero, is placed to catch the light coming through the door's transparent glass panel.

The mausoleum for the Asociación de Reporters de La Habana is a paraboloid of reinforced concrete enclosed by two facades of green glass (fig. 25). Max Borges Jr. and Enrique Borges designed a sumptuous chapel for Emilio Núñez Gálvez utilizing the most advanced technology of the moment to make the concrete vault, covering it with pieces of stoneware glazed with copper powder, creating the image of a golden mantle, while a symbolic tomb is placed below it, on axis with the center of the overall composition (fig. 26). This is an accomplishment of great aesthetic value, as it shimmers in the sun or moonlight.

Rita Longa sculpted a highly stylized relief in white marble of the *Piedad*, which forms the shape of a heart against a background of black marble, for the Aguilera family tomb (fig. 27). The work stands on a smooth black block that forms the

Fig. 23. Juan José Sicre, *La muerte de Ignacio Agramonte*, bronze high relief, 1944, mausoleum of the Veterans of the Wars of Independence. Photograph by Richard Weston, 1995.

Fig. 24. Eugenio Batista, tomb of Raúl de Zárraga, ca. 1950. Photograph by Richard Weston, 1995.

Fig. 25. Mausoleum of the Asociación de Reporters de La Habana, ca. 1950. Photograph by Raúl L. Rodríguez, 1990.

altar, placed within a roofless chapel that may be seen from the street through the monument's grillework gates. These gates, of a simple design, are attached to walls paneled in black marble.

Architectural typology is central to the study of the Cristóbal Colón Cemetery, one of the most important funerary sites in the Americas because of the wealth of its artistic diversity; in 1987 it was declared a National Monument of the Cuban Republic. In addition it is the final resting place of many generations that shaped the country's history. Its potential value as a historic, artistic, and urban center makes it worthy of being considered as a museum, especially now, since 1996 marks its 125th anniversary. □

Fig. 26. Max Borges Jr. and
Enrique Borges, tomb of
Emilio Núñez Gálvez,
ca. 1950. Photograph by
Raúl L. Rodríguez, 1990.

Fig. 27. Rita Longa, *Piedad*,
Aguilera family tomb, ca. 1950.
Photograph by Cathy Leff, 1992.

Fig. 1. Étienne-Sulpice Hallet, Cementerio General de La Habana (Espada Cemetery), 1806. From Frédéric Miahle, *Vista del Cementerio General de la Ciudad de La Habana*, lithograph, ca. 1839; reproduced in Emilio Cueto, *Miahle's Colonial Cuba* (Miami: The Historical Association of Southern Florida, 1994), 18.

Étienne-Sulpice Hallet and the Espada Cemetery: A Note

By Narciso G. Menocal

Narciso G. Menocal is a professor of architectural history in the Department of Art History, University of Wisconsin-Madison. He has been a recipient of Buell and Guggenheim Fellowships and has published and lectured widely on Louis Sullivan and Frank Lloyd Wright. His most recent publication is *The Tobacco Industry in Cuba and Florida: Its Golden Age in Lithography and Architecture* (Miami: Cuban National Heritage, 1995).

Hallet (or Allet, as the name is often spelled) is an elusive figure to Cuban scholars; not even his first name appears in their publications.[1] Yet he was responsible for introducing Neoclassical architecture in Havana, early in the nineteenth century. The first monument in that style was his Cementerio General de La Habana, generally known as the Cementerio Espada (Espada Cemetery) inasmuch as it had been commissioned by Bishop Juan José Díaz de Espada y Landa (1756–1832; bishop of Havana, 1802–1832) (fig. 1).

Information on Hallet is scanty, especially concerning his Cuban sojourn — insufficient even to round out a biographical sketch. Available facts, however, place him in wider context than heretofore. Étienne-Sulpice Hallet (ca. 1760–1825), born and trained in France, arrived in Richmond, Virginia, in 1788 to teach in an ill-fated Academy of Sciences and Fine Arts promoted by the French painter Alexandre-Marie Quesnay du Beaurepaire (1755–1820), but he soon moved to Philadelphia.[2] Stranded there and eking out a poor living, he saw the competition for a national capitol, called for 15 July 1792, as an opportunity to improve his condition.

His submission would have been standard in the Europe of his day. It was a Neoclassical building with a center block capped by a tall dome and with wings containing the House and the Senate. Thomas Jefferson, who saw the competition as an excellent opportunity for advancing his cause in favor of public buildings in the Roman Classical style, suggested that Hallet should change his design to a "temple" solution. The peristyled exterior of the new design found favor with the commission appointed by Congress to supervise the buildings of the federal capital, then in the making, but they objected to the plan. Nevertheless, since Hallet was the only professionally trained architect in the country, he was retained to make new studies.

1. For information on Hallet in Cuban publications, see mainly Antonio de Gordon, *Datos históricos acerca de los cementerios de la ciudad de La Habana* (Havana: Imprenta de J. Huguet, 1901), 13; Evelio Govantes, "Vicente Escobar, uno de los precursores de la pintura en Cuba," in Emilio Roig de Leuchsenring, ed., *Cuadernos de historia habanera* 13 (Havana: Municipio de La Habana, 1937), 94; and Guy Pérez de Cisneros, *Características de la evolución de la pintura en Cuba* (Havana: Dirección General de Cultura, Ministerio de Educación, 1959), 64.

2. For Hallet in English, see Wells Bennett, "Stephen Hallet and His Designs for the National Capitol, 1791–94," *Journal of the American Institute of Architects* 4 (1916): 290–295, 324–330, 376–383, 411–418; Fiske Kimball and Wells Bennett, "William Thornton and the Design of the United States Capitol," *Art Studies* 1(1923): 76–92; Daniel D. Rieff, "Hallet, Étienne-Sulpice," in Adolf K. Placzek, ed., *Macmillan Encyclopedia of Architects* (New York: The Free Press, 1982), 2:298; and Glenn Brown, *History of the United States Capitol* (1900–1903; New York: DaCapo Press, 1970). For Quesnay du Beaurepaire, see Mantle Fielding, *Dictionary of American Painters, Sculptors and Engravers* (Philadelphia: Printed for the Subscribers, 1926), 292.

In the meantime Dr. William Thornton presented a late entry, which, according to Jefferson, "captivated the eyes and the judgment of all."[3] After a few corrections Thornton's design won General Washington's approval on 31 January 1793. On 11 March the commissioners decided to split the prize between Hallet and Thornton — building the capitol according to Thornton's design and retaining Hallet (who by then had designed five different schemes) as superintendent of construction, with an annual salary of four hundred pounds sterling. A need for correcting inaccuracies in Thornton's drawings allowed Hallet an opportunity to change the design to the point of imposing his own work on it, begin foundations, and lay the cornerstone on 18 September. President Washington realized the extent of the changes in the spring of 1794 and expressed his disapproval. After prolonged friction, the commissioners discharged Hallet on 15 November 1794. He lingered for about a year and a half and left Washington in August 1796. Little is known of the rest of his life other than he was in Havana by 1800, later returned to New York, was there by 1812, and died in New Rochelle in 1825.

Bishop Espada is the other important character in the story.[4] Born on 20 April 1756 in Arroyave, Álava (Spain), he took holy orders after studies at the University of Salamanca. A protegé of Manuel Godoy, prime minister to Charles IV, Espada moved within Spanish Enlightenment circles and reputedly was a friend of Goya. He was appointed to the see of Havana in 1800 and arrived there in 1802.

Since he was highly interested in the arts, once in Havana, Espada more than likely became impatient with what he perceived as a hopelessly unfashionable colonial cathedral, albeit one completed only twenty-five years earlier. As a first measure, he proceeded to decorate the chancel with frescoes, and to that end he availed himself of the talents of a Brescian painter, Giuseppe Perovani (ca. 1765–1835), who, like Hallet, had arrived in Havana via Philadelphia. Perovani's paintings for the cathedral were finished by early 1806, as suggested by an ode published in the *Papel Periódico* of 4 February 1806 (fig. 2).[5] Eight years later Espada continued his reform of the cathedral "to new style" by installing Neoclassical side altars in place of the old Baroque ones. In 1820 he had a new main altar designed, and some time later, at an unspecified date, he had the wooden *mudéjar* ceilings concealed under plaster vaults. Hallet had already left Havana when all this work was done.[6]

Other of Espada's achievements in favor of the arts were, in 1815, to bring the painter Jean-Baptiste Vermay (1784–1833) to Havana and, in 1828, to commission José María de la Torre with the design of the Templete, a monument in

3. Brown, *History of the United States Capitol*, 1:8.

4. For Bishop Espada's biography, see Jacobo de la Pezuela, *Diccionario geográfico, estadístico, histórico de la Isla de Cuba* (Madrid: Imprenta del Establecimiento de Mellado, 1863), 2:300; Francisco Calcagno, *Diccionario biográfico cubano* (New York: Imprenta y Librería de N. Ponce de León, 1878), 261–263; and Esteban Roldán, ed., *Cuba en la mano* (La Habana: Úcar García, 1940), 870–871. For his involvement in politics, see Miguel Figueroa, *Religión y política en la Cuba del siglo XIX: el Obispo Espada visto a la luz de los archivos romanos, 1802–1832* (Miami: Ediciones Universal, 1975).

5. Mentioned in Calcagno, *Diccionario*, 497.

6. Tradition ascribes to Hallet the Neoclassical altars in the cathedral, but their designers and chronology have been established by María Elena Martín and Eduardo Luis Rodríguez, *Guía de arquitectura: La Habana colonial (1519–1898)* (Seville: Junta de Andalucía, 1993), 75–76. The side altars (1814) were the work of P. Abad Villarreal, and the main altar (1820) was designed by A. Solá. The name of the person in charge of building the plaster vaults and their date are unknown. The present masonry vaults were constructed during the restoration undertaken ca. 1950 by the architect Cristóbal Martínez Márquez during the bishopric of Manuel Arteaga y Betancourt.

the shape of a Classical temple that marks the site of the first Mass in the city. Espada was also interested in improving Havana by other means. He gave large sums of money to the Foundlings Hospice and the Hospital for the Insane, desiccated the marshes of the Campo de Marte near the city, revitalized the moribund girls' school of San Francisco de Sales, and caused the reform of the San Carlos Seminary, promoting the first courses ever in Cuba on political economy, physics, and chemistry, all taught by José Antonio Saco (1797–1879), one of the major figures of the Cuban Enlightenment. He also encouraged the teachings of Father Félix Varela (1788–1853), who introduced speculative and pragmatic intellectual methods to the teaching of philosophy in the seminary. Espada died in Havana on 13 August 1832, a death deeply mourned by many.

While Hallet may have designed the Espada Cemetery early on, work was delayed through early 1804. In the summer of 1802, shortly after his arrival on 27 February, the bishop had fallen ill with yellow fever. Moreover, a large number of people raised religious objections to the idea of burying the dead other than in churches, a custom Espada opposed on grounds of public hygiene. It was Espada who, as bishop, underwrote the cost of the project—thirty-nine thousand *pesos*—and who brought it to completion, inaugurating the new cemetery on 2 February 1806.[7]

The Espada Cemetery was located about a mile west of the city, near the shore, next to the lepers' hospital of San Lázaro (for the plan, cf. Aruca, fig. 2, this issue). The site was a rectangle surrounded by a high wall, 150 *varas* north to south (411 feet and 9 inches) by 100 *varas* east to west (274 feet and 9 inches). The main axis ran from the gate, on the south side, to the chapel, on the far north side. The area was divided into four sections by two paths forming a cross. A pyramid stood at each end of the east-west path and an obelisk in imitation jasper marked the location of the underground ossuary at each of the four corners of the cemetery.

The portal and the chapel were the two major monuments. The portal, designed as a triumphal arch ten *varas* wide (27 feet and 2 inches), featured Tuscan pilasters and an almost square gate. Above the entrance a lunette framed a bronze relief with figures representing Time and Eternity; in between them was a vase of perfume to signify that time destroys everything and turns it into smoke. Left and right of the central lunette, rectangular panels enclosed representations of Religion and Medicine, respectively, an iconographical choice that speaks volumes of Bishop Espada's enlightenment, a fact further supported by the inscription on the gate, which dedicated the premises *A la Religión; A la Salud Pública* (To Religion [and] Public Health) and dated the work as of 1805. Beyond, the chapel, looking almost like an Etruscan temple, featured a pedimented facade supported on four Tuscan columns, the whole painted a light yellow with black striations to resemble marble, a standard device used throughout the Baroque and Neoclassical periods, yet heretofore unknown in Havana.[8] Inside, the altar was a simple block of stone supporting a crucifix of ebony and ivory. The paintings for the chapel, by Perovani, were

7. Gordon, *Datos históricos acerca de los cementerios*, 13.

8. The now-demolished Convent of Santa Teresa, on O'Reilly Street, had a Neoclassical temple-like portal supported on a pair of unfluted Greek Doric columns of exaggerated entasis, of the kind made popular by French architects of the late eighteenth century but stylistically completely out of place in Havana. A second similar pair of unfluted Greek Doric columns, this time flanked by pilasters and surmounted by a blind lunette — the whole creating a severely Neoclassical version of the Palladian motif—frame to this day the entrance to the Convent of Santa Clara, on Cuba Street. It is very possible that these two works were designed by Hallet.

finished in 1810. They consisted of a *Final Judgment* on the rear wall, an *Ascension of the Lord* on the ceiling, eight blindfolded matronly figures holding Neoclassical vases of perfume, and representations of Faith, Hope, and Charity above the door.

By 1840 the Espada Cemetery was insufficient for a growing city; there were 151,896 bodies buried in it.[9] In 1844 a project for erecting walls with niches for burial was approved and built in 1845.[10] In 1849 adjacent land was purchased for new walls with niches, and the area of the cemetery was increased from the 15,000 original square *varas* to 43,215 square *varas* (cf. Bretos, fig. 17, this issue). In 1865 an annex for the burial of non-Catholics was created through the purchase of two lots, one 112 *varas* long by 12 *varas* wide and the other 60 *varas* long by 8 *varas* wide.[11] In spite of these additions, the Espada Cemetery was still too small for Havana. It was closed on 3 November 1878 inasmuch as the new Cristóbal Colón Cemetery was already in use; all remains were transferred to the new cemetery in 1901 (cf. Bretos, fig. 18, this issue).[12] A wall on the corner of Vapor and Hospital Streets is all that remains of the old cemetery. □

9. Pezuela, *Diccionario*, 3:152.

10. Gordon, *Datos históricos acerca de los cementerios*, 15.

11. Ibid., 17.

12. Ibid., 17–18.

Fig. 4. Ingenio Manaca, near Trinidad. From a lithograph by Édouard Laplante, 1857. Photograph courtesy Division of Prints and

The Architecture of American Sugar Mills: The United Fruit Company

By Felipe J. Préstamo

Translated by Narciso G. Menocal and Edward Shaw

Felipe J. Préstamo is a professor at the University of Miami School of Architecture, Coral Gables, Florida. His most recent publication is *Cuba: arquitectura y urbanismo* **(Miami: Ediciones Universal, 1995).**

The sugar industry, which depended on slave labor through the third quarter of the nineteenth century,[1] developed first around Havana and later spread to the center of the island. After 1898 it expanded toward the eastern end of Cuba, at the time an isolated area traditionally rich in lumber and agricultural produce.[2] Early in the sixteenth century Diego Velázquez, the island's first governor, introduced into Cuba sugarcane that the Spaniards had brought from the Canary Islands to Santo Domingo.[3] Production developed quickly along the edges of an aqueduct finished in 1596, when Havana had a population of less than five thousand. Those early mills either used hydraulic power produced by the waterway or traction supplied by animals. The growing industry caught the attention of Governor Juan Maldonado Barnuevo, for in a 1598 report to the king, he offered suggestions for financing sugar concerns. Historian Irene Wright called this document "the birth certificate of the Cuban sugar industry."[4]

The older, smaller manual mills were known as *trapiches* (fig. 1) and the new, larger ones were called *ingenios* (sugar mills), a term in use throughout the nineteenth century. *Ingenios* were developed around a *batey* — the central, open space around which various structures housing the industrial and administrative activities of the mill were located. The term was originally used by the Indians to denote the plaza at the center of their village. In time *ingenios* became increasingly mechanized, complex, and efficient. As a result of these developments the city of Matanzas, sixty miles to the east of Havana, established by one of the coast's best natural ports, became the largest exporter of sugar in the world in the middle of the nineteenth century.[5]

Sugar warehouses were built around 1850 on the banks of the San Juan River in Matanzas to accommodate the new industry. These warehouses, small when compared to those in Havana, differed from others in that their upper-floors were designed as residences for sugar-mill owners (fig. 2). The houses fronted the street that ran parallel to the river. From the street the building looked like a Neoclassical mansion, with a *piano nobile* designed in ways so that the

Fig. 1. A seventeenth-century trapiche. From Leví Marrero, *Geografía de Cuba* **(Miami: La Moderna Poesía, 1981), 205.**

1. Manuel Moreno Fraginals, *El ingenio: complejo económico social cubano del azúcar*, 3 vols. (Havana: Comisión Nacional de la UNESCO, 1964). Volume 1 gives the early history of the sugar industry.
2. Leví Marrero, *Cuba: economía y sociedad* (Madrid: Editorial Playor, 1973), 2:311–320.
3. Marrero, *Cuba*, 2:309–310.
4. Irene Aloha Wright, *El establecimiento de la industria azucarera en Cuba* (Havana: La Reforma Social, n.d.); also in "The Commencement of the Sugar Cane Industry in America," *American Historical Review*, vol. 21 (n.d.): 755–780.
5. Leví Marrero, *Geografía de Cuba* (Miami: La Moderna Poesía, 1981), 473–474.

commercial activity of the San Juan River did not interfere with the sophisticated ambiance of the buildings.[6]

Another urbanistic and architectural consequence directly related to the sugar industry boom appears in the area around the city of Trinidad. One of the first seven towns founded by Diego Velázquez in 1514, Trinidad grew slowly due to its geographical isolation from Havana, but the eastward expansion of the sugar industry finally reached the region in the nineteenth century. In 1861 there were two thousand mills operating in Cuba, each producing small quantities of sugar, often of poor quality.[7] Fifty mills were operating at this time on the outskirts of Trinidad. By the beginning of the twentieth century, only one of those mills still functioned.[8]

Trinidad, with a population of 14,400 in 1861, was a regional center connected to the rest of Cuba mainly by sea, through the port of Casilda, a few kilometers away. Isolation was a predominant factor in the local economy. Wealthy families improved the city, financed parks and thoroughfares, and built churches and residences reflecting the taste of the elite. This same character is reflected in the plazas, such as La Placita, which, like others in the city, was first paved with donations from Trinidad's sugar-producing families (fig. 3). The families that owned land and mills were instrumental in deciding the architectural profile of Trinidad, introducing the style of their preference on such a scale that they created an urban image that still persists.[9]

The interest in architecture manifested by the owners of the mills in Trinidad can be seen in the grounds (*batey*) of the Ingenio Manaca, a mill belonging to

6. Jacobo de la Pezuela, *Diccionario geográfico, estadístico, histórico de la Isla de Cuba* (Madrid: Imprenta de Establecimiento de Mellado, 1863), 3:87–89.

7. Ibid., 1:187–192.

8. Marrero, *Geografía*, 207.

9. Joaquín E. Weiss, *La arquitectura cubana del siglo XIX* (Havana: Publicaciones de la Junta Nacional de Arqueología y Etnología, 1960), xlii–xliii.

Fig. 3. La Placita, Trinidad.

From a 1910 photograph.

Courtesy of Division of Prints

and Photographs, U.S. Library

of Congress, Washington D.C.

Fig. 5. Iznaga Tower, remains

of Ingenio Manaca, near

Trinidad. Photograph courtesy

of Division of Prints and

Photographs, U.S. Library of

Congress, Washington, D.C.

the Hernández de Iznaga family (fig. 4). The *batey* at the Manaca mill mixed remnants of indigenous architecture with the Cuban version of the Baroque. One unique detail was the observation tower, later called the Iznaga Tower, 148 feet high, the tallest in all of colonial Cuba (fig. 5). In contrast, the industrial buildings, such as those that housed the boilers and served for storage, were made of wood, while brick was used for houses.[10] But such an interest in the design of *bateyes* dwindled at the end of the nineteenth century, when the sugar industry faced serious economic difficulties. From then on the sugar companies built their infrastructures with utilitarian criteria, abandoning the attention to architectural or aesthetic detail found at the Ingenio Manaca.

Sugar production in Cuba underwent a great transformation between 1818 and 1898. During that period the number of mills was reduced from over two thousand to about four hundred. At the same time the total production of the country increased, reaching one million tons for the first time in 1894.[11] A series of adverse economic and political factors affected the sugar industry at the turn of the century. Competition in the world marketplace for sugar increased at the same time that Cuba's share of that market decreased from 24.3 percent of the world's total production in 1860 to just 14.2 percent in 1895.[12] International competition created great pressure to increase the efficiency of the country's industrial plants. The abolition of slavery in 1886 increased labor costs, and a need to incorporate an ever-evolving technology produced by the industrial revolution made broader demands on capital for operating and modernizing mills.[13] In addition to these external factors, the War of Independence destroyed much of the rural economy, and after the brief Spanish-American War the island

10. Édouard Laplante, *Ingenio Manaca*, lithograph, in Justo Germán Cantero, *Los ingenios: colección de vistas de los principales ingenios de azúcar de la Isla de Cuba* (Havana: Litografía de Luis Marquier, 1857), 85.

11. Ramiro Guerra, *La industria azucarera* (Havana: Cultural S.A., 1927), 90–95.

12. Ibid., 75–79.

13. Moreno Fraginals, *El ingenio*, 2:186–207.

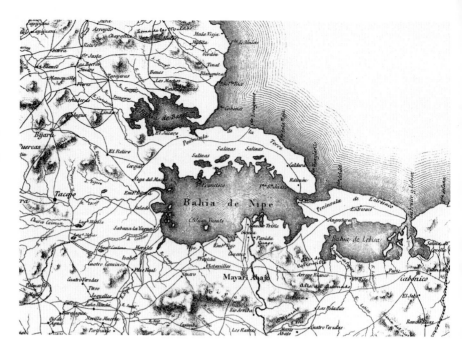

Fig. 6. Region of the Bay of Nipe and Banes. Detail of map *Croquis de la Provincia de Santiago de Cuba, Estado mayor de la Capitanía de Cuba*, enlarged and stamped in colors by the Depósito de Guerra, 1897. Photograph courtesy of Division of Geography, Land, and Maps, U.S. Library of Congress, Washington, D.C.

was occupied by the United States in 1899. In this period, and as a result of these processes, a new sugar producer appeared: *el central azucarero*, the integrated sugar mill. The high cost involved in modernizing the traditional mills, and their inefficiency, created conditions that allowed for the consolidation of smaller mills into a larger central one. This new "modern sugar mill" (now known as *el central*) not only produced sugar but in many instances also exported it directly.

Prior to the American occupation in 1899, sugar mills were owned mainly by Cubans and Spaniards, but after 1898 American investors developed a series of mills that, in scale, operation, and location, differed substantially from others built at the end of the nineteenth century.[14] Reconstruction of sugar-producing areas affected by the war, the introduction of new production techniques, and the use of the railroad as part of the transportation network designed, built, and operated by the industry required an amount of capital not readily available to Cuban investors. This new stage of development, dominated by large American corporations, created a much larger *central,* a gigantic productive unit housed in buildings with an iron structure and metallic siding and roofing, with several large chimneys, the focal point of a rail network that traversed the cane fields. At the same time the mill was easily accessible to ships that carried the sugar to world markets. They were often built next to piers in a port, in contrast to their nineteenth-century counterparts, usually located at the center of areas of cane production. This new model required the control over, or the outright ownership of, vast extensions of land in order to assure the raw material (sugarcane) in large quantities. It also required ownership and operation of deep-water ports.

Starting in 1898, a number of American companies developed these new sugar mills and to that effect bought large tracts of land for planting sugarcane. In 1950, out of a total of sixty-five *centrales* in the provinces of Camagüey and

14. Marrero, *Geografía*, 209–211.

Oriente, twenty-eight were owned by American companies. Eighteen of those mills were established between 1898 and 1915; the others between 1916 and 1921.[15] Two of these mills represent the basic characteristics of the *latifundio*, a plantation system considered to be the foundation of the sugar industry for the twentieth century. These were El Central Boston, founded in 1901 in the town of Banes, and El Central Preston, founded in 1904 near the town of Mayarí,[16] both belonging to the United Fruit Company, with headquarters in Boston, Massachusetts. The two *centrales* were located near the Bay of Nipe on Cuba's northeast coast, a region composed of a broad coastal plain where sugarcane could be grown, bordered to the south by mountains rich in minerals and forests. At the center of the region is the Bay of Nipe, the largest in Cuba, with two well-protected bays, Banes to the west and Lebiza to the east, both with excellent port facilities. Christopher Columbus described the area during his first voyage, traveling from San Salvador, and he was obviously impressed by the beauty of the landscape. In his diary he wrote, "Not myself, nor a thousand men together, could describe these beautiful ports and coastlines."[17] Although in reality Columbus did not discover the Bay of Nipe, there is no doubt that the United Fruit Company certainly did four hundred years later. They colonized its coast, changing the region's landscape and its economy (fig. 6).

The United Fruit Company, formed on 30 March 1899, was established in New Jersey "as a single corporation"[18] because of advantageous tax legislation in that state. This new firm was the result of the consolidation of various companies dedicated to selling imported fruit in the United States: Boston Fruit Company, Tropical Trading and Transport Company, Colombian Land Company, and Snyder Banana Company. The creation of the United Fruit Company (UFC) was the idea of three businessmen: Lorenzo Dow Baker, Andrew W. Preston, and Minor C. Keith. Lorenzo Dow Baker, who began his business career as the captain and owner of the *Telegraph*, a schooner that carried bananas from Jamaica to New York in 1870, later became one of the founders of the Great White Fleet, UFC's shipping branch.[19] Baker founded the Boston Fruit Company in 1885 with a banana salesman named Andrew W. Preston and a group of investors. Ten years later they were all rich, thanks to the boom in the banana market.[20] Andrew Preston was the first chairman of UFC.

The third founding member, Minor C. Keith, built railroads in Central America. *Fortune* described him as "a little man with a head like an apple and the eyes of a fanatic."[21] His sole interest was building railroads, and when his railway in Costa Rica did not have enough passengers to make a profit, he planted bananas in order to use his freight cars to transport fruit. Keith had economic difficulties throughout the 1890s and finally completed negotiations with Andrew Preston for the creation of UFC. The United Fruit Company, therefore, started out in business with the experience of fruit producers who knew well the technical aspects of agricultural operations. The company also counted on

15. Ibid., 211–213.

16. Ibid., 634.

17. Bjorn Landstrom, *Columbus: The Story of Don Cristóbal Colón* (New York: Macmillan, 1966), 84.

18. Frederick Upham Adams, *Conquest of the Tropics* (New York: Doubleday and Co., 1914), 82.

19. Thomas P. McCann, *An American Company: The Tragedy of the United Fruit* (New York: Crown Publishers, Inc., 1976), 14.

20. Ibid., 15.

21. Ibid., 16.

Fig. 7. Santa Marta Hospital, Colombia. From Frederick Upham Adams, *Conquest of the Tropics* (New York: Doubleday and Co., 1914), 280.

the talents of builders of railroads and operators of ships. These were the principal ingredients present at the founding of what was to become a veritable banana empire.[22]

United Fruit Company operated a central office in Boston, where the company defined its operational policies. In addition there were different divisions in different places. The Boston and Preston divisions were responsible for all the activities of the two mills, reporting directly to the headquarters in Boston. According to former UFC employees who worked in Aruba and Costa Rica, decisions concerning new building projects came from Boston along with budgets and preliminary plans. Local technical departments designed and built facilities following guidelines set by UFC. In the opinions of many past workers of UFC and of historians who have researched the period from the end of the nineteenth century and beginning of the twentieth, the architectural typology common to UFC projects may have been influenced by the building styles favored by English companies operating in Jamaica and Barbados, two islands frequently visited by New Englanders. The admiration that the original directors of UFC felt for the British Empire is evident from the chronicles of the period.

The operations of UFC in Cuba were eased by previous investments made by the Boston Fruit Company, which had acquired partnerships in a number of Cuban companies that produced bananas in the Banes area. When the United Fruit Company was created, the properties of the Boston Fruit Company became a part of UFC's holdings. The variations in world markets, both for fruit and sugar, brought UFC to plan the building of its first *central*, the Boston, which started operating in 1901. In its first annual report, UFC described the Central Boston: "The mill will have the capacity to press [grind] 15,000 tons of sugarcane a day; the experts consider this to be one of the best equipped mills in Cuba."[23]

The report informed stockholders that the company owned 60,330 acres mostly dedicated to sugarcane, a very large amount of land, considering the Cuban economy at the beginning of the century. United Fruit Company's sugar production was based on a carefully designed vertical organization that controlled production, transport, warehousing, and distribution. The administrative structure, on the other hand, extended "horizontally, covering all the offices and

22. See Charles Wilson, *Empire in Green and Gold: The Story of American Trade* (New York: Holt and Co., 1912); May Stacy and Galo Plaza, *La United Fruit Company en América Latina* (Mexico, D.F.: Imprenta Nuevo Mundo, S.A., 1959); and Charles D. J. Kopner and Jay Henry Soothill, *El imperio del banano* (Mexico, D.F.: Ediciones del Caribe, 1949).

23. United Fruit Company, ed., *First Annual Report* (Boston: United Fruit Company, 1900), 7.

service centers."[24] In addition it included the possession of extensive tracts of sugarcane fields, land held in reserve, and the development of other services.[25]

While UFC reports make careful references to systems of production, they pay scant attention to architectural design and the construction of buildings. It is evident that architecture was not one of United Fruit Company's primary concerns. Architectural design at both Central Boston, named for the corporation's home city, and Central Preston, which was given the name of the president of UFC, Andrew W. Preston, was a topic never mentioned in the company's annual reports.

The archives of the company in Boston were disposed of after the sale of different units of production to other companies in the 1960s. The archives of UFC in Cuba were deposited at the Central Preston, now called Guatemala, where they are inaccessible. Therefore, the only information available about the architecture of UFC is to be found in old photographs taken at certain installations and published in the sources referred to in this article and in the collective memory of its former employees.

Fig. 8. United Fruit Company hospital at Bocas del Toro, Panama. From Frederick Upham Adams, *Conquest of the Tropics* (New York: Doubleday and Co., 1914), 22.

Refurbishing the sites and building a potable water system and hospitals were important initial activities in the development of UFC plantations. It had become evident to the company that the failure of French builders at the Panama Canal was due in large part to the unhealthy conditions found there. That realization influenced the decision to have the most modern sanitary facilities in the new sugar mills. Initially, in the 1890s, the United Fruit Company's hospitals in the Caribbean were planned and operated by experts brought over from Java, India, and the tropical regions of Africa, people who had worked with different British companies or in the administration of the British Empire.[26] Hospitals were important to the positive image that UFC wanted to project both in the tropics and in the United States. Models were established; for instance, the Santa Marta Hospital in Colombia was duplicated in Tela, Honduras (fig. 7). Hospitals were always sited in high places, and the exaggerated scale of the elevations of the floors made the buildings even more impressive. They had exterior doorways, staircases, and columns forming part of a composition that was more refined than those of the administration buildings and living quarters for local workers, who had low incomes. The hospital at Bocas del Toro, Panama, offers an outstanding example of tropical landscaping, set dramatically against its environment, dominated by the Caribbean coast (fig. 8). A similar example occurred with the hospital at Puerto Limón, Costa Rica, where the same vernacular architecture is produced in carefully designed and maintained gardens (fig. 9). This hospital, initially designed as a small building, was expanded to one hundred beds when pavilions were added continuing the same architectural vernacular style in wood. The hospital thus developed into an important health center within UFC operations. The first hospital at Central Boston was similar to these, although smaller, with only fifty beds. Nevertheless, it was a two-story building offering an image of grandeur that was very important to the company (fig. 10).

Another building type repeated at banana plantations owned by the company was the plantation office building, with a typology depending on the scale of the installation (fig. 11). Their exaggerated proportions are more symbolic of

24. Oscar Zanetti and Alejando García, *United Fruit Company: un caso del dominio imperialista en Cuba* (Havana: Editorial Ciencias Sociales, 1976), 104–105.

25. Ibid., 105–109.

26. Adams, *Conquest*, 268.

Fig. 9. Hospital grounds,
Puerto Limón, Costa Rica.
From Frederick Upham Adams,
Conquest of the Tropics
(New York: Doubleday and
Co., 1914), 283.

Fig. 10. Typical small hospital
of the United Fruit Company,
location unknown. From
Frederick Upham Adams,
Conquest of the Tropics
(New York: Doubleday and
Co., 1914), 269.

the company's power than of the administrative functions that were carried out in the buildings. Wide galleries not only protected employees from both sun and rain but also created an image of opulence previously unknown in the region. The building's structure was simple. Wood from local sawmills was used following no prefabrication standards. In most cases the roof consisted of metallic sheets of galvanized zinc. United Fruit Company's administration buildings were unornamented, and even the verandahs of the structures' wide galleries were extremely simple.

An executive of UFC and his family posed in the garden in front of an imposing home, an example of the residential architecture of the banana plantations in Central America (fig. 12). (If we were to add the Union Jack, this photograph could be incorporated into the history of the British Empire.) The house, built on a grand scale, is surrounded by wide galleries, with no ornamentation; a variation in the spacing of the wooden columns on the ground floor indicates the entrance from the garden, through a stone staircase. The roof is made of sheet metal. This typology of the villa was opulent in scale but, as standard with UFC structures, very easy to build using local methods and materials.

At the other extreme of the company's residential typology were the "sanitary cottages." These were small wooden houses that had galvanized-zinc roofing, with a gallery in front and occasionally along one side, sited in small groups, clustered together, and tucked in the banana groves (fig. 13). The extensive and elaborate gardens of the executives' homes were substituted by small areas for planting so each resident could have his own vegetable garden, a popular feature at plantations.

The experience UFC acquired during the development of the banana industry in Colombia, Costa Rica, Jamaica, Panama, Honduras, Dominican Republic, and Cuba provided the foundations for developing the Boston and Preston sugar mills. The first settlement in Banes was called *el barrio americano* (the American neighborhood) by the Cubans. It consisted of rectangular blocks, wide streets, and two or three types of houses. An administrative building and a small hospital at the entrance to the compound were connected to the village of Banes by a dirt road and narrow bridge. There was substantial contrast

Fig. 13. Example of a "sanitary cottage" erected by United Fruit Company in the tropics, location unknown. From Frederick Upham Adams, _Conquest of the Tropics_ (New York: Doubleday and Co., 1914), 293.

between the two neighborhoods in Banes. The chaotic conditions of Banes's main street, at the end of the bridge, can be compared to the orderly entrance to *el barrio americano* (figs. 14 and 15).

When UFC decided to build its first *central*, the Boston, the company chose a site by the sea, on a key called Macabí, seven miles from Banes. This decision meant that two urban centers were to evolve, Banes and Macabí, both to be integrated into the operations of the Central Boston. Banes developed as the UFC headquarters, with the hospital, administrative building, general store, American Club, and residences of personnel from the United States and high-ranking Cuban executives of the company. The other center, Macabí, next to the sea and close to the mill, called El Coloso (The Colossus) by local residents, was primarily composed of production workers' homes. This was the mill's *batey*.

The Central American typology of the UFC buildings was not applied with precision; it underwent certain transformations. The homes of the top executives were designed without the standard impressive gardens, even though the houses were large (fig. 16). The commercial center was built with a wide sidewalk and a large rustic porch. The hospital did not have the gardens found at other UFC towns in the Caribbean.

The *batey* at the Central Boston did, however, maintain the character of the company's other settlements. Preston Street (named in honor of Andrew Preston) was lined with wooden houses, which, instead of the gallery previously used in the Caribbean, had wide porches elevated three or four feet above the sidewalk (figs. 17 and 18). On the other hand, the wooden columns, sheet-metal roofs, and windows and doors are identical to those of the banana plantation houses in Costa Rica and Panama.

The experience gained in design, construction, and operation at the Boston mill were put to good use by UFC in developing the second (and last) UFC *central* in Cuba, the Preston. There were seven miles between *el barrio americano* in Banes, the administrative center for the Banes division, and the mill itself, at Macabí Key, where workers' housing, other buildings, and piers were

Fig. 14. Bridge over the Banes River, 1909. From Victor Amat Osorio, *Banes (1953–1958) estampas de mi tierra y de mi sol* (Miami: New Ideas Printing, Inc., 1981), 295.

Fig. 15. Entrance to *el barrio americano*, 1916. From Victor Amat Osorio, *Banes (1953–1958) estampas de mi tierra y de mi sol* (Miami: New Ideas Printing, Inc., 1981), 10.

Fig. 16. Residence of an American official in *el barrio americano*, Banes, 1922. From Oscar Zanetti y Alejando García, *United Fruit Company: un caso del dominio imperialista en Cuba.* (Havana: Editorial Ciencias Sociales, 1976), Fig. 26 (n.p.).

Fig. 17. Residences along Preston Street, *batey* of Central Boston, Macabí, 1932. From Victor Amat Osorio, *Banes (1953–1958) estampas de mi tierra y de mi sol* (Miami: New Ideas Printing, Inc., 1981), 276.

Fig. 18. Example of residence with elevated porch, *batey* of Central Boston, Macabí, 1932. From Victor Amat Osorio, *Banes (1953–1958) estampas de mi tierra y de mi sol* (Miami: Ideas New Printing, Inc., 1981), 276.

located. This distance created serious communication problems at a time when the telephone was still inefficient and the best means of transportation was the railroad.

The Preston mill was inaugurated in 1904, three years after the Boston, and was designed and developed as an industrial city. The center of the industrial-residential complex was *el central*: a grouping of gigantic metallic structures, with galvanized-zinc roofs. In 1907 it was the second largest mill in Cuba (and in the world) in sugar production.[27] Extensive rail lines radiated in semicircles around the mill itself. Taking advantage of the topography of the area, they created terraces which visually and functionally separated the residential areas at the Preston mill (figs. 19 and 20).

The urban design of the *batey* at the Preston mill was remarkable. It is a well-known fact that the two elements vital in determining the aesthetic quality of a city are its profile against the horizon and the clarity with which its points of access can be perceived. In the case of the Preston *batey*, these two considerations were clearly defined. Located at the edge of the Bay of Nipe, the largest in the Antilles, the mill constituted a landmark that dominated the horizon both from land and sea (fig. 21). The accesses to Preston were clearly established. Then the extensive cane fields created a green belt around the *batey* and the settlement's principal access, the road to the towns of Antilla and Mayarí. This composition offered a unique image, with the mill and hills defining the entrance to the Bay of Nipe as the backdrop and the residential areas emerging out of stands of lush trees. The rail lines, with their strong geometric design, gave a clear sense of direction to the corridors supplying access to the *batey*.

The internal structure of the *batey* in the residential areas was established hierarchically, ranging from tree-lined streets in neighborhoods where the executives lived to the simple streets of the workers' quarters (figs. 22, 23, and 24). Tree-covered areas and green spaces, varying in size and always beautifully maintained, created an urban image. Gardens with a wide variety of flowers also added accents of color in different corners of the *batey*. Even in marginal areas, where the scale of the houses or public green spaces was minimal, the level of maintenance and sanitation was excellent, and water, electricity, and public health were available to all residents (figs. 25 and 26). In this environment, large wooden houses, of one or two floors, with spacious porches and gardens, were aligned along the length of streets, while in the distance the mill dominated the urban landscape with its immense scale (fig. 27).

In addition to the industrial-rail center and residential areas, the Central Preston had the most complete system of urban services in the region, including a Methodist church, built and maintained by UFC. The church also operated a school built by the company and supervised by the Cuban Ministry of Education. The church building was clearly a descendent of the traditional architecture of New England in its use of wood, the design of the roof, and the central tower that rose above the entrance (fig. 28).

Residents were offered a variety of services usually found only in large cities. Commercial activities included bakeries, drugstores, and a laundry with a home-delivery service — all operated by UFC (fig. 29). This complex and efficient system of services differentiated the UFC mills from nearby villages, which

27. The Jaronú mill in Camagüey Province was the first.

Fig. 19. Central Preston. From United Fruit Company, Preston Division, 1944 Report, n.p.

ig. 20. View of rail lines of

entral Preston. From United

ruit Company, Preston

Division, 1944 Report, n.p.

Fig. 21. Central Preston with view of the Bay of Nipe. From United Fruit Company, Preston Division

Fig. 23. Residential street for executive employees, Central Preston. From United Fruit Company, Preston Division, 1944 Report, n.p.

Fig. 22. Residential area and Bay of Nipe, Central Preston. From United Fruit Company, Preston Division, 1944 Report, n.p.

Fig. 24. Residential street for mid-level employees, Central Preston. From United Fruit Company,

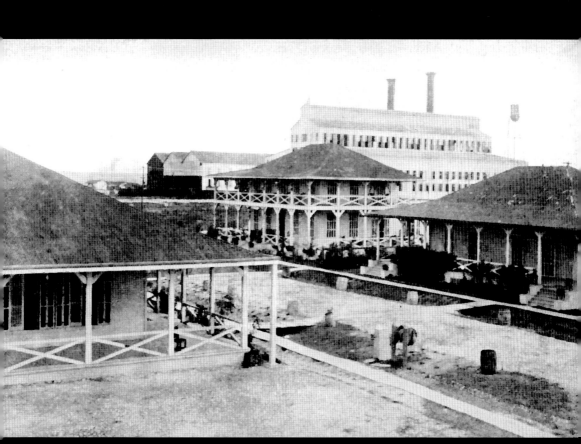

Fig. 26. Typical residence of agricultural worker, Central Preston. From United Fruit Company, Preston Division, 1944 Report, n.p.

Fig. 25. Residential street for agricultural workers, Central Preston. From United Fruit Company, Preston Division, 1944 Report, n.p.

Fig. 28. Methodist church, *batey*, Central Preston. From United Fruit Company, Preston Division, 1944 Report, n.p.

Fig. 29. Laundry service delivery truck, Central Preston. From Oscar Zanetti and Alejando García, *United Fruit Company: un caso del dominio imperialista en Cuba* (Havana: Editorial Ciencias Sociales, 1976), n.p.

lacked these amenities (not to mention a contrast with the solid economic situation of the company itself).

Life at the Preston mill was much more luxurious than at the Boston, with two clubs at the center of the *batey*. One of them, the American Club, had rooms and suites for unmarried American employees and company guests (figs. 30 and 31). Built of wood, the club looked like a large barrack, although the interior was very well appointed, with imposing dining rooms, game rooms, and large bedrooms on the second floor. The other club, for Cuban employees, was more modest and had no bedrooms, but there were playing fields and a salon for parties. While the reception room was smaller than the one at the American Club, it was an intensively active center for Preston's social life (fig. 32).

The residential areas in the Preston mill were segregated according to the level of the company's employees, following the precedent established in the Central Boston and plantations throughout Central America. Moreover, such was the norm for American and Cuban sugar mills at that time. Residential areas were remodeled in 1940 using brick walls specially manufactured by UFC and roofing of wood and ceramic tiles. Other residential sections, for Cuban employees or industrial and agricultural workers, were similar to those in the Central Boston but were better planned and maintained.

The Preston mill represented the culmination of economic development and urbanization initiated at the end of the nineteenth century by the founders of UFC. The "empire in green and gold" (a metaphor of the day signifying the wealth of the United Fruit Company in sugarcane and bananas) transformed entire regions not only urbanizing them but also creating political and economic controversies that still affect life in the Americas. In this long political and

Fig. 30. American Club, Central Preston. From United Fruit Company, Preston Division, 1944 Report, n.p.

Fig. 31. Interior lounge, American Club, Central Preston. From United Fruit Company, Preston Division, 1944 Report, n.p.

Fig. 33. La Llave hardware store, Banes. From Victor Amat Osorio, *Banes (1953–1958) estampas de mi tierra y de mi sol* (Miami: New Ideas Printing, Inc., 1981), 20.

technological process, the Preston mill should be considered as the best example of UFC's urbanistic model, in spite of the socio-economic segregation evident in residential arrangements.

The task of locating mills in a tropical setting, the finding of solutions for establishing regional transport networks and shipping routes, the well-planned infrastructure (dams, telephone lines, and electric energy networks), and the public health and sanitation systems created a model that offered a quality of living difficult to find in other rural areas in the Caribbean. This kind of architectural and urban design never received recognition in Cuba. The Preston mill was considered "just another American mill." The residential typology, one that included landscaping and houses with large terraces, was never considered an alternative for Banes, or for Cuba in general — a rejection due to Spanish influence (and European influence in general). A 1914 photograph of the La Llave hardware store in Banes, located near the main entrance to *el barrio americano*, shows a building with a classical colonnade along a large porch (fig. 33). This structure, built when UFC dominated Banes's economy, was totally foreign to the company's architectural vocabulary. The same attitude may be found in the use of brick masonry — a more permanent construction material — in contrast to the wooden plank, considered by Cubans to be a transitory material, typically used in utilitarian and inexpensive buildings.

In summary, American sugar mills should be studied for their architectural and urbanistic efficiency. Because of their foreignness, they had little influence on the architecture and town planning of Banes, Mayarí, and Antilla. In contrast, earlier sugar mills developed by Cubans in Matanzas and Trinidad, although much less efficient, left a lasting mark on the nation's architectural heritage. □

Fig. 32. Cuban Club, Central Preston. From United Fruit Company, Preston Division, 1944 Report, n.p.

Fig. 1. Four *jai alai* players,
Havana Jai Alai Court. The
figure in the center is General
Leonard Wood, American military governor in Havana.

Imaging Cuba under the American Flag: Charles Edward Doty in Havana, 1899–1902

By Miguel A. Bretos

Miguel A. Bretos is counselor for Latino affairs at the Smithsonian Institution. A specialist in the history of Hispanics in the United States, he has published and lectured extensively on the history of colonial Latin American architecture. He holds a Ph.D. from Vanderbilt University.

Eighteen ninety-eight was the "Imperial Year" in American history; the year of the Spanish-American War and the annexation of Hawaii. For the first time, the United States overflowed the confines of North America to occupy and, in some cases, annex islands beyond the seas and peoples of profound otherness. This created problems in justifying and explaining these events and generated an unprecedented demand for words and pictures about the new possessions and their inhabitants.

The National Anthropological Archives at the Smithsonian Institution contain an important collection of photographs taken in Cuba during the first American occupation of the island (1899–1902). Most pertain to Havana and environs. A few were taken in neighboring districts like Matanzas; some as far away as the Isle of Pines. There are approximately 270 Cuba-related items in diverse formats, including full- and half-size glass-plate negatives and, in some cases, contemporary prints. The latter bear a stamp with their creator's name and title: "Charles E. Doty, Official Photographer, Office [of the] Chief Engineer, Division of Cuba, Havana."[1]

It is not clear to what extent the materials at the Smithsonian are typical of Doty's range and his entire production. There is no information in the archives as to why this group of images holds together or how it found its way to the institution. In all probability it was part of a transfer of government materials to the Bureau of American Ethnology some time in the past. We know that in 1913 a group of plates was under the control of Major William M. Black, formerly the commander of U.S. Engineers in the Havana district (1899–1902).[2] Since Major Black, Doty's supervising officer, was interested in the preservation and diffusion of the record of his achievements in Cuba, it is just possible that he may have played a role in the conveyance of these materials to the Smithsonian, but this is purely speculative.

Little is known of Charles Edward Doty's early life.[3] He descended from a family that had come to America on the *Mayflower* and grew up in the Cincinnati,

Photographs by Charles Edward Doty. Courtesy of the National Anthropological Archives, National Museum of Natural History, Smithsonian Institution.

1. National Anthropological Archives, National Museum of Natural History, Smithsonian Institution, Photographic Lot 73-26A. The file is a miscellany that includes some thirty-five photographs made by Doty in the Philippines after 1904, a few photographs by Miles and Gómez de la Carrera that are roughly contemporary with the Doty material, and a handful of very interesting earlier views of Cienfuegos from the Cotera studio (ca. 1880).

2. "American Progress in Havana," *National Geographic Magazine* 13 (March 1913), 97.

3. Doty's biographical information has been gleaned from James R. Glenn, *Guide to the National Anthropological Archives, Smithsonian Institution* (Washington: Smithsonian Institution, 1996), 99, and his army dossier at the National Archives. National Archives and Records Administration, Washington, D.C., Adjutant General's Office Records, Records Group 94, 161474 and 202591. The latter is the source of all quotations.

Ohio, area. He must have learned the photographic trade through an apprenticeship, as was common practice in his day. Early in his career, he was employed as a portrait photographer in Hamilton, Ohio, and worked at a photoengraver's shop.

On 15 February 1898, the U.S.S. *Maine* blew up in Havana, and Congress declared war on Spain on 25 April. Like many young Americans, Doty answered the call of duty. On 5 June he enrolled in Company C, Second Engineers, U.S. Volunteers, in Cincinnati. A few weeks later Private Doty was stationed at Fort Sheridan and subsequently detailed as a photographer to the U.S. Army base in Augusta, Georgia. He spent the better part of the winter of 1898–1899 making blueprints at the Augusta engineers' depot while the rest of his company went to Havana. Frustrated by his dead-end job, he applied to the office of the Adjutant General, U.S. Army, for an honorable discharge. "I am married," he explained in a letter dated 20 January 1899, "and desire to return to my wife and child, who need my support, besides having an aged mother who depends greatly upon me for assistance."

Subsequent events suggest that however sincere the young soldier's concern for his family's well-being may have been, his immediate objective was to get to Cuba, where the action was. He must have knocked at several doors and tried several approaches. On 22 January Captain T.L. Huston of the Engineers' Corps endorsed a transfer: "Private Doty is an *expert* photographer," he argued, "and is required very badly to photograph fortifications." Huston must have thought very highly of Doty's skills. He was even more emphatic in a second letter, written on 4 February, to Major William M. Black, Chief Engineer at Havana. "Private Doty," he wrote, "could be used to great advantage by Lt. [George] Purington in his survey of fortifications, which photographic work is now being done by an amateur." And then, he could take "many views in and about Havana...of much historical value."

Doty's application was turned down in spite of his superior's strong backing, but his cause continued to move informally up the ranks. On 20 February General William Ludlow, the corps commandant, overruled the earlier decision and ordered Doty to report to his company in Cuba, "where his services could be very useful in the work of mapping fortifications." A week later, the eagerly awaited order arrived from the War Department in Washington. Charles Edward Doty was on his way to the Pearl of the Antilles. He arrived in Havana in March 1899 and remained there until 1902. On 15 April 1899 he was discharged from the Army, remaining as a contract photographer assigned to the Office of the Chief Engineer and the Public Works Department in the Cuban capital.

Our photographer traveled to Washington in 1902 as a member of General Leonard Wood's staff, helping the outgoing military governor prepare his reports. One of Doty's pictures depicts the general, a fan of the Basque game, at the Havana Jai Alai Court wielding a *cesta* and surrounded by four muscular *pelotaris* (fig. 1).[4] Doty intended to return to Cuba and left most of his personal effects in Havana, with the result that his luggage was lost. He had to replace his army discharge certificate and other personal documents later at some personal inconvenience. He entered the Philippine civil service in 1904, serving as a photoengraver with the Bureau of Engraving and Printing in Manila. The Philippine capital was to be his home until his retirement in 1920, except for the period 1907–1912. He was in Cuba again between 1907 and 1909, during the second

4. Herman Hagedorn, *Leonard Wood: A Biography*, 2 vols. (New York: Putnam, 1931), I, opposite 352.

American occupation. No Cuban photographs from this later period, if any existed, have found their way to the Smithsonian. Evidence at the National Archives shows that in 1909 he was living in Washington, D.C., listing his address as 1637 R Street, N.W., a house that still stands.[5] Fittingly, it is now a Spanish restaurant. He died in 1921.

The Doty collection at the Smithsonian is not unique. Similar materials exist at the National Archives and the Library of Congress, to name but two. Many photographic images saw contemporaneous publication in the stream of books and albums that appeared during the war year and its aftermath.[6] Perhaps the best known of such "1898 books" is José M. Olivares's *Our Islands and Their People as Seen with Camera and Pencil*, with photographs by Walter B. Townsend, Frederick W. Fout, and George E. Dotter.[7]

Although extraordinary both in scope and quality, the inventory of images from the period is not neutral. On the whole these are images of empire thoroughly suffused with messages of Anglo-Saxon racial and cultural superiority and the justification of colonial rule. One might expect that the approaching centennial of the Spanish-American War and the annexation of Hawaii will stimulate scholarly and curatorial interest in this opulent mine of visual information.[8]

Unlike later conflicts, relatively little of this considerable photographic output deals with war operations. Combat reporters like William Didwiddie of *Harper's Weekly* and J.C. Hemment of the Hearst organization carried cameras with them, but they seem to have used them sparingly.[9] Perhaps one of the reasons for the camera's absence from combat situations in 1898 was the obvious one that the war was over quickly. For all the bluster of Teddy Roosevelt's charge at San Juan Hill, the most significant battles of the war in Cuba had been conducted by Cuban guerrillas since 1895.[10] Naval encounters like those at Santiago and Manila Bay, though decisive, were difficult to photograph. Action

5. National Archives, A.G.O., Records Group 94, 202591.

6. The following is a selective list of "new possessions" books published in 1898 and 1899 alone that contain significant photographic material. American Art Association, *Catalogue of 500 Large Photographs.... Views Taken by the Special Photographic Outfit with the United States Army during 1898 and 1899, Illustrating the Scenic Beauty of Puerto Rico* (New York: American Art Association, 1899); James Baldwin, *Our New Possessions: Cuba, Puerto Rico, Hawaii, Philippines* (New York: American Book Company, 1899); A. M. Church, ed., *Picturesque Cuba, Porto Rico, Hawaii, and the Philippines: A Photographic Panorama of Our New Possessions* (Springfield, Ohio: Mast, Crowell and Kirkpatrick, 1898); Richard Harding Davis, *The Cuban and Porto Rican Campaigns* (New York: Scribner's and Sons, 1898); James Dewell, *Down in Puerto Rico with a Kodak* (New Haven: The Record Publishing Company, 1898); Murat Halstead, *Pictorial History of America's New Possessions* (Chicago: The Dominion Company, 1898) and *Our New Possessions: Natural Riches, Industrial Resources of Cuba, Porto Rico, Hawaii, the Ladrones, and the Philippine Islands* (Chicago: The Dominion Company, 1898); F. Tennyson Neely, *Neely's Panorama of Our New Possessions* (New York: Neely Publishing Company, 1898); and Trumbull White, *Our New Possessions* (Boston: Adams, 1898).

7. José M. Olivares, *Our Islands and Their People as Seen with Camera and Pencil*, ed. William S. Bryan, 2 vols. (St. Louis: N. D. Thompson Publishing Co., 1899). For a modern, perceptive interpretation of this work, see Lanny Thompson Womacks, *Our Islands and Their People: Constructing the Other Puerto Rican* (Río Piedras: University of Puerto Rico, 1994).

8. A good example of the possibilities of this material is the recent University of Puerto Rico's exhibit, *Archipiélago imperial: imágenes de Cuba, Puerto Rico, Hawai'i y Filipinas bajo el dominio estadounidense, 1898–1914*, curated by Lanny Thompson Womacks. The exhibition anticipated the 1998 commemoration.

9. Jorge Lewinski. *The Camera at War: A History of War Photography from 1848 to the Present Day* (London: W. Allen & Co., 1978), 53.

10. For background on the war in Cuba since 1895, see Louis Pérez Jr., *Cuba: Between Reform and Revolution* (Oxford: Oxford University Press, 1988.)

Fig. 2. General Calixto García's funeral cortege, Havana.

takes in moving ships were beyond the practical capabilities of existing technologies. The classic battle images of 1898, therefore, must remain the preserve of illustrators like Howard Chandler Christie, Edward Kirby, and Frederic Remington.

From the Cuban perspective, photographs of people, places, and events taken under U.S. auspices during the war and the American occupation are one of the richest visual sources for the nineteenth century. They hold extraordinary significance for the history of the Cuban nation and for the history of photography on the island, a field in which seminal scholarship has emerged during the last two decades.

Photography began in Cuba not long after Daguerre. Americans played a critical role from the outset. On 3 January 1841 George Washington Halsey announced that he was "completely qualified to do portraits of ladies and gentlemen in a room or in the large roof garden of the house at number 26 Obispo Street" in Havana. A few months later, R.W. Holt boasted that he could produce portraits "three times larger than any previously known daguerreotypes…[costing] the same as Mr. Halsey's: one ounce [of gold; a coin of the day]."[11] From this early start the art of the camera flourished in nineteenth-century Cuba. The first Cuban photographer was Manuel Arteaga, "a native to this island just arrived from Paris," offering daguerreotypes at 71 Lamparilla Street in 1844. By 1860 eight studios or galleries were listed in the colony's capital.[12]

The souvenir views offered by Charles DeForest Fredricks are one of the most significant ensembles of Cuban images from the second half of the 1800s. Fredricks's involvement with Cuba began in the 1850s. In 1857 he opened an affiliate of his New York photographic firm in Havana (Fredricks and Penabert, 98 Obispo Street). A recent scholar of Fredricks's oeuvre, Robert M. Levine, has

11. *Salon and Picturesque Photography in Cuba, 1860–1920: The Ramiro Fernández Collection* (Daytona Beach, Fla.: Museum of Arts and Sciences, n.d.), 5.

12. Ibid.

argued that his static, depopulated views of prestigious urban settings emphasizing "affluence, good taste in the European manner, material progress and orderliness," reflected the ideological needs of the upper class who, presumably, bought his products.[13] Just as likely, Fredricks's deserted tableaux reflected the extraordinary difficulty of preventing blur, given the limitations of the photographic equipment of his day. By the same token, some of Fredricks's images mirrored the genteel, stable world evoked by lithographers like Frédéric Miahle. One only needs to view Miahle's and Fredricks's version of the Cuban *quitrín* side by side to accept the weight of this argument.

Doty's photographs bear comparison with those of Fredricks. They are both the views of a foreigner — a Yankee. Neither penetrates intimate spaces or explores human dimensions. In Fredricks's day this may have been a function of technical limitations. By the end of the century, however, equipment had progressed enough to permit a much wider range of movement. Doty took full advantage of it when he chose to, but such was not always the case. His takes of *mambí* troops entering Havana or General Calixto García's funeral cortege are essentially snapshots, and good ones at that (fig. 2). His main subject, however, was buildings, fortifications, streets, and city squares, not necessarily the people that inhabited them. His output — or perhaps more accurately, what portion of it survived in official files — reveals a fine craftsman attuned to the specific product that his superiors or employers demanded. One surmises, for example, that the intent of his multiple views of Havana street crossings, thoroughfares, and city squares may well be documenting the condition of the pavement. His point of view is essentially that of the Engineers' Corps or the Public Works Department. By the same token, when his camera was trained on the *habaneros* of his day, he could turn out moving and informative images.

Fig. 3. Corner of Apodaca and

Suárez Streets, Havana.

Students of urban history will find much of interest in Doty's photographs. For example, there are no less than twenty neatly identified studies of important street crossings in old Havana: Muralla and Bernaza, Revillagigedo and Alcantarilla, Águila and Virtudes, Tacón and O'Reilly, Apodaca and Suárez, and many others (figs. 3 and 4). To that must be added numerous views of urban thoroughfares (Calzada del Cerro, Calzada de Jesús del Monte) (fig. 5), squares and buildings (Plaza de Albear, Manzana de Gómez) (figs. 6 and 7), and suburban settings (Calzada de Palatino, Quinta de los Molinos) (figs. 8 and 9). Taken as a whole, this is an important body of documentation about late colonial Havana's urban design and aesthetics.

Numerous images in Doty's portfolio document the fortifications of Havana. That, after all, was his original assignment in Cuba. There are extraordinary shots of the colonial bastions that made the Cuban capital a formidable bulwark of empire: El Morro, La Cabaña, La Punta, La Fuerza, La Chorrera, and the old city walls (fig. 10). The aesthetic value of stone carvings and decoration is evident

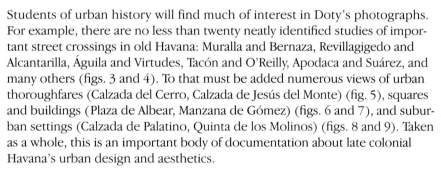

13. Robert M. Levine, *Cuba in the 1850s: Through the Lens of Charles DeForest Fredricks* (Tampa: University of South Florida Press, 1990). There is a risk in reading too much into photographs or, for that matter, any other art work. One of Fredricks's views, featured in Levine's book, shows a building with a flag (plate 16). The flag is slightly blurred. Levine speculates on page 48 that "the presence of the slightly blurred flag suggests a consular or ambassadorial [!] residence, and also shows that the camera was sufficiently advanced to allow the photographer to show street diversity if he so desired." A close examination of the building reveals a sign: "Colegio Público Para 50 Pupilos." Clearly, neither the function of the building nor the presence of the Spanish flag is a mystery. Indeed, the blur produced by the very slight movement of the flag — it is almost limp, in fact — suggests that any movement, however minor, was a real problem for photographers of Fredricks's generation, regardless of the ideology of the upper classes.

Fig. 4. Corner of Águila and Virtudes Streets, Havana.

Fig. 5. Calzada de Jesús del
Monte after paving, Havana,
February 1901.

Fig. 6. Plaza de Albear, Havana.

in a handful of excellent close-ups of Spanish architectural heraldic devices (fig. 11). From time to time Doty manages to bring in a picturesque note, as when he depicts a string of fishing nets hung out to dry against a classical Morro Castle skyline (fig. 12).

Though less imposing, the defensive system built by the Spanish in Cuba since 1868 held great interest for U.S. authorities and, consequently, for Doty. The works were put in place in the wake of the Ten Years' War (1868–1878) in order to keep Cuban insurgencies bottled up far away from populated centers. Such was the purpose of the Júcaro-Morón and Mariel-Majana *trochas* in Puerto Príncipe and Pinar del Río, respectively. They were the Maginot lines of their day, and just as useless. To the Spaniards' discomfiture, the Afro-Cuban general Antonio Maceo successfully penetrated both *trochas* with light cavalry during his *Invasión* of the western districts in 1896. Having traversed one thousand kilometers all the way from Oriente to Mantua, near Cuba's western tip, Maceo was killed in action near Havana on 7 December 1896.

Like the *trochas*, the capital's outer perimeter was heavily defended by a chain of dugouts, bivouacs, snipers' nests, trenches, *fortines* (blockhouses), and barbed wire entanglements (fig. 13). It was Havana's guarantee against insurgent forays. Doty's camera gives us a glimpse of the ring of cement, steel, and barbed wire with which the Spanish sought but failed to bring the Cuban insurgency under control — or, at least, keep it at bay (fig. 14). How these fortifications would have fared against American regulars we will never know, of course. The war ended too quickly to yield an answer.

Fig. 7. Manzana de Gómez, Havana.

Fig. 8. Calzada de Palatino,

Havana, 23 November 1899.

Fig. 9. Garden and fountain at the Quinta de los Molinos, Havana.

Fig. 10. La Cabaña Fortress, detail, Havana.

Fig. 11. Hapsburg royal coat of arms at La Fuerza Castle, stone carving, Havana.

Fig. 12. Nets drying near Morro Castle, Havana.

Fig. 13. _Fortín_ near Havana.

Part of a chain of fortifications

deployed throughout Cuba.

Blockhouses like this one

were designed to contain the

insurgency for independence

from Spain.

Public works and sanitation were matters of profound interest to the U.S. military government and to Doty's immediate superiors. By any accounts, the American regime in Cuba achieved remarkable results in both fields, especially in Havana. Unpaved streets were resurfaced and sealed throughout the capital and new sewer lines installed. (Two consecutive views of the Calzada de Jesús del Monte make the point neatly.) The city's seaside promenade, the Malecón, was laid from the Punta esplanade, where it met the Prado, to Lealtad Street. Ancient monuments were recontextualized in newly formulated urban spaces, and the city was scrubbed down. All of this was dutifully recorded by Doty's camera.

The contrast between Spanish colonial squalor and the wonders of the American proconsulate could not be more evident. A "before and after" sequence of the environs of the Punta Castle show the transit from a jumble to a modernized and redesigned corner of the urban grid. Doty's first photograph of the subject shows the ancient fortress hemmed in by later and lesser structures (fig. 15). Another photograph, dating from May 1902 (when the Republic was inaugurated), shows it released from encroachments and breathing freely amidst a park (fig. 16). In the foreground the historical marker from one of the vanished buildings has been preserved on a segment of wall picturesquely set out in the middle of a lawn. It is a setting befitting the sweeping new Malecón at its confluence with the handsome Prado and the future Avenida del Puerto.

Havana's poor sanitation was a commonplace of nineteenth-century travel literature. Cleaning up the Cuban capital had important domestic implications for U.S. policymakers. Rightly or wrongly, Havana, a city of 250,000 by 1898, was universally believed to export disease to the southern and eastern ports of the United States, where summer visitations of yellow fever were common. Havana's germs were New Orleans's runs and Savannah's fevers.

By the time of the American occupation, the city's sinister reputation as a nursery of dreaded tropical ailments was heightened by the calamities of war. Like Matanzas, Cárdenas, and other cities in western Cuba, Havana, in 1898, had a large homeless population. This was a consequence of Captain General Valeriano Weyler's "reconcentration" policy and the near impunity with which Cuban forces operated in the countryside. Driven by war, the rural desperate flocked to the towns, swelling the numbers of the urban poor. Numerous Spanish soldiers were quartered in Havana, many of them sick. Neglect and overuse had damaged the capital's urban infrastructure. Sewers and drains had been choked by years of refuse. The water supply was at risk. That the U.S. authorities made a significant dent in these complex problems is beyond question. That it would become one of the most important _pièces justificatives_ of the American occupation and a staple of U.S. propaganda was equally certain. The need for images was compelling.

Fig. 14. Wire entanglement near

Havana. Barbed wire was used

extensively by the Spanish in

their network of _trochas_ and

field fortifications.

One of the sanitation techniques used by U.S. authorities was cleaning environmental surfaces with bichloride of mercury and "electrozone," a cheap cleaning agent made by the electrolysis of seawater. Some thirty-three thousand gallons of electrozone would be used in a single day and sixteen thousand houses cleaned this way in a month. Major William Black was credited as one of the architects of the cleaning strategy. No wonder that his photographer dutifully recorded the huge iron tanks of the mighty stuff, mounted on horse-drawn wagons as cleaning crews wound their way through the old city's streets.

Some of Doty's photographs were published in the March 1913 _National Geographic Magazine_.[14] The unsigned article conveyed in words and pictures

14. "American Progress in Havana," 97–108.

Fig. 15. Environs of the Punta Castle before redevelopment, Havana.

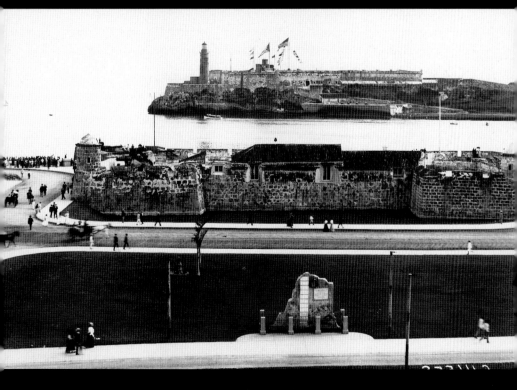

Fig. 16. Environs of the Punta Castle after redevelopment, May 1902. Encroaching structures have been demolished and a historical marker preserved in a picturesque setting. Morro Castle is in the background.

Fig. 17. Niches at the Espada Cemetery, Havana.

a glowing account of American success in sanitizing and beautifying the capital in the short span of three years. The contrast "between the Havana of the past and the Havana of today" could not be more dramatic. The article laid much of the credit for that stupendous achievement at Major Black's feet. It was Black, in fact, who loaned the photographs to *National Geographic.*

The dichotomy between perceived Spanish backwardness and American modernity is unmistakable in Doty's images. Views of the Espada Cemetery prior to its demolition underline the sharp contrast between American reticence towards, and the presumed Spanish familiarity with, and even enjoyment of, the macabre (fig. 17). Surely few spots could be more unhygienic and shocking to American sensibilities than an open-air vertical file for corpses. A further view reveals a pile of skulls and bones: the *fosa común,* or ossuary, at Havana's Cristóbal Colón Cemetery, where remains buried in the old Espada Cemetery since 1806 were transferred in 1901 and gathered into mountains and valleys of skulls, femurs, clavicles, and ribs (fig. 18).

Fig. 18. Ossuary, Cristóbal Colón Cemetery, Havana.

This dramatic imagery is not unique to Doty's repertoire. Every American photographer of the time and place seems to have been fascinated by the startling customs that accounted for this macabre topography. There are several views of these horrid landscapes in the National Archives of the United States.[15] Olivares's book *Our Islands and Their People* shows the common graves at Aguadilla, Puerto Rico, with a "Spanish gentleman" holding a skull

15. See, for example, Miguel A. Bretos, "Al volver a la patria añorada," *Cuban Heritage* 1, no.2 (1987), 28.

Fig. 20. The *garrote*, detail.

in either hand. In the far distance, a cross marks the point where Columbus landed — a telling juxtaposition.[16] Farther along there is a view of a rural cemetery in Luzón, the Philippines. The caskets have been removed from a row of niches, doubtless a step towards the impending demolition of the unhygienic eyesore. A casket with a "mummy" has been propped up against a corner wall, the contents fully exposed. The caption is eloquent: "This mummy, which is said to be more than two centuries old, has a merry expression on his face, as if he were delighted at the coming of the Americans."[17]

The same fascination is evident in Doty's vivid study of the *garrote*, the executioner's screw. Many a Cuban patriot's neck was crushed by this implacable machine. The sinister appliance is shown atop the scaffold, like a throne of Death (fig. 19). Doty's camera then zooms in to capture in crisp detail the steel yoke — front and rear views — and the screw that snapped the victim's cervical vertebrae like an outsize nutcracker (fig. 20). Finally — might this not also be telling? — the head of a black man is shown, fitted with the deadly mechanism (fig. 21).

Fig. 19. The *garrote*, Havana.

Mapping fortifications, documenting street crossings, and providing visual evidence of advancing public hygiene may not be the best way to get people into a photographic frame. Nevertheless, Doty managed to provide compelling images of the Cuban people under the American occupation. A *guajiro* (peasant) family stands in front of a *bohío* thatched with palm fronds (fig. 22). The father wears a straw hat and a thick moustache. His twelve children line up to his left and right, in front of the hut that is their home. Some hold hands. Their rank in the family pecking order is neatly signified by their clothing. The oldest girls wear dresses and shoes, the younger ones dresses but no shoes. The oldest boys wear shirts, pants, shoes, and hats. The three younger brothers are stark naked, their distended bellies proclaiming the presence of intestinal parasites. For all their obvious poverty, the family has an air of dignity. A clothesline laden

Fig. 21. Demonstration of the use of the *garrote*.

16. Olivares, *Our Islands*, 1:337.

17. Ibid., 2:732.

Fig. 22. A *guajiro* family.

Fig. 23. "Home of Poor Cubans," Havana.

Fig. 24. *Reconcentrados*, victims of Spanish repression.

with scrubbed white garments reveals industry and a concern for hygiene — but where is the mother?

Another family group, labeled "Home of Poor Cubans," reveals a different scene (fig. 23). The setting now is a masonry structure that has known better times; a deeply shaded *portal*. In the center of the picture, a mother holds a child. She is young and quite beautiful despite her dirty dress, which, like her hair, seeks after fashion. Her child is impeccably clean and wears his hair in a Kewpie topknot. Who are the other two women? Who is the man lying on the floor, one of his shoes removed for comfort? Are these refugees from better times and places? A further frame shows a group of famished *reconcentrados*, the victims of Spain's systematic repression of the Cuban rebellion. They are black and look dejected (fig. 24). A homeless man — a Chinese — makes do in a cave, possibly the Cueva del Indio in nearby Matanzas, a known abode for the otherwise homeless (fig. 25). A vendor peddles his wares in the street (fig. 26).

Doty's final days in Cuba must have been hectic. Regardless of his personal feelings about the future of the island, a matter about which we have no information at all, he must have shared in the excitement of a nation preparing for a historic transit. On 18 May 1902 his most important appointment was with the man of the hour, Cuban President-elect Tomás Estrada Palma, who sat for a portrait on an elaborate wicker rocking chair (fig. 27). Don Tomás wears a dark three-piece woolen suit and a watch chain. There are two additional group portraits showing the soon-to-be chief executive with what looks

Fig. 25. A Chinese man in his cave abode near Matanzas.

Fig. 26. A street vendor in Havana.

Fig. 27. Tomás Estrada Palma, the first president of Cuba (1902–1906). This portrait was made by Doty

Fig. 28. The American flag is lowered

Fig. 29. The entrance to the Havana harbor channel on 20 May 1902. A crowd gathers at the recently completed Malecón.

Fig. 30. O'Reilly Street decorated for Independence Day, 20 May 1902, Havana.

like a delegation of visiting Americans. Though diminutive by comparison, the Cuban leader looks cocky and confident. There is no intimation that his presidency would end up in crisis and the Americans would be back barely four years later.

Approximately a dozen photographs document the transfer of sovereignty from the United States to the Cuban Republic on 20 May 1902. It was a bright day in Havana. Exactly at noon, the Stars and Stripes came down simultaneously from Morro Castle and the Palace of the Captains General. The Cuban flag—*la Bandera de la Estrella Solitaria*—was hoisted in its place. Doty caught the solemn instant before the American flag was lowered over El Morro (fig. 28). He perched his camera on the castle wall facing the harbor channel, catching an unusual angle of the old lighthouse dedicated by Leopoldo O'Donnell, the nineteenth-century Irish-Spanish Captain General. In another photograph, a crowd at La Punta watches the gaily bannered vessels sailing into the narrow harbor channel (fig. 29).

A striking aspect of the festivities were the triumphal arches and other decorations rigged up in Havana streets to salute the singular occasion. The city was beribboned with bunting, and hung with palm fronds (fig. 30). An arch at the corner of Muralla and Bernaza saluted Don Tomás (fig. 31). His bust figures prominently at the apex, framed by two Cuban flags spangled with incandescent bulbs. Marbleized surfaces suggest elegance and opulence. A personification of Cuba emerging from a shell, surrounded by a sunburst, holding the Law in her right hand and a wreath of laurel over Cuba's coat of arms in her left, sits precariously on a lintel. The lintel bears the coats of arms of the European powers (including Spain in the place of honor) while those of

Fig. 31. Triumphal arch at Muralla and Bernaza Streets, Independence Day, 20 May 1902, Havana. Note the incandescent bulbs on the Cuban flags above.

the American republics are arranged along the semicircle of the arch: Cuba is taking its place among free nations.

Another arch at Obispo Street, one of the city's main commercial thoroughfares, hailed the Cuban Republic (fig. 32). At the gable, Industry and Commerce, flanked by views of Morro Castle and a typical Cuban palm grove, attend a triumphant personification of Cuba. One thinks of an enormous cigar box label. Medallions of José Martí and Antonio Maceo on either side — Maceo holds the place of honor — complete the ensemble. Garlands of incandescent bulbs highlight the parapet and cornices. Those who witnessed the displays must have thought them fit to welcome a new era of freedom and prosperity. Almost a century later, Cubans are still striving for those elusive goals. □

Note

Thanks are due to Dr. John Homiak, Director, National Anthropological Archives, Smithsonian Institution, and his staff for their support and assistance at all stages of this project.

SOCIAL

OL. III NUM. 3
ARZO, 1918
EINTA CENTAVOS

The Years of *Social*

By María Luisa Lobo Montalvo and Zoila Lapique Becali

Translated by Narciso G. Menocal and Edward Shaw

María Luisa Lobo Montalvo has worked extensively on art collections in Cuba and Kenya and produced films in Peru. She has assembled one of the largest photographic archives on Cuban architecture and decorative arts and is working on a book on the architecture of Havana.

Zoila Lapique Becali is a research librarian at the Biblioteca Nacional, Havana. She has published widely on nineteenth- and early- twentieth-century Cuban periodicals and has written extensively on Cuban culture, particularly on music and engravings.

◀

Fig. 1. Conrado W. Massaguer, cover of *Social*, March 1918.

Social, considered at its time as the best periodical in Latin America, was a luxurious publication, profusely illustrated with drawings, caricatures, photographs, works of art, graphics, and musical scores (fig. 1). Founded in January 1916 by its director, the illustrator and caricaturist Conrado Walter Massaguer, the magazine was geared to a specific audience of wealthy Cubans, who, in those early years of the Republic, had left behind their old colonial ways and wanted to catch up with the world's high bourgeoisie. At the same time they looked forward to adopting the practical manner of living of the United States, with its notions of comfort. At first there was imitation, but later there was a definite local flair (fig. 2). The economic boom of the period made all of this possible.

In the first issue (January 1916) the editors explained their objectives: "The magazine will be dedicated to describing our great social events, art exhibits, and fashion shows by means of the pencil or the camera lens." The content of the publication, nevertheless, was of a much broader scope. It included permanent sections on Cuban architecture, interior decoration, high fashion and design, and reviews of social events. Besides these, articles on literature, visual arts, music, opera, ballet, and film were featured as well as on such sports as motoring, yachting, rowing, and tennis. Graphics were a vital part of the publication.

Massaguer, along with Rafael Blanco (1885–1955) and Armando Maribona (1894–1963), belonged to a group of caricaturists and illustrators who early in the twentieth century reacted against nineteenth-century standards (fig. 3). Their work differed from the deformed French style that attempted to incorporate the lineal impressionism typical of periodicals of the period. Even the best nineteenth-century illustrators in Cuba, like Victor Patricio de Landaluze, had been influenced by French caricaturists, especially Léandre, whose characters showed enormous heads set on small, weak bodies, like puppets or stuffed figures.

Massaguer's style is different. Sober, brief lines prevail in his work. His agile, precise strokes always captured the outstanding traits of a subject with remarkable aesthetic economy. Most characteristically, he was always humorous and good natured. His work echoes his dictum, "simplify by exaggerating" (fig. 4). With a gregarious personality and an amiable and generous character, he was incapable of giving anyone pain or overdramatizing. Quite correctly, Bernardo Barros called him "the Mark Twain of caricature." And while there is a degree of North American influence in his work, he achieved an unmistakably personal style that also expressed his Cubanness (fig. 5).

Of all the humorists and illustrators of the period, Massaguer carried on the line started by the journalist and caricaturist Ricardo de la Torriente. Torriente, working in the city of Matanzas, drew caricatures for *El Album* (1885), but he left for the United States because of his involvement with the cause of Cuban independence. Later, back in Cuba, Torriente continued his work on political satire at *La Política Cómica* (1906–1935), of which he was editor, director, and illustrator. That weekly was made popular by his character of "Liborio," who symbolized Cubans and their country as Uncle Sam did in the United States or John Bull in England.[1] But Torriente's importance was only insular, while Massaguer's transcended globally, recognized for his agile drawings of world

1. In the early years of the Republic (1903), the secretary of health used Ricardo de la Torriente's popular figure of Liborio for a massive campaign for public hygiene. It was the first time a caricature of a fictional character was used in billboard ads and for advertisements in the press.

leaders as much as for his contributions to important foreign periodicals. With the perspective of years, we look back at whom we remember as an outgoing and charming small, stocky man with a round face and smiling eyes. He usually enjoyed a cigar while taking notes and making sketches of situations, personalities, or of everything good and agreeable that crossed his path. Also, at times, things that deserved to be criticized would become the subject of a humoristic drawing pervaded with appealing mockery. As we read in *Social*, Massaguer asked people, when they discovered that he was sketching them, to let him draw them simply, without any affected and unnatural posturing. The caricatures that Massaguer and his friend singer Enrico Caruso, also an excellent draftsman, did of each other will serve as examples (figs. 6 and 7). Massaguer made most of his drawings furtively, his sketches were "notes taken treacherously," and he always set out with a pencil small enough to hide in the palm of the hand (fig. 8). His hand was tireless, and his work never needed correction.

Conrado Walter Massaguer y Díaz was born in Cárdenas on 3 March 1889. In 1896 his family emigrated to Mérida, Yucatán, and he lived there until 1902, when he was sent to study at the New York Military Academy. He returned to Havana in 1905, but his family sent him back to the Yucatán from 1906 to 1908. Completely self-taught in art, he published his first caricatures in two Mérida magazines, *La Campana* and *La Arcadia*, and in a local newspaper, *El Diario Yucateco*. Early in 1908 he returned to Havana, where, through the help of the journalist Víctor Muñoz, he worked as a baseball illustrator at *El Mundo,* a Havana newspaper. Concurrently, he contributed to *El Fígaro, Cuba y América, El Tiempo, El Hogar,* and *Letras*. In 1910 he founded Mercurio, his first advertising agency, with Laureano Rodríguez Castells as his partner. The following year he had his first one-man exhibition of caricatures at Havana's Ateneo, of which he was a member of the board of directors since the preceding year. In 1912 his first drawings depicting Broadway were published in the United States in the Sunday supplement of the *New York American Journal*. In 1913, with his brother Oscar, he founded *Gráfico*, which was published until 1918. Then came *Social* in 1916, and in January 1919, *Pulgarcito*, a children's magazine. In June of that same year the first number of *Carteles*, a weekly magazine, was released. This was another joint publication of the

CARUSO por MASSAGUER.

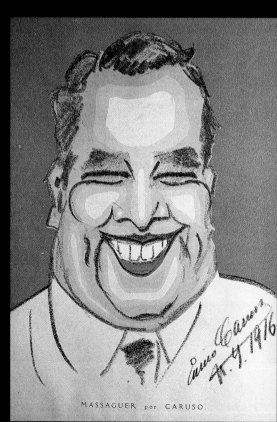

MASSAGUER por CARUSO.

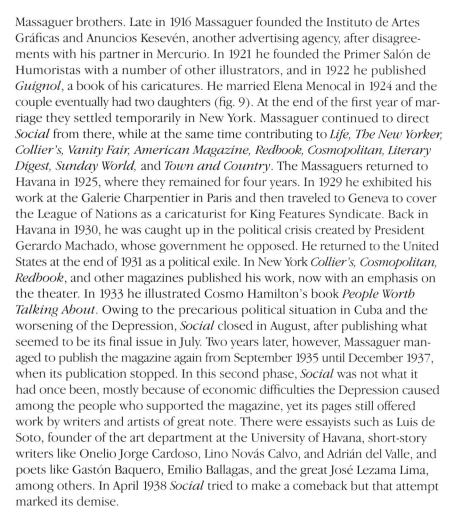

Massaguer brothers. Late in 1916 Massaguer founded the Instituto de Artes Gráficas and Anuncios Keseven, another advertising agency, after disagreements with his partner in Mercurio. In 1921 he founded the Primer Salón de Humoristas with a number of other illustrators, and in 1922 he published *Guignol*, a book of his caricatures. He married Elena Menocal in 1924 and the couple eventually had two daughters (fig. 9). At the end of the first year of marriage they settled temporarily in New York. Massaguer continued to direct *Social* from there, while at the same time contributing to *Life, The New Yorker, Collier's, Vanity Fair, American Magazine, Redbook, Cosmopolitan, Literary Digest, Sunday World,* and *Town and Country*. The Massaguers returned to Havana in 1925, where they remained for four years. In 1929 he exhibited his work at the Galerie Charpentier in Paris and then traveled to Geneva to cover the League of Nations as a caricaturist for King Features Syndicate. Back in Havana in 1930, he was caught up in the political crisis created by President Gerardo Machado, whose government he opposed. He returned to the United States at the end of 1931 as a political exile. In New York *Collier's, Cosmopolitan, Redbook*, and other magazines published his work, now with an emphasis on the theater. In 1933 he illustrated Cosmo Hamilton's book *People Worth Talking About*. Owing to the precarious political situation in Cuba and the worsening of the Depression, *Social* closed in August, after publishing what seemed to be its final issue in July. Two years later, however, Massaguer managed to publish the magazine again from September 1935 until December 1937, when its publication stopped. In this second phase, *Social* was not what it had once been, mostly because of economic difficulties the Depression caused among the people who supported the magazine, yet its pages still offered work by writers and artists of great note. There were essayists such as Luis de Soto, founder of the art department at the University of Havana, short-story writers like Onelio Jorge Cardoso, Lino Novás Calvo, and Adrián del Valle, and poets like Gastón Baquero, Emilio Ballagas, and the great José Lezama Lima, among others. In April 1938 *Social* tried to make a comeback but that attempt marked its demise.

Massaguer worked tirelessly for each issue of *Social*. He designed the cover and did full-page drawings in watercolor or crayon to illustrate literary texts or some

Fig. 11. Conrado W. Massaguer,

Guillermo de Blanck y

Menocal, caricature,

Social, October 1919.

Fig. 10. Conrado W. Massaguer,

Regatas de Varadero, Social,

August 1916.

other special topic. In addition, he drew small caricatures of familiar personalities at events or social gatherings not only to illustrate a chronicle but also to reflect its atmosphere with singular wit (fig. 10).

There was a full-page caricature of a Cuban or foreign personality in each "Ellos," a section on men (fig. 11). Later, the magazine added a section called "Ellas" dedicated to women who deserved recognition because of their social or artistic prominence. Further developing this idea, Massaguer created feminine characters to criticize what he felt were reprehensible customs of the high society in which he himself moved. In 1916 "Nena" appeared in *Social* with a drawing of the character and a text written by the artist (fig. 12). After obtaining an American education, Nena returned to Cuba with no prejudices. Back among her old friends, she wisely appraised some of their hypocritical attitudes, such as marrying for money or abandoning friends because their families had lost their wealth.

During *Social*'s first year, Massaguer introduced another female character whom he called the "Massa-Girl." This was the first inkling of an idea he developed

Fig. 12. Conrado W. Massaguer,

Nena, Social, **June 1916.**

Fig. 13. Conrado W. Massaguer,

La muy mona **(The cutest),**

Social, **September 1925.**

further in 1925. The name Massa-Girl was a play on words, since *masa*, taken from his surname, meant the female body, or flesh in Cuban slang. The girl he drew was young and pretty, very much into the styles of her time: she loved sports, led an independent life, smoked and drank in public places, dressed in the latest fashions, and was, in summary, a Creole flapper based on the model of those American girls recently emancipated at the end of World War One. The Massa-Girl, then, broke with rigid social conventions and rules in the style of characters designed by Marjorie (Neysa) McMein (1887–1949), whose advertisements and covers of top magazines, such as *McCall's, The Saturday Evening Post*, and others, spread images of chic modern girls who quickly replaced the image of baby-doll beauty. Massaguer's imagery, however, is different from that of the original flapper. His drawings are composed of lighter, simpler lines, with a tendency toward caricature, and charged with irony and humor. Occasionally he would turn his humor around and make fun of girls who aspired to the image of the Massa-Girl but would never make it (fig. 13).

While Massaguer was less prone than some of his contemporaries to social and political criticism in his caricatures, he has left some remarkable contributions in this area. Although *Social* was geared to a definite kind of reader, Massaguer, nevertheless, drew, in 1923, two political cartoons: *Veinte y un años* (Twenty-One Years) and *¡Dios mío! ¡Qué solos se quedan los muertos!* (My Lord! How Lonely the Dead Remain!). The first referred to the anniversary of the establishment of the Republic on 20 May 1902. The drawing represents Cuba as a young and sad girl dressed in torn and threadworn clothes, covered with patches. The patches conceal all the problems facing the nation at that moment. In spite of its simplicity it shows emotive and reflexive strength. In the second instance Massaguer used the famous lines of the Spanish poet Becquer as caption for a drawing in which a young Cuban contemplates several tombstones in a cemetery where civic conscience, idealism, sacrifice, Cubanism, patriotism, and nationalism are all buried (fig. 14).

Social had a long editorial life. Its best moment was the magazine's first stage (1916–1933). Well-known foreign and local artists, including those of the avant-garde, contributed to the monthly, no matter what their political tendencies happened to be. Thus the magazine became the spokesman of modernity, covering Cubism, Futurism, Art Deco, African art, and Japanese prints. Until 1927 when the *revista de avance* [sic], directed by Juan Marinello, Jorge Mañach, Francisco Ichaso, Alejo Carpentier, and Martí Casanova, made its appearance, *Social* was the only voice of the avant-garde.

The covers were always outstanding for their drawings; and their color and typography, all done by Massaguer, were equally exceptional. In the early years the designs were usually of two types. One consisted of a small figurative drawing, framed each month by a different geometric border set in a background of contrasting colors. For the other Massaguer would use the entire field for his figures, always in search of something that would be suggestive, usually a barb aimed at the public to which the magazine was directed. There were allusions to certain parties held in the best homes of Havana, sports, theatrical performances, or fashion and travel, generally designed according to the season (fig. 15). Patriotic celebrations and holidays were also the subjects on covers (fig. 16). The January cover was always reserved for the publication's anniversary.

Artistic influences varied. Russian decorative art reached *Social*'s audience when Massaguer drew a cover titled *La invasión rusa* (The Russian Invasion), alluding to the famous company of Ivan Torzoff, which was the furor of Havana. Another example was his drawing of *Los húsares negros* (The Black Hussars),

**Fig. 15. Conrado W. Massaguer,
cover of *Social*, July 1919.**

**Fig. 14. Conrado W. Massaguer,
*¡Dios mío! ¡Qué solos se
quedan los muertos!*, Social,
November 1923.**

a theme that inspired Jorge Mañach to do a beautiful page to accompany
the musical piece of the same title. At the end of the 1920s Art Deco design
invaded the magazine with large straight planes that cut and superimposed
upon themselves, forming sharp edges (fig. 17). Echoes of Mexican muralism
resonated in *Social* at the time it was beginning to influence local painters and
sculptors. Then, by the 1930s, Cuba was identifying its colonial past with
a genuinely national and autochthonous spirit. This revival was a source of
inspiration to Massaguer, who captured it on covers and in drawings and caricatures (fig. 18).

Fig. 16. Conrado W. Massaguer,

cover of *Social*, November 1918.

In the early 1920s the interior of the magazine was designed by Rafael Ángel Surí, a painter and an illustrator now unjustly forgotten. Under his direction a varied graphic repertory for the design of the table of contents was adopted, with one theme for each issue. In 1922, for example, Surí designed a series based on the twelve motifs of the zodiac, *Motivos del zodíaco*. On the upper part of the page he drew small female nudes with long curling hair. The drawings were done in pen and ink, and a loose and wavy line predominated, reminding us that the artist was still under the influence of Art Nouveau. The finely drawn female figures, looking like Tanagra figurines, stand by the zodiac's animal symbols and the logotype for the corresponding month.

Along with Surí, other graphic artists and illustrators, such as Rafael Lillo Botet, Enrique García Cabrera, José Manuel Acosta, José Hurtado de Mendoza, and Enrique Riverón, a painter who introduced Cubism into his drawing and his humor, worked for the magazine (fig. 19). José Manuel Acosta, the Cubist painter, did a caricature of Jorge Mañach, shaping his face out of curved lines and cubes. But of all the graphic artists Massaguer invited to contribute to *Social*, the most outstanding was Jaime Valls, born in Catalonia. His drawings are soft, elegant, and light, with a great economy of line. Other artists who illustrated *Social* were the Spaniard Alejandro Sánchez Felipe, who did ink drawings of

SOCIAL

MARZO 1927
C. W. MASSAGUER, DIRECTOR
LA HABANA, CUBA

Fig. 17. Anonymous [Esperanza

Durruthy?], cover of *Social*,

March 1927.

◀

▶

Fig. 18. Conrado W. Massaguer,

cover of *Social*, April 1932.

Fig. 19. Enrique Riverón,

Artículos de importación

(Imported Articles), *Social*,

November 1923.

colonial architecture, and Ernesto de Blanck Martín, who did mezzotints of scenes of Old Havana.

Several pictures appeared in 1932 made jointly by painters Mario Carreño, Antonio Aguilar, and López Méndez, who signed the works with an anagram. In 1936 a number of important Cuban artists did illustrations for *Social*'s calendar. These were García Cabrera, Mario Carreño, Enrique Caravia, Vergara, and Her-Car, the artistic name used by José Hernández Cárdenas (1904–1957), an excellent painter, illustrator and, above all, caricaturist. In the final years of the publication a drawing and a comic strip by Horacio Rodríguez Suriá (1908–1975) appeared. Finally, the graphic work of Jorge Mañach, the distinguished Cuban writer, should be acknowledged, especially his caricature of José Manuel Acosta and his self-portrait.

Fig. 20. Conrado W. Massaguer,

logotype, *Social*.

Fig. 21. Leopoldo Romañach, *La*

hija del pescador (The

Fisherman's Daughter), Salón

de 1917. *Social*, February 1917.

Among the graphic sections of the magazine, the logo, designed by Massaguer, was full of irony and elegantly reflected the essence of the publication: it consisted of a heraldic shield on which a peacock and a mask stood out (fig. 20). The magazine also reproduced foreign engravings and lithographs of Cuba or by Cubans from the eighteenth, nineteenth, and twentieth centuries, as well as sketches and original drawings of scenes of life in Havana and landscapes of other places in the country. It illustrated Havana's annual Salón de Pintura (fig. 21), as well as published music of Cuban and foreign composers of the nineteenth and twentieth centuries, including works in small formats by Debussy, Stravinsky, Satie, Ravel, Honegger, and Villa-Lobos. It also exposed its audience to the work of such avant-garde Cuban composers as Alejandro García Caturla and Amadeo Roldán, who borrowed elements from black music and expressed them in a universal, contemporary language.

Advertisements, both Cuban and foreign, were aimed at an audience with a high purchasing power. Luxury motor cars of American and European make, sold in Havana by local agencies, were the most advertised product in the 1910s and 1920s. "Havana, which is progressing with giant steps in every field, is today one of the cities that, in proportion, has the most automobiles in the world," *Social* boasted in February 1916 (fig. 22). Montalvo y Corrales sold uniforms for the chauffeurs of those automobiles (fig. 23). Advertisements for elegant clothing and shoe stores for both men and women also filled many pages, as did promotions for home appliances (gas and electric stoves, electric refrigerators, phonographs, lamps, ceramic artifacts, tiles, and accessories for bathrooms), imported or nationally made furniture, high-fashion boutiques, cruise lines, food and beverages, and the leading brands of cigars and cigarettes (fig. 24).

These advertisements were of two types. One was conventional, with or without an image, either dependent on text and typographic decoration or illustrated with photographs or representative drawings. The other style introduced novelties in design: large or small areas contrasted in a solid color — generally black on the white of the paper — and a use of halftones or color. The aim was to achieve a compositional synthesis of the main image, be it a photograph, drawing, or combination of both. The object advertised was

left,

Fig. 22. Advertisement for White automobiles, *Social*, February 1917.

right,

Fig. 23. Conrado W. Massaguer, advertisement for Montalvo y Corrales, *Social*, February 1917.

Fig. 24. Advertisement for General Electric Company, *Social*, December 1928.

highlighted in the foreground with a faded scenic background, usually depicting some well-known corner of Havana. The drawings, done in modern lines, emphasized the curvilinear and were accompanied by a brief text carrying a direct message to the consumer.

Massaguer designed advertisements for his own agency—Anuncios Keseven— and many of them appeared in *Social* along with those coming from other Cuban and international design studios and agencies. Beginning with the first issues of the publication, Massaguer used in ads popular characters like Liborio, which assured instant impact. In 1916 he presented Nena in an ad: "A bit of friendly advice, Nena uses Gripol." Massaguer's style was taken up by other commercial artists and extended quickly to other publications.

Massaguer complemented the graphic content of the magazine with illustrated coverage of the city's important social events. It was the custom in Havana, as in many other places, to hold costume balls during Carnival. Two especially brilliant ones were held during the 1916 season: the Baile Rojo (Red Ball), given by Lili Hidalgo de Conill, in February, and the Bal Watteau, offered by Mina Pérez-Chaumont de Truffin, in March. Both reviews, presented in the March and April issues, show a complete and systematic treatment of the topic. In the first instance Massaguer announced the motif of the party on the magazine's cover with a dandy dressed in red escorting a lady in fancy dress (fig. 25). Inside, a double-page caricature, also by Massaguer, captured the leading personalities of Havana's society decked out in reds. Massaguer's advertisements for Enger motor cars and Larrañaga cigars (which used as its text Kipling's verse "There's peace in a Larrañaga") were also designed around the theme of the ball (figs. 26 and 27). An article titled "Male Styles" not only referred to the guests but also explained the origins of the English term "hunting pink."

For the feature article on the party Massaguer selected photographs of the site of the ball and published decorations of the palm garden of Sra. Hidalgo de Conill's mother's mansion on the corner of Paseo and 13th Streets in El Vedado, built by architect Leonardo Morales.[2] The tennis court was specially decorated

2. The Conills also owned a splendid residence, built in 1869, in the Reparto de las Murallas, in Old Havana, on Teniente Rey Street between Cristo and Villegas, on the Plaza del Cristo.

SOCIAL

VOL I.   MARZO, 1916   No. 3

"Hay Placidez en un Larrañaga"

Fig. 26. Conrado W. Massaguer,

advertisement for Larrañaga

cigars, *Social*, March 1916.

Fig. 27. Conrado W. Massaguer,

advertisement for Enger auto-

mobiles, *Social*, March 1916.

with garlands and lighting for the splendid dinner served during the party. The covers of the menus were each done in watercolor. Massaguer showed several of the guests in their dazzling costumes (fig. 28) and a photographic portrait of the hostess was set off by a decorated border. She is elegantly dressed as a Russian ballerina, so beautiful that she seems to have escaped from Diaghilev's Ballet Russes, "Pavlova transported to El Vedado." Sra. Hidalgo de Conill stands with her arms crossed behind her neck, as if she had been surprised in the moment of spinning into a pirouette (fig. 29). Although the image cannot capture the brilliant colors of the gown, the article gives all of the details, likening the colors of the costume to the tones of the palette of Léon Bakst, the great designer of theatrical wardrobes and set designs. There are other portraits decorated with vignettes done in pencil of the women guests and their elaborate costumes, which they were allowed to choose at will or whim and were made by famous dressmakers from all over the world. Male guests, on the other hand, were dressed in tails with red vests and black breeches, tight at the knees, black silk stockings, and pumps of black patent leather with gold buckles. There were three orchestras and every guest received a carefully chosen present. "A ball that never ends, an elegance that is enrapturing, a luxury that casts its spell, a beauty that bewitches; the men in their red tails; the ladies in period gowns, all so admirably classical, of exquisite taste, of supreme chic," *Social* reported.[3]

The Bal Watteau was the other grand costume party of 1916. It was held at Villa Mina and was offered by Mina Pérez-Chaumont and her husband Regino Truffin, honorary consul to the Russian Empire in Havana. The Truffin residence, located at 72nd Street and 45th Avenue in Marianao, had enormous gardens with impressive stands of trees.[4] *Social* reviewed the event with delight, indicating that "Havana society spent a month feeling as if it were back in the eighteenth century" and no one talked about anything but *paniers*, powdered wigs, and Pompadour *crétonne*. The chronicler proclaimed that the entire atmosphere appeared to be lifted intact right out of eighteenth-century France, but then, also, "Three orchestras filled the evening with gay waltzes and one-steps and, to add more flavor to the party, an animated *farandole*. The guests danced in circles, ran across the lawns, there was a reveille at dawn; no additional detail could make this original *fête champêtre* more amusing…. A delicious menu was served at two in the morning…and the feast was animated by a live show in the little open-air theater."

The table of contents of the April 1916 issue of *Social* reflects the dimensions of the coverage the magazine gave to the Bal Watteau. For the cover Massaguer drew a very funny picture (fig. 30). A girl young enough for this to be her first ball stands stiff and awkward, apparently at a loss and bewildered by the concurrent attention of two mature, worldly gentlemen. In the frontispiece he

3. "It is a brilliant parade that brings memories back to life…. María Ruiz de Carvajal — the young Marquesa de Pinar del Río — in the sumptuous costume of an Arabian princess; Lolita Morales de del Valle — as María Leszczynska, Queen of France, superbly decked out in jewels; Mercedes Montalvo, as a butterfly; María Dolores Machín de Upmann, as a Grecian; Loló Larrea de Sarrá, as Night; María Louisa Gómez Mena de Cagigas escaped from a Watteau; María Luisa Menocal de Argüelles, a graceful *maja* straight out of a tapestry at the Escorial; Susanita de Cárdenas de Arango, who comes directly from the Court of Louis XV; the Sritas. Cámara: María Francisca, as a Persian and Gracia, as Madness;…Rosario Arango, as a Lady of the Court of Charlemagne; Rosita Sardiñas, as Diana the Huntress;…such a poetic entourage, a procession of fairies…. And presiding over the admirable gathering — the ideal individual, as dignity personified — Mariana Seva de Menocal." From Rafael María Angulo, "Después del baile," (After the Ball) *Social* 1 (March 1916).

4. In 1952 the Tropicana nightclub was installed there. Architect Max Borges Jr. integrated the house and its garden into the design of the cabaret in a highly organic way. He was awarded the Gold Medal of the College of Architects in 1953 for this achievement.

Fig. 28. Ana María Menocal and María Radelat de Fontanills at the Baile Rojo, photographs, *Social*, March 1916.

Fig. 29. Lili Hidalgo de Conill at the Baile Rojo, photograph, *Social*, March 1916.

Fig. 30. Conrado W. Massaguer, cover of *Social*, April 1916.

placed a photograph of Sra. Mina Pérez-Chaumont de Truffin "dressed in the historic Louis XV-style gown that she wore at her Bal Watteau," framed with decorative borders (fig. 31). Massaguer also published a series of allegorical verses written by Gustavo Sánchez Galarraga, titled *Siglo XVIII* (The Eighteenth Century), illustrated with pencil drawings. Among those photographed at the ball were Matilde, Regina, and Regino Truffin, María Luisa Gómez Mena de Cagigas, Sra. de Ferrara, and Sra. Goicoechea. All of these illustrations were accompanied by pen-and-ink-vignettes (fig. 32). For the "Ellos" section, Massaguer did a caricature of Regino Truffin (fig. 33). He also did *Como comienzan los chismecitos* (How Tidbits of Gossip Originate), an amusing pencil drawing about what went on in the garden (fig. 34). "El milagro de los pájaros" (The Miracle of the Birds), an eighteenth-century short story, was also published in the April issue. In the "Decorative Arts" section, there was a photograph of the

Fig. 31. Mina Perez-Chaumont
de Truffin at the Bal Watteau,
photograph, *Social*, April 1916.

Sra. MINA PEREZ-CHAUMONT DE TRUFFIN

Vistiendo el histórico traje Louis XV, que lució en su Bal-Watteau el diez y ocho
del pasado mes.

Fot. Irving T. Adams, de Boston.

Fig. 32. María Luisa Gómez
Mena de Cagigas at the Bal
Watteau, photograph, *Social*,
April 1916.

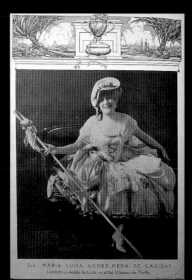

Sra. MARIA LUISA GOMEZ-MENA DE CAGIGAS

Luciendo un modelo de Lucile, en el Bal-Watteau che Truffin.

Fig. 34. Conrado W. Massaguer,

Como comienzan los chis-

mecitos, *Social*, April 1916.

Prince de Condé's salon at the Château of Chantilly, decorated in Louis XV style (the upholstery of the chairs are based on paintings by Watteau), and in "Men's Fashions" the theme was the clothing worn by political personalities of the eighteenth century.

The way of life, and up to a certain point even the private lives, of this social class, was made, if not public, at least known to the reading public who bought *Social*. Architecture, interior decoration, and fashion sections — both men's and women's—were the vehicles through which this information was furnished.

The large suburban homes in El Vedado, Miramar, La Víbora, El Cerro, and Country Club Park, designed by firms like Morales y Mata and Rafecas y Toñarely during the first period of *Social*, were subject matter for "Arte Arquitectónico," the monthly page dedicated to architecture (fig. 35). These residences were inspired by eighteenth-century classicism as well as by Beaux-Arts architecture in the United States, yet those styles were adapted to the needs of the tropics with large outside galleries with porticoes. The design of the houses also took into consideration twentieth-century living conditions as well as the need for sequences of reception rooms. These numerous houses represented a new and important landmark in the history of Cuban architecture (fig. 36).

The section on architectural art ran parallel to the health of the national economy. When the magazine was launched in 1916 the country was enjoying the effects of a boom produced by the high price of sugar during World War One; one page every month was dedicated to new Havana houses (fig. 37). The practice of showing one or two new residences in every issue continued until April 1921, a date that marked the abrupt fall in the postwar price of sugar. The construction business was severely affected by the recession and *Social* did not publish another new house until December. In 1922 new building types were added, such as hotels, schools, office buildings, monuments, clubs, and only occasionally, a new residence. (fig. 38).[5]

Interior decoration came to Havana under the influence of styles imported from the United States, mainly through the firm of H. F. Huber of New York. Mister and Mrs. Huber traveled frequently to Cuba, both on pleasure and business trips, and developed an extensive network of friends there. The firm eventually opened a branch in Havana and was given a number of commissions, the first being the decoration of the home of banker Herman Upmann in El Vedado. Other foreign firms soon followed, setting up shop in Havana, and decorating public buildings and the city's great residences. Tiffany and Company of New York created vitraux for shop windows and lamp designs for homes. Jansen's of Paris also opened a branch in Havana, taking advantage of capable local artisans.

Teodoro Bailey opened a studio on the elegant Paseo del Prado, dedicated to "artistic furniture and interior decoration" and Massaguer selected him to write the "Arte Arquitectónico" section. In it Bailey advised readers about function and use in decoration, discussing the demands of each room, the use of furniture, and of the upholstery and accessories that should be included in each decoration. Bailey's contributions were interrupted, probably because of a trip. On returning he wrote a long article for the April 1924 issue on "La influencia

5. We wish to thank Mr. Carlos Gles, a tireless investigator of Cuban architecture of the first third of the twentieth century and a great connoisseur of the architectural contribution of *Social*, for his very generous and valuable cooperation supplying information on the subject. In the opinion of Gles the residential architecture that appeared in *Social* suffered a change around 1925, which divides the magazine's coverage of the subject into two periods. The first, although frankly classical in terms of form, is picturesque when one considers the compositions of volumes designed to be seen from a side instead of frontally, as had been the norm during the nineteenth century and the first decade of the twentieth, except for large monumental corner buildings, like those on the ring. The principal examples of this period are the following residences: Josefina García viuda de Mesa (13 between C and D, Vedado), Pablo G. Mendoza (Paseo corner to 15, Vedado), Herman Upmann (17 corner to K, Vedado), Marquesa viuda de la Real Proclamación (17 corner to 6, Vedado), José Ignacio Lezama (17 corner to L, Vedado), Elvira Cil viuda de Sánchez (23 corner to B, Vedado), Frank Seigle (13 corner to E, Vedado), and Eduardo Montalvo (9 between 6 and 41, Alturas de Miramar). All of these houses are by Morales y Mata or Morales y Compañía. Other houses of this period are those of Juan Gelats (17 corner to H, Vedado, by Rafecas & Toñarely), Fausto Menocal (N corner to 25, Vedado, by Emilio de Soto) and Luis Menocal (G between 21 and 23, Vedado, by Herminio Lauderman). The second period is eclectic and stylisms proliferated. Thus, one finds Second Empire details in the Pedro Marín residence (Calzada corner to G, Vedado, designed by Francisco Centurión, ca. 1919–1923); the Carlos Miguel de Céspedes residence (Marina corner to Malecón, by César Guerra, 1926) is Neo-Gothic; the Eduardo Chibás residence (H corner to 17, Vedado, by Morales y Compañía, 1926) is Neo-Plateresque, and Morales y Compañía's own building (República 470, Havana, 1926) is Neo-Florentine. Finally, two houses introduced new styles that were to become extremely popular up until World War Two. The Juan Pedro Baró and Catalina Lasa residence (Paseo between 17 and 19, Vedado, by Govantes y Cabarrocas, 1927) was the first in Havana in the Art Deco style, and the residence of the Countess Buenavista (6 corner to Quinta Avenida, Miramar, by Morales y Compañía, 1928) initiated the Neo-Colonial style.

del arte antiguo español" (The Influence of Old Spanish Art). He illustrated it with a design that emphasized the use of wood for paneling dining room walls from floor to ceiling, following prevalent vogues in the United States and Europe. In more modest homes, he argued, "an identical effect can be achieved by adding wooden molding to the wall, then completing the idea of paneling with a coat of paint similar to that of the wood," a practice perpetuated in Havana for many years.

This eminent decorator therefore popularized Spanish styles, which had always been latent, both in architecture and in interior decoration. In those years, and even later, a taste for the Spanish Renaissance style spread in Havana, especially in architectural ornamentation and furniture. Work of great quality was achieved in that mode, all done in fine Cuban woods. Early in the 1920s, articles by a writer who signed himself as Casamejor (Betterhome) appeared in this section of *Social*, but we have been unable to determine who the author was. The campaign initiated by the magazine to incorporate interior decoration into architecture, added to the work of the decorators themselves, achieved its aims. It encouraged owners of new houses and commercial buildings to have interior decorators designing their new premises.

The topic of fashion also became important for *Social* when the writer Alejo Carpentier, under the pseudonym of Jaqueline, edited a column called "Cosas de Paris S.M. la Moda" (Things from Paris: Her Majesty the Fashion), from November 1924 to June 1927. Earlier, in the January 1922 issue, an advertisement asked, "What do you want to buy in Paris?" and answered, "If you wish to buy something that you cannot find on your trip to New York or in your expeditions to our shops here in Havana, write to Sra. Irene de Arlés, 3, rue Cimarosa, Paris, France. She is our representative in the French capital for everything related to purchases. Send her a letter today with your inquiries or order whatever you want. This magazine offers these services to its readers, absolutely free." We believe that the person hidden behind this pseudonym might have been the writer and fashion designer Ana María Borrero, a young woman who belonged to a distinguished family of Cuban intellectuals, who was soon to alternate with Alejo Carpentier in sending the magazine delicious chronicles on Parisian fashion. She later opened a fashion design and dressmaking shop in Havana, and with her taste, she helped many people who were not wealthy to dress elegantly.

When Ana María Borrero was announced as a contributor, *Social* presented her enthusiastically to readers in an extensive article. The first fashion report bearing her signature, published in January 1925, was an interview with Jean Patou, held during a long boat journey the two shared between France and New York. The famous fashion designer confided, "My Cuban clients constitute my biggest illusion. They have just the right lines, and besides, they are beautiful. But you must agree with me that chic cannot originate in tropical lands. Any of the ladies that forego frequent visits to Paris, would lose, without realizing it, the proper sense of perfect elegance."[6] Ana María Borrero would always maintain her contacts with the Maison Patou.

6. Ana María Borrero, "De la moda femenina: el viaje de Jean Patou a los Estados Unidos," *Social* 10 (January 1925): 58–61.

Fig. 35. Morales y Mata, Guillermo Lawton residence,

Social, January 1916.

Fig. 36. Morales y Mata, Pablo G. Mendoza residence,

Social, February 1916.

Arte Arquitectónico

Vista de los puentes desde una de las terrazas.

Gran salón de recepciones.

(Fotos Buendía)

Una de las escaleras de entrada.

El mes pasado, y con una suntuosa recepción, se inauguró el magnífico edificio que en la Playa de Marianao acaba de construir el notable arquitecto señor Goyeneche, para el Havana

Yacht Club, nuestra aristocrática y prestigiosa sociedad.

Varios aspectos de ese espléndido palacio que honra a su constructor y a nuestra capital, ofrecemos aquí.

Aspecto general de la nueva casa del Havana Yacht Club.

49

Fig. 37. Morales y Mata, Herman Upmann residence,

Social, June 1916.

Fig. 38. Rafael Goyeneche, Havana Yacht Club,

Social, February 1925.

Written in elegant, fluid, and charming prose, her articles on fashion were enjoyed by many readers. One of the most delightful of her pieces was "Lo que dice Paris..." (What Paris is Saying...), about the latest fashions for the summer of 1925, or another, titled "Viajes de placer" (Traveling for Pleasure), in which she recommended the proper selection of clothing, and warned against taking things that would not be used. Another article, "Los trajes iguales" (Identical Dresses), suggested criteria of selection for a woman faced with the styles imposed by some fourteen couturiers in Paris. She also explained the mystery of how fashion designers protect their designs each season from being copied. She commented that Jean Patou had an under-the-table pact with imitators, since he felt that additional publicity for his designs was important to their worldwide diffusion.

Ana María Borrero divided women into three groups: those who need to copy, those who do not wish to be copied, and those who care neither to copy nor be copied. According to the writer, those of the third category "are the truly elegant women. They are not interested in the least in copying and couldn't care less if they are copied. They are elegant in their own right, and they take much less interest in clothing than people think. They have no problem in opening their wardrobes to everyone." Two years later, in 1927, Jean Patou presented his models at El Encanto, one of Havana's best department stores, where he offered a "magnificent collection, including evening wear." The photographic coverage devoted to the Maison Patou was a visual gift for *Social*'s readers.

These chronicles did not appear regularly, because Ana María Borrero herself was probably busy getting ready to open her own fashion house, late in 1927. Nevertheless, other articles by her continued to come out in *Social* at the same time that the advertisements for her high-fashion shop at O'Reilly 51 appeared in the last issues of 1927.[7] Toward the end of the 1920s and in the early 1930s, *Social* also published fashion designs from Paris by Lucien Lelong, Worth, Louise Boulanger, Maggie Rouff, and hats by Germaine Paige. During the 1930s, dresses and accessories were modeled by young ladies from Cuba's best society. In February 1932 an article referred to the death of designer Esperanza Durruthy, in New York. She was described as "a brilliant Cuban artist, a valued contributor to this magazine, in whose pages her designs often appeared. In this issue we publish the last design that she sent us from her residence in the Babel de Hierro (The Iron Babel; New York). She also drew one of our covers several months ago with the singular grace and good taste that characterized all her work." This young artist was an important contributor and her death a distressing loss (fig. 39). Havana, however, could still count on the talent of Ana María Borrero, with her shop, and of the equally famous Ismael Bernabeu, the fashion designer with a long and refined career behind him, still working with his sisters, first at Aguacate Street in Old Havana and later in his fashion house in El Vedado.

7. These chronicles were widely read because from·1910 to 1930 a select group of women ordered their clothes and accessories directly from the most famous couturiers in Paris or New York. Others, forming a broader circle, were dressed either by designers operating out of Havana who followed the styles set by the city's leading shops or by clothing boutiques in the largest department stores. Others still made use of smaller independent dressmakers. This elegant world of fashion was first clustered around Obispo and O'Reilly Streets and the wide Paseo del Prado, where the most luxurious fashion houses were found. Later, the fashion area spread to San Rafael, Neptuno, and Galiano Streets, as one can see from the advertisements published in the press at the time. The successful La Casa Grande and El Encanto, soon to become the two largest store chains on the island, were located on Galiano Street.

But *Social* was far more than just a magazine for Cuba's wealthy class; it acted as well as a vehicle of cultural renewal. Its pages revealed the complex process of change in this challenging period, one that was both contradictory and filled with hope. To that end the magazine emphasized the importance of new art forms and contemporary artistic doctrines, above all in literature.[8] Well-known authors, however, were not the only force that gave the magazine its quality. *Social* also published less known work, such as *Fantoches* (Puppets) (1926), a Cuban novel in twelve chapters written by eleven different authors.[9] The novel ran from January 1926 for eleven consecutive months. Another novel, *Cinco soluciones a un triángulo amoroso* (Five Solutions to a Love Triangle), began in the January 1927 issue. It was written by six authors.[10] Both works were illustrated by the best graphic artists of the moment.

Everything in the publication was interconnected: if there was a literary piece or the reproduction of a painting, sculpture, or musical score, it would be accompanied by a chronicle or text about the author. Moreover, Alejo Carpentier, then in Paris, would file brilliant reports on whatever happened in literature and the arts, including film. *Social* was "the journalistic organ of Cuba's young intellectuals," as Emilio Roig de Leuchsenring, the publication's literary editor, expressed in his "Notas" of the February 1925 issue. Beyond this, the magazine was also a vehicle for the diffusion of ideas of El grupo minorista, an association of intellectuals, writers, and artists, from both the right and the left, established in 1923. The group gathered occasionally at banquets or at meetings to examine and attempt to influence the country's policies, reform public life, and lead on issues of art and literature. Although the group had no specific publication through which to accomplish its aims, nor a definite program, its projects were known because almost all of its members worked at important publications, but mostly at *Social*—both Massaguer and Emilio Roig de Leuchsenring were *minoristas*, as the members called themselves. In the June 1927 issue the group published its manifesto giving the reasons for its existence and outlining a nationalist ideology.[11]

The works of Emilio Roig de Leuchsenring (1889–1964) in *Social* deserves special mention. Linked with Massaguer by a solid friendship built up over decades shared in journalism, Roig contributed to one of the first issues of *Social* in 1916 with a section titled "Cartas" (Letters), signed with the pseudonym of Milio. These articles were criticisms of customs reigning in a Havana struggling to

8. Collaborations that stand out are those by José María Chacón y Calvo, Enrique Hernández Miyares, Enrique José Varona, Alfonso Hernández Catá, Héctor de Saavedra, François García de Cisneros, Luis Rodríguez Embil, Enrique Serpa, José Zacarías Tallet, Ramiro Guerra, Juan Marinello, Rubén Martínez Villena, Mariano Brull, Alejo Carpentier, José Antonio Fernández de Castro, Bernardo Barros, Fernando Ortíz, Emeterio Santovenia, Carolina Poncet, María and Aurora Villar Buceta, Gonzalo de Quesada y Miranda, and Álvaro de la Iglesia.

9. The writers who took part were: Carlos Loveira, who wrote the first and final chapters; Guillermo Martínez Márquez; Alberto Lamar Schweyer; Jorge Mañach; Federico de Ibarzábal; Alfonso Hernández Catá; Arturo Alfonso Roselló; Rubén Martínez Villena; Enrique Serpa; Max Henríquez Ureña; and Emilio Roig de Leuchsenring.

10. The writers were: Introduction, Guillermo Martínez Márquez; Solution 1, Jésus J. López; Solution 2, Enrique Serpa; Solution 3, Ofelia Rodríguez Acosta; Solution 4, Carlos Loveira; Solution 5, ending, Emilio Roig de Leuchsenring.

11. The document also explained the Protesta de los trece (Protest of the Thirteen). This is the name given to the act of protest against the administration of President Alfredo Zayas, held on 19 March 1923, by a group of young intellectuals, against the purchase by the government of the former Convent of Santa Clara, considered a jewel of Cuban architecture of the seventeenth century, and which the government planned to tear down and use the land to build new facilities. La Protesta de los trece triggered a debate on the convent, which was saved and still stands today as one of the main monuments of colonial Havana.

rise above its colonial lethargy. They were written by Roig in the style of the Cuban *costumbristas* (folkloric chroniclers) of the nineteenth century. Hermann is another of the pseudonyms that Emilio Roig used in the "Acotaciones Literarias" (Literary Annotations) section of the magazine, which appeared between 1919 and 1923. He continued to write for the magazine even after he became its literary editor in 1918. During this new phase he contributed numerous articles on local customs and history under the pen name of Cristóbal de La Habana. Even after he ended his editorship, Roig's work continued to appear in the magazine. *Social* also had important foreign contributors, among them Rubén Darío, Alfonso Reyes, Gabriela Mistral, José Vasconcelos, Paul Valéry, Juan Ramón Jiménez, Federico García Lorca, Alfonsina Storni, Langston Hughes, Alejandro Casona, Juana de Ibarbouru, Paul Claudel, Vicente Blasco Ibáñez, Manuel and Antonio Machado, Rufino Blanco Fombona, José Santos Chocano, Max Henríquez Ureña, Enrique González Martínez, Francis de Miomandre, and Miguel de Unamuno.

Fig. 39. Esperanza Durruthy,

design for evening gown,

***Social*, February 1932.**

Massaguer's work has never been fully evaluated. His contribution has been acclaimed in Cuba as a humorist, illustrator, and caricaturist, but this knowledge has not spread abroad. Neither has anyone properly measured his influence on younger generations of Cuban artists, such as Juan David, whose forceful work appeared in the pages of *Social* in 1936 and 1937. His contributions to the theory of humor also awaits study. In that respect "La taquigrafía del retrato" (The Shorthand of Portraiture), which he published in the November 1927 issue of *Social*, is important. In that article he explained the characteristics of the genre and listed the most important Cuban and foreign artists. In first place was Sirio (García), an excellent Cuban caricaturist who lived in Madrid, where he contributed to the leading newspapers and magazines. Other Cubans Massaguer mentioned were Rafael Blanco, Abela (also a painter), and Her-Car. From Latin America he named Málaga Grenet (a Mexican contributor to *Vanity Fair*), Covarrubias, Toño Salazar, and from more distant lands: Sem, Sime, Bagaría, and Fruch.

The contribution of the Instituto de Artes Gráficas (founded at the end of 1916) to the development of graphic arts in Cuba also deserves study. *Social* moved its offices to the institute, and a few months later (January 1917) Massaguer brought the magazine out in full color. Neither his work as a publicist nor as editor of other important magazines (such as *Gráfico* [1913–1918], a weekly with international news, illustrated with photos, and *Carteles* [June 1919], of which he became assistant director, and later, artistic director) has been studied. In 1925 Massaguer participated in the edition of *Libro de Cuba* (The Book of Cuba), an essential reference book for anyone interested in Cuba from pre–Columbian times to the date of publication. After *Social* closed in 1937, Massaguer returned, ten years later, as editor of *Desfile* (Parade) magazine (1947), but times were different, and the magazine closed after several months. From then on he limited his contributions to caricatures and drawings for national and international publications. Among these one stands out: *El doble-nueve* (The Double-Nine) (1943) depicting Roosevelt and Churchill playing a game of dominoes against Mussolini and Hitler while Stalin and Hirohito look on. A work of important propaganda for the Allied cause, it was published the world over (fig. 40). During this later stage of his life, he became a caricaturist for the daily *Información*, from 1945 to 1949, and, as of 1949, he contributed weekly sections called "Massaguerías" and "Massaguericaturas" to *El Mundo*. There he also did a column called "En esta Habana nuestra" (In this Havana of Ours). In 1944 he was decorated Caballero in the Orden Nacional Carlos Manuel de Céspedes, a Comendador of the Orden Nacional

Fig. 40. Conrado W. Massaguer, *El doble-nueve*, **watercolor and ink, 1943.**

de la Cruz Roja, and not long after was made Caballero of the Orden de Finlay. In 1952 he accepted the post of director of public relations of the Cuban Institute of Tourism. In 1956 he published his *Autobiografía* (Autobiography). Conrado Massaguer died in Havana on 18 October 1965.

Because of his personal, colloquial style, the motto of *El Esquife,* a small Havana broadsheet dedicated to humor, published during the first period of freedom of the press (1812), could have as well applied to him: "Witty criticisms correct better than solemn and bitter diatribe." That was his method as an artist, editor, publicist, journalist, and, above all, educator during a significant part of the history of the Cuban Republic. □

TRINIDAD, EPISCOPAL PRO-CATHEDRAL, HAVANA, CUBA (C. G. & F.)

Drawn by Mr. Goodhue

Fig. 1. Bertram Grosvenor Goodhue, Santísima Trinidad Episcopal Cathedral, drawing, Havana, 1905 (demolished). From Bertram Grosvenor

American Architects in Cuba: 1900–1930

By José A. Gelabert-Navia

José A. Gelabert-Navia is a practicing architect and associate professor at the University of Miami School of Architecture, Coral Gables, Florida. His work has received awards from the American Institute of Architects and has been exhibited, most recently at the Museum of Contemporary Art, North Miami, Florida, whose new facility he designed in collaboration with Charles Gwathmey.

When the Cuban Republic was established in 1902, following the Spanish-American War and the U.S. military occupation, the stage was set for the influx of immigration and foreign investment that had not taken place during the final half-century of Spanish domination. Spanish immigrants came in numbers unparalleled in the first four hundred years of colonization: two hundred thousand alone arrived between the period of 1902 to 1910. According to Hugh Thomas: "The Spanish migration to Cuba between 1511 and 1899 was, without a doubt, smaller than the one reached between 1900 and 1925."[1] With them came many architects, artisans, sculptors, and builders who learned their trade under the mantle of turn-of-the-century *modernismo* in Spain. The North American immigrants also came, but in far fewer numbers. They settled in Havana and the Isle of Pines (which many sought to annex to the United States). The United States replaced Spain as the major influence on Cuba from 1900 on. Browsing through *Social*, a remarkable magazine edited by Conrado W. Massaguer (1889–1965) between 1916 and 1933, one can see how extraordinary and widespread this fascination with the United States really was. Amid articles on current movements in music and literature were advertisements highlighting banking, real estate, and shopping opportunities available to Cubans in the United States. *Social* went so far as to open an office in the McAlpin Hotel in New York to facilitate these exchanges.

In the space of twenty-five years, the work of North American architects in Cuba would move from the profoundly "regional" design of Bertram Goodhue's Santísima Trinidad Episcopal Cathedral (1905) to the universal classical style of McKim, Mead and White's Hotel Nacional (1930). The profusion of detail of Goodhue's facade gradually gave way to the Spanish colonial quotations present in Kenneth Murchison's Central Railway Station (1912) and Barclay, Parsons and Klapp's Customs House (1914). By the 1920s Schultze and Weaver all but reduced the regional interpretation to a series of refined decorative details. The programmatic charge was clearly to move away from the reserved Cuban Baroque prevalent during the period of the Spanish colony and into the fashionable Beaux-Arts style that was flourishing in the United States following the success of the World Columbian Exposition of 1893, which had become synonymous with the Gilded Age.

---

1. Hugh Thomas, *Cuba, la lucha por la libertad* (Barcelona: Ediciones Grijalbo, S.A., 1974), 647. See also Manuel Moreno Fraginals, *La historia como arma y otros estudios sobre ingenios y plantaciones* (Barcelona: Crítica, 1983).

Economically and politically, the period came to a close with the stock market crash of 1929 and its aftermath. If Beaux-Arts Classicism would finally fade out of fashion, the search for international inspiration and recognition would not. With few exceptions, in the three decades that followed, architectural practice in Cuba remained a reflection of international currents — Art Moderne in the 1930s and the International Style in the years before the Revolution of 1959.

Bertram Grosvenor Goodhue (1869–1924) was the first major American architect to design a building in Cuba. The Santísima Trinidad Episcopal Cathedral, of Havana, designed in 1905, had a four-bay nave and a two-bay chancel (fig. 1). The walls of the church were windowless, only the structural piers provided any articulation. Light came from clerestory windows with paneled surrounds that continued the lines of the structure below. Goodhue concentrated Churrigueresque decoration on the facade and the upper section of the bell tower. As was his style, details only alluded to a tradition rather than quoting directly from it. We have no record of the architect ever having visited Cuba or being acquainted firsthand with its architecture. In fact, there were no Churrigueresque buildings in colonial Cuba. The style of the Santísima Trinidad probably owed more to Goodhue's interest in Mexican architecture, recorded in two publications for which he produced drawings: *Mexican Memories* (1892) and *Spanish Colonial Architecture* (1901), written in collaboration with Sylvester Baxter and Henry Greenwood Peabody. On the other hand, his design for the Santísima Trinidad was his first attempt at incorporating a Spanish colonial style into his work, anticipating the much more publicized designs for the 1911–1914 Panama-California Exhibition in San Diego, California.

Since the turn of the century the Episcopal Church was making inroads in Cuba. To embark on a major project such as a full-fledged cathedral, given that the Protestant Church was still struggling to gain converts and the North American presence only numbered about 10 percent of the total 261,000 foreign immigrants, was a bold move, though not unusual for the aggressive efforts at spreading the Protestant faith.[2] Richard Oliver speculates that "the commission may have come to Goodhue through his friendship with [James W.] Gillespie, who owned a house in Mariel, Cuba,"[3] and for whom Goodhue had designed a home in Montecito, California, in 1902. Gillespie, a lifelong friend and patron, sponsored and accompanied Goodhue on his first extended travel overseas when they both went to Isfahan, Shiraz, and Samarkand in 1902.[4] It would seem fitting that it would also be Gillespie who would promote his first work abroad, a building that traditionally became known as "*la iglesia de los americanos*" (the church of the Americans). Goodhue went on to design another building for the Episcopal Church in Cuba — the Todos los Santos Church in Guantánamo, which was not built (fig. 2).

At the time Goodhue began designing his church, Cuba gained privileged access to the U.S. market through a reciprocal trade agreement that reduced tariffs for sugar exports to the United States by 20 percent in return for reductions of up to 40 percent on a range of U.S. imports to the island. The price of sugar remained high during the second decade of the century, in great measure

---

2. Early commissions of the Czech-American architect Antonin Nechodoma were Protestant churches for the Dominican Republic and Puerto Rico. See Thomas S. Marvel, *Antonin Nechodoma* (Gainesville: University of Florida Press, 1994).

3. Richard Oliver, *Bertram Grosvenor Goodhue* (New York: The Architectural History Foundation, 1983), 86.

4. Ibid., 41.

Fig. 2. Bertram Grosvenor Goodhue, proposed Episcopal Church of Todos los Santos, drawing, Guantánamo, 1905. From Bertram Grosvenor Goodhue, *A Book of Architectural and Decorative Drawings* (New York: The Architectural Book Publishing Company, 1914), 43.

because of the international crisis created by World War One. Other Cuban goods, such as tobacco, rum, and nickel, would find new markets in the United States, while foreign investment on the island increased. In 1910 José Miguel Gómez became Cuba's first freely elected president following the second U.S. intervention. Gómez, who was known for his political skills, sought foreign investment. A political scandal concerning the exchange of the site of the former colonial Arsenal for the site of the former Villanueva Railway Station became central to that legacy.

Havana boasted one of the greatest boatyards in the Spanish Empire, the Arsenal. At the beginning of the twentieth century it became a far cry from its heyday in the eighteenth, when it claimed to be the finest in the New World. The Villanueva Railway Station, built in 1837, stood outside the Old City, near the Puerta de Tierra and the Puerta de Monserrate, and belonged to the United Railway Company.[5] Like the Arsenal, it had become an eyesore, and now was in the way of an expanding Havana. The British investors who had acquired the Villanueva Railway Station as part of the transaction that gave them control of the Havana United Railways proposed to President Gómez a trade of their site for what eventually turned out to be a much larger one at the Arsenal. In addition, the British company promised a new and elegant train station with shops, warehouses, and an elevated railway so as not to interfere with street traffic. The old Villanueva station was to be replaced by five new buildings, parks, and a new incineration plant, all at a cost of $6.5 million.[6] Only the station was built.

The building commission engaged New York architect Kenneth McKenzie Murchison (1872–1939), who designed the project in 1910. Murchison had a reputation as a designer of railway facilities, having won the competition for Baltimore's Pennsylvania Station in 1909, completed in 1911.[7] He also designed a number of stations for the Long Island, Union, and Erie-Lackawanna lines before and after receiving the commission for the Havana station, including the Scranton (1908), Long Beach (1910), Manhattan Beach (1910), Johnstown

5. Thomas, *Cuba*, 660.

6. Herminio Portell-Vilá, *Nueva historia de la República de Cuba* (Miami: La Moderna Poesía, 1985), 153.

7. Allen Freeman, "Restoring the Remaining Railroad Extravaganzas," *Architecture* (June 1988): 92.

(1915), Lehigh Valley (1915), and Lackawanna (1917) stations. Murchison later won the competition for the Union Terminal Building in Jacksonville, Florida (1916–1919).[8] In all likelihood it was the relationship to the Union line, which operated the Havana line prior to the British acquisition, that resulted in Murchison being awarded the commission for that project.

The Central Railway Station, completed in 1912, was one of the final hurrahs of that particularly nineteenth-century building type, the monumental railway station, which had so captured the imagination of architects schooled in the Beaux-Arts (fig. 3). Murchison's design, however, was quite different from the cavernous fantasies of New York, with its allusions to Roman baths, or London's cathedrals of wrought iron and glass. As in his earlier project for Baltimore, the architect produced a reserved, laconic piece that did much to recall the Spartan classicism characteristic of the architecture of Renaissance Spain. The building has a tripartite division, with the baggage room and café flanking the main waiting room. As is typical in most terminal stations, the tracks are perpendicular to the exit concourse. The main entrance is modest and pragmatic but made prominent by two monumental towers that recall La Giralda in Seville. The towers, containing bathrooms, stairs, and elevators, are rusticated at the base and rise with a minimum of openings, decoration being reserved for a series of diagonal rows of shells along the central portion and a coat of arms below the upper balcony. This feature, with its stone balusters and brackets and Serlian window above, became a favorite motif of both Schultze and Weaver and McKim, Mead and White in the 1920s. Even today, the station rises above the fabric of Old Havana, its twin towers acting as beacons and locators for all the city to see.

In sharp contrast to the austere elegance of the train station stands the old Customs House, or Aduana, designed by Barclay, Parsons and Klapp (fig. 4). It sits at the corner of Amargura and San Pedro Streets in Old Havana. Like the train station, it represented an urban intervention at a scale rarely seen during

8. Richard Martin, "Jacksonville, Florida's Union Terminal Building," *Historical Society Bulletin* (May–June 1989): 33–36.

Fig. 4. Barclay, Parsons and Klapp, Customs House, Havana, 1914. From a postcard. Courtesy of Otto G. Richter Library, University of Miami, Coral Gables, Florida, Cuban Collection. (Address: Amargura corner to San Pedro.)

the Spanish colony, breaking away from the tightly knit urban texture of the old core of the city. The structure was built on a full city block in front of San Francisco Wharf, the most active in the port. The building's main characteristic is its long arcade, running the entire length of the wharf and punctuated by a central section with two towers at either end.

The architects seemed unable to cope with the extraordinary length of the building, trying hopelessly to break it up with various changes in height, a pedimented entrance, and finally the twin towers. Like a train with cars placed out of sequence, the design is awkward and ill-proportioned and the transitions in height are largely unresolved. The details, though interesting, bear little relationship to the ensemble, with the arcades remaining too low for the mass above them. The towers are much less successful than the elegant ones of the train station, almost incidental to the lower portion of the building. The Islamic flavor of the details owed more to the reinvented Hispano-Moorish tradition that the United States was trying to establish in their public building program for the Caribbean than to a true understanding of either culture.

By the middle of the nineteenth century the old core of the city, La Habana Vieja (Old Havana), was bursting at the seams. The tearing down of the city walls by the train station and the Arsenal opened the western limits of the city. La Habana Vieja remained as the center of trade but not as the preferred choice for housing for the emerging native-born ruling class. New villas and palaces began to rise in the areas of El Cerro and El Vedado, beyond the original fortified walls. Two of the most prominent members of the haute bourgeoisie were Manuel Carvajal and Margarita Mendoza, Marqueses de Avilés. In 1915 they commissioned Thomas Hastings to design a residence at Seventeenth and I Streets in El Vedado.[9]

Thomas Hastings (1860–1929) was born in New York City, studied at Columbia University, and afterwards went to Paris, where he attended the École des Beaux-Arts in the Atelier André (later Laloux), until 1884. He returned to New

9. In the February 1916 issue of *Social*, there is a project for the same house by Félix Cabarrocas, who in time became Cuba's preeminent classical architect.

York where he worked for a little over one year with McKim, Mead and White before the commission for Henry Flagler's Ponce de León Hotel (1889) in St. Augustine, Florida, allowed him and his colleague, John Carrère, to set up an independent practice. They later designed there the Alcázar Hotel and the Presbyterian and Methodist churches before returning to New York City in 1887 and establishing one of the preeminent classicist practices in the United States, one that included the building of the New York Public Library (1911).

In *Les annales* the French writer Paul Morand wrote derisively about the monumental residences that dotted El Vedado as "*des Petits Trianons en beurre*." The notable Cuban architect and historian José María Bens Arrarte, outraged by this comment, suggested in a 1929 article that Morand listen to the advice of the French poet and novelist Paul Geraldy, who in 1925 had also begun to see pearls amid the ostentation of the Riviera and Biarritz.[10] One such similar pearl in Havana was the house at Seventeenth and I.

Hastings unquestionably was one of the pivotal figures of the so-called American Renaissance style, and the mansion admirably displays his hand. The house is composed of a major central element with a single-story pavilion on either side (fig. 5). The main block has a tripartite organization formed by the parlor, living room, and dining room. In the right pavilion are the service areas and kitchen. In the left pavilion an L-shaped arcade wraps around the library and parlor and ends at the dining room (fig. 6). In its day it had Pompeian-style frescoes on its deep crimson walls. This was perhaps the most outstanding feature of the building and certainly a daring move in Hastings's style of this period.

The house is set back from Seventeenth Street, allowing a full view of the structure and its towering two-story portico and colossal Corinthian columns, mirrored by twin royal palm trees in the forecourt. Marble steps lead to a wrought-iron chancel flanked by a pair of bronze dogs cast from the originals at the Château de Chantilly. For many years this remained the most idiosyncratic detail of the house (fig. 7).

10. José María Bens Arrarte, "La arquitectura en La Habana del 1928," *Social* 14 (January 1929): 24, 78.

The design of the house is an excellent example of Hastings's style. In the architect's 1929 obituary, Francis S. Swales wrote: "Mr. Hastings chiefly was credited with the creating and fostering of fine technique and that kind of designing which adheres closely to precedent. He recognized that France in the eighteenth century did better with the combination of architecture and landscape accessories than had been done previously or since, and he chose the monuments of the periods of the Louis as the models upon which to base all his designs whenever they provided a precedent that could be adapted."[11]

The vestibule, in Caen stone, pays, nevertheless, a classical homage to the Antillean *medio punto* (fig. 8).[12] On one side of the foyer is the library, on the other, a spectacular staircase with an elaborate wrought-iron railing and a monumental stained-glass window around the curved landing. There are two consoles in the vestibule: one, in marble, held a copy of Canova's portrait of Paulina Borghese; the other, in grey lacquer, held two tall bronze candelabra. Renée García Kohly, writing in *Social* in 1930, also described a series of unusual oriental green carpets and two Wedgwood porcelain vases.[13]

Two enormous bronze candleholders and vases with fresh palms helped to lead the way into the central hall. This room contained a sofa, two large chairs upholstered by Jansen of Paris, and a single table in the center.[14] Beyond, at the end, a marble sculpture surrounded by the vegetation of the garden was visible. The house, while not outwardly deviating from the classicism that characterized Hastings's work, showed the architect's ability to make sophisticated references to regional details — a characteristic that drew Flagler to him

11. Francis S. Swales, Thomas Hastings's obituary, *Pencil Points* (December 1929): 10.

12. The term *medio punto*, particularly in the Dominican Republic and Puerto Rico, describes a series of screening devices that create a partial separation between the foyer and the hall. See Jorge Rigau, *Puerto Rico 1900* (New York: Rizzoli, 1992). [This use of the term *medio punto* is different from that associated with Cuban colonial architecture, a semicircular fan of colored glass above a door or window.]

13. Renée García Kohly, "El Palacete de los Marqueses de Avilés," *Social* 15 (June 1930): 31–35.

14. In later years Jansen would be commissioned by the second owner of the house, Isabel Falla de Suero, to substantially refurbish the interiors. Many details date from that alteration.

Fig. 9. Carrère and Hastings, residence of the Marqueses de Avilés, dining room, Havana, 1915. Photograph by Tetsuo Fukaya, 1994.

Fig. 10. Carrère and Hastings, residence of the Marqueses de Avilés, doorway on second-floor terrace, Havana, 1915. Photograph by Tetsuo Fukaya, 1994.

twenty-five years earlier. Hastings, who later designed a Spanish Revival mansion on the shores of the Hudson River in upstate New York, was now drawing as well from tropical influences by paying homage to the most Cuban of architectural devices: the *portal*.

The parlor had gilded furniture upholstered with Aubusson fabric and an Aubusson carpet. The piano, which had a gold patina, was surrounded by mirrors and screens with portraits and graceful bibelots. The most striking element of the room was a large lamp with medallions of Baccarat crystal. The living room and dining room are Adamesque in style (fig. 9). On the second floor three bedrooms open to a sitting area, in turn leading to a second-story terrace located above the arcade (fig. 10).

The house stayed in the hands of the Mendoza family for only a few years after the death of the Marqués de Avilés. It was then purchased circa 1932 by David Suero and his wife, Isabel, a daughter of a sugar planter, Laureano Falla Gutiérrez.

A period of reciprocal benefits encouraging Cuba to concentrate its trade and fortunes with the United States peaked between February and May 1920, when the world price of sugar rose to a record of 22.5 cents per pound and fortunes were made overnight. Since the first decade of the century, banks began to appear in the old section of Havana along the traditionally merchant streets of Obispo and O'Reilly. One of the chief institutions of this period was the National City Bank of New York. Its main office was designed in 1925 at O'Reilly and Compostela Streets by Walker and Gillette, designers of the bank's headquarters at 55 Wall Street (fig. 11).[15] The firm had been established in New York City for over a decade prior to receiving the commission. Their practice ranged from eclectic country houses in upstate New York to stately Manhattan *pieds-à-terre*, but by 1914 they began to design banks, eventually becoming the

15. The importance of the relationship between the bank and the government of Gerardo Machado is clear from the fact that in 1925, during a rare visit to New York, President Machado took time to attend a reception at the bank's headquarters hosted by its president, Charles Mitchell. Thomas, *Cuba*, 323.

Fig. 11. Walker and Gillette,

National City Bank of

New York, Havana, 1925.

Photograph author's

collection. (Address: O'Reilly

402 corner to Compostela.)

Fig. 11. Walker and Gillette, National City Bank of New York, Havana, 1925. Photograph author's collection. (Address: O'Reilly 402 corner to Compostela.)

official architects of National City Bank;[16] the October 1930 issue of *Architectural Record* illustrates branches built in New York City, Brooklyn, Buenos Aires, and Panama City. The Havana bank borrowed its majestic and monumental colonnade from its Wall Street counterpart, but now reduced to a single story, using the typology of the temple. The building has a tripartite organization with the central element containing a portico framed by four colossal Corinthian columns behind which are three doorways with matching oculi above. The portico comes out to the edge of the street, providing a covered entrance. The design was not innovative in its use of elements, nor did it alter the organization of an already standard plan typical of many banks of this period. However, its firm and assured use of the classical language was unique, especially in its reaffirmation of the grid of Old Havana and in the way it turned an all-important corner by means of a monumental two-story pilaster. In 1925 this design set the course for a brief period of sober classicism in the architecture of Havana.

President Gerardo Machado (1925–1933) developed an ambitious public works program. This included building a central highway connecting the whole island, constructing a capitol that sought to rival its United States counterpart, and launching numerous other engineering and construction projects largely concentrated in Havana. Wishing to project an image of stability, Machado was host to the Sexta Conferencia Internacional Americana, of 1928, attended by President Calvin Coolidge. It was in this climate that the Cuban American Realty Company, known in Cuba as the Sindicato Nacional, traveled to New York City to engage the firm of Schultze and Weaver to design several projects in Havana. Leonard Schultze (born in Chicago, 1877; died 1951) had studied architecture under E. Léonard Masquerey at the Metropolitan Museum School. He was the chief designer and office manager of Warren and Wetmore (of Grand Central Station fame) when he left to form his own firm with Major Spenser Fullerton Weaver (born in Philadelphia, 1880; died 1939), an engineer with substantial contacts in New York financial circles.

16. Alwyn T. Covell, "Variety in Architectural Practice," *Architectural Record* (April 1914): 277–355.

Fig. 12. Schultze and Weaver,

Sevilla Biltmore Hotel,

view from Paseo del Prado,

Havana, 1921. Photograph

author's collection. (Address:

Trocadero 55–59 between

Prado and Zulueta.)

Schultze and Weaver's first design for Havana consisted of a major addition to the Sevilla Biltmore Hotel, in 1921 (fig. 12).[17] The hotel was built on a narrow lot, barely one hundred feet wide, on Havana's most prestigious street, the Paseo del Prado.

Schultze and Weaver were faced with the daunting task of providing an interesting sequence from the street to the elevator lobby, almost 144 feet away. They did this by creating an interior street, five meters wide, that opened to a series of ten shops with a mezzanine above. This device, similar to the French *passages* and Spanish *pasajes*, also became fashionable in late-nineteenth-century Havana, as in the Hotel Pasaje. Schultze and Weaver arranged a sequence that began at the street arcade and continued along the vaulted foyer, leading to an interior courtyard. The arcade was composed of five limestone arches on either side with a glazed sash and an iron frame within. The idea was clever, creating three sources of light within the tight constraints of an interior lot. There were two light wells above the mezzanine, left and right of the courtyard next to the

17. First designed and constructed by the firm of Arellano y Mendoza in 1908.

adjoining properties. The third produced a dramatic atrium at the center of the hotel, providing light as well as cross ventilation to all the hotel rooms, four by six meters each. Cross ventilation was essential at the time, and the architects addressed this need throughout, even including operating sashes above the doorways of the arcade's shops. The interiors were all of carved limestone and stucco. A series of ornate wrought-iron gates and wooden screens with compositional ornaments now surrounded the existing patio (fig. 13), predating the Moorish motifs that the firm used successfully in the Miami Biltmore Hotel three years later.

The building, 145 feet high to the bottom of the roof terrace (almost exactly its depth), has eight floors above the base, plus the roof facilities. The base carries five arches, broken up by a progression of flat openings following the first and last bay. The windows above feature alternating triangular and segmental pediments. The roof terrace has a series of large windows on wood frames. For all windows Schultze and Weaver used the vernacular *persianas* (wood louvers) but framed them in classical moldings of cast cement.

Fig. 13. Schultze and Weaver,

Sevilla Biltmore Hotel, original

courtyard, Havana, 1921.

Photograph Narciso Menocal

collection.

The Sevilla Biltmore's most singular attribute, however, was its roof terrace (fig. 14), of which Joseph Hergersheimer wrote in his 1921 travel memoir of Havana:

> The audience melted away — I was unable to discover if they were flattered or annoyed — and I found myself actually seated at one of the small tables on the fringe of the dansant at the Sevilla. The Cascade Orchestra from the Biltmore, their necks hung with the imitation wreaths of Hawaii, were playing a musical pastiche of many lands and a single purpose; and there among the girls from the New York Follies and girls on follies of their own, colliding with race track touts from Jefferson Park and suave predatory gentlemen from San Francisco, I found a whole section of young Cuba.[18]

The room featured a curious mix of colossal Corinthian pilasters with an elaborate, almost feminine, Spanish faience tile wainscot and base. The balusters were made of cast stone, with travertine marble railing. The ceilings were coffered with quatrefoil inserts.

18. Joseph Hergersheimer, *San Cristóbal de La Habana* (London: William Heinemann, 1921), 69.

Fig. 15. George Duncan, Torre del Reloj, monument drawn on photograph, Miramar, Marianao, Havana, 1920. Photograph Narciso Menocal collection. (Address: 5ª Avenida corner to 10, Miramar.)

Fig. 16. Schultze and Weaver, La Concha, Marianao, Havana, 1928. Photograph Narciso Menocal collection. (Address: 5ª Avenida between 112 and 116, Miramar.)

Fig. 17. Schultze and Weaver, Cuba-American Jockey Club, Marianao, Havana, 1928. Photograph Narciso Menocal collection. (Address: Avenida 63 between 106 and 108, Marianao.)

Schultze and Weaver later became the preeminent designers of hotels in the United States, responsible for the Biltmore (1924) and Roney Plaza (1925) in Miami, as well as the most famous hotel of its day, New York's Waldorf-Astoria (1931). They were a natural choice to give form to Havana's elegant society, which frequented the Waldorf when visiting New York. As the architects of the Biltmore-Bowman chain, they were actively involved in all of the developments with which this firm would participate in Havana, providing plush hotels and private seaside clubs to a society that was "rushing to live," to borrow Bens Arrarte's phrase, "in English and in motor cars."[19]

Between 1915 and 1930 a number of suburban developments appeared west of Havana. They were made possible by the new bridge that connected El Vedado with Miramar. The most significant of these suburbs was owned by José López Rodríguez and Ramón González de Mendoza. Carlos Miguel de Céspedes, in association with José Manuel Cortina, also formed a company called Cortina y Céspedes Real Estate, with offices at O'Reilly 33. Their most significant development was La Playa, in Marianao, where they commissioned the projects for El Casino and La Concha.

Typical of the principles of the suburban City Beautiful, the street layout was picturesque, incorporating natural design features such as trees and lakes as well as urban monuments, like George Duncan's 1920 Torre del Reloj, in Miramar (fig. 15). During his tenure as secretary of public works for President Machado, Céspedes continued to promote the area, and the Havana Biltmore Yacht and Country Club came into being. Along with Carlos Manuel de la Cruz and José Manuel Cortina, Céspedes formed the Cuban American Realty Company, which commissioned Schultze and Weaver to design La Concha, a beach resort popular with the working classes (fig. 16), the Cuba-American Jockey Club (fig. 17), as well as an unbuilt project for the Biltmore hotel chain, all in 1928.

Their unquestioned masterpiece, however, was the Casino Nacional (fig. 18). Plans were completed in 1928, and, as in Schultze and Weaver's other projects for Havana, the project was an addition to an existing structure consisting of a

19. Bens Arrarte, "La arquitectura," 24.

Fig. 18. Schultze and Weaver, Casino Nacional, front view, Marianao, Havana, 1928 (demolished). From a postcard.

oseph Pubillones collection.

Fig. 19. Rafael Goyeneche, Casino Nacional, Marianao, Havana, 1920. Fountain by Aldo Gamba. Photograph Narciso Menocal collection.

vestibule, foyer, men's and women's restrooms, coatroom, and porte-cochere. It was designed by Lloyd Morgan (1892–1970), who joined the firm as chief designer in 1926 and was made a partner in 1928. Morgan, winner of the Paris Prize in 1921, studied at the École des Beaux-Arts under Victor Laloux and was responsible for the firm's designs executed that year.

The limitations of the program did not prevent the architects from dramatically changing the face of an eight-year-old building, one that had been rapidly put together in time for the 1920 social season. The original structure, a French château, was designed by Rafael Goyeneche (fig. 19), a successful Mexican architect active in Cuba. Morgan's intervention cleverly maintained all the typological elements of Goyeneche's design, such as the porte-cochere, while cladding the building with a classical grandeur similar to that of its counterparts in the south of France and Monte Carlo. Morgan's design was stark, elegant, and imposing on the exterior. Goyeneche's building had a front pavilion enclosing a monumental stair that ascended for a half-level to the main foyer and descended a similar distance to the basement. The new porte-cochere extended the line of the building frontward by twenty feet and disguised its vehicular function by glazing a central element of an arched window, also twenty-five feet in height, and two sidelights that towered seventeen feet above the ground. This triumphal arch motif was completed by two ornamental cast-stone panels. Adapting the colossal scale that they had already used in the Cuba-American Jockey Club, Schultze and Weaver designed a grand circular approach, on axis with a fountain by Aldo Gamba, since moved to the Tropicana nightclub.

The building was clad in imitation stone panels. The floors were of Tennessee marble in the vestibule and foyer and Cuban tile in the service areas. The structure was made up of steel I-beams over the long spans, holding up wooden trusses made up of four-by-six-inch members above.

The sequence from the porte-cochere to the remodeled dining rooms was an exercise in some of the most elaborate ornamentation to emerge from Schultze and Weaver's office, with mirrors in gilded metal frames surrounding a series of ornamental painted plaques. Coming through the vestibule, one was greeted by four stunning Doric pilasters in cast imitation Caen stone (fig. 20). The walls at either side of the pilasters were canted and sloped inward, gradually stepping into the doorway. This was a rare experiment in the Neo-Egyptian style that enjoyed a brief popularity in the United States and which would find stronger definition during the Art Moderne thirties. The pilasters had a series of ornamental fluted bands below the chair rail, punctuated by individual inserts. The columns were painted in sharp contrast to the monochromatic exterior. Past the vestibule, Morgan produced a second tripartite composition (fig. 21). Here, only the central bay was open, yet partially screened by an undulating folding metal grille in polished silver and gold. Niches were carved at either side, repeating the mirror-on-metal-frame motif of the vestibule. Cleverly, the architects had repeated the same motif of the previous room, only this time one had only the reflection and not the actual ornament.

Schultze and Weaver also redesigned the interiors of the existing dance floor and main dining room. Working with a continuous height of twenty-four feet, they produced a series of ceiling coffers, breaking up the uniform height of the roof into a series of repetitive bays. The wood floors were refinished and a plaster ceiling depicting images of flowers, tropical vegetation, and bucolic goddesses was added. The wall reliefs drew upon conventionalized images of palm fronds, from which a garland of gilded and silvered coins cascaded. At either side the design was framed by still another floral relief surrounded by

Fig. 20. Schultze and Weaver,

Casino Nacional, vestibule,

Marianao, Havana, 1928. From

a postcard. Joseph Pubillones

collection.

black marble with gold inserts. The medallion crowning the arches contained the Cuban coat of arms. The bar was the jewel of the building and perhaps one of the most unique interiors ever produced in Havana (fig. 22). The room was surrounded by a tile wainscot that extended into the bar itself. This motif had already been used in the Sevilla Biltmore years before, only here it flowed gracefully into the mirrored-frame motif and into the composition of ornamented pilasters cast in the shape of palm trees, complete with coconuts, that rose and turned into the Cuban sky.

Between 1900 and 1930 Cuba provided a setting where North American architects could refine and enrich their work. Their commissions in Havana allowed Schultze and Weaver to experiment with an ornamentation and detailing that prefigured much of their work in Miami and Los Angeles; Murchison's Central Railway Station was the watershed that made him perhaps the most idiosyncratic designer of train stations; Bertram Goodhue's church was his turning point from the Gothic to the Spanish Revival, a move that established the latter as an accepted style in a country that had largely forgotten its Hispanic past.

Sitting at the bar in the Casino Nacional, one could have agreed with Hergersheimer that,

> Although for the best, I was even then a little late, I was glad that I had seen the city when I did, just as I was glad to have known Venice before the Campanile fell, and the Virginian Highlands when they had not been modernized. [But then, he also wrote:] When I was young I had looked in vain for a perpetual Havana, hoping for nothing more, and now when my youth was dead, I had found the perfection of my desire. But as always, the discovery was too late; I couldn't stay in the covered paseos, the plazas and the flambeau-trees and royal palms; nor idle in a room of Moorish tiles with a dripping fountain, over a magic drink; my time for the actualities of charming liberty, the possession of unaccounted days, was gone. But this mood was nothing more than a gesture, a sentiment, thrown back to romance.[20] □

20. Hergersheimer, *San Cristóbal*, 70–71, 186.

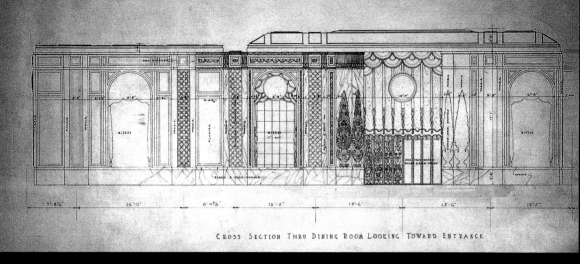

CROSS SECTION THRU DINING ROOM LOOKING TOWARD ENTRANCE

Fig. 21. Schultze and Weaver, Casino Nacional, foyer section, Marianao, Havana, 1928. The Mitchell Wolfson Jr. Collection, The Wolfsonian, Miami Beach, Florida, and Genoa, Italy.

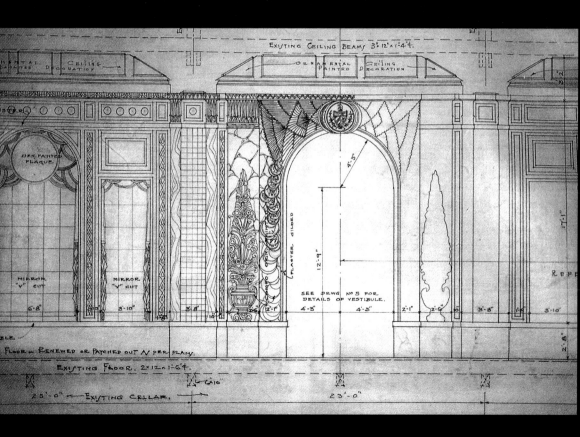

Fig. 22. Schultze and Weaver, Casino Nacional, detail of bar, Marianao, Havana, 1928. The Mitchell Wolfson Jr. Collection, The Wolfsonian, Miami Beach, Florida, and Genoa, Italy.

Fig. 1. Arbol de la Fraternidad Americana, dedicated on 24 February 1928, Havana. Photograph Secretaría de Obras Públicas de Cuba.

The City as Landscape:
Jean Claude Nicolas Forestier and the Great Urban Works of Havana, 1925–1930

By Jean-François Lejeune

Translated by John Beusterien and Narciso G. Menocal

Jean-François Lejeune is a Belgian-born architect and author. He is an associate professor at the University of Miami School of Architecture, Coral Gables, Florida, and editor of the academic journal *The New City*. His research and publications focus on the history of the Garden City Movement and on colonial and twentieth-century urbanism in the Caribbean and Latin America.

On 16 January 1928 the Sexta Conferencia Internacional Americana opened in Havana with President Calvin Coolidge and twenty-one Latin American heads of state attending. Within forty days President Gerardo Machado y Morales and the secretary of public works, Doctor Carlos Miguel de Céspedes, inaugurated a number of great public spaces. Those works made up the first phase of a program that would transform the colonial image of the city into a metropolitan vision in tune with the ambitions of the Republic. At the head of a French-Cuban team of architects, engineers, and artists, the French landscape architect Jean Claude Nicolas Forestier made his mark on that program with his designs for the Plaza de la Fraternidad, the esplanade of the Avenida de las Misiones, the extension of the Malecón, the Plaza del Maine, and the great staircase of the university. The Capitolio (Capitol), originally expected to serve as the conference headquarters, remained unfinished, but the metallic structure of its dome dominated over the new Parque de la Fraternidad Americana, built upon the site of the former Campo de Marte.

Five weeks later, on 24 February, the commemorative Tree of the Fraternidad Americana, a cottonwood ironically called by *Social* the "poor *ceiba*," was planted at the center of the park, in line with the transversal axis of the Capitolio (fig. 1)[1]. The act was symbolically admirable but socially ambiguous since the conference had not resolved a conflict between political theory—the unanimous respect for the independence of every nation—and pragmatic reality—the support given by many to the military occupation of Nicaragua by the United States. Forestier and his team surrounded the tree with a magnificent bronze circular grille—a *reja*—elevated on steps and decorated with the coats of arms of all member countries. In a moment of genuine understanding of the history of the Caribbean, they not only evoked the foundation of the city and the first Mass celebrated under a similar *ceiba* four hundred years earlier, on the shore of the bay (in the place today marked by the Templete), but they elevated the tree to the dimension of a monument (fig. 2).

The same unique fusion of nature, architecture, and city was later achieved by Forestier at the nearby Parque Central, the republican forum where the vegetal columns of royal palm trees he planted echo the porticoes of *La ciudad de las columnas* (The City of Columns),[2] and even more so in his reconstruction of the Paseo del Prado. Out of this illustrious avenue lined with the last palaces

---

1. *Social* 13 (October 1928): 25. The seed of the tree had been planted at the official inauguration of the Republic in 1902. For the conference, see *Diario de la Sexta Conferencia Internacional Americana* (Havana: Impr. de Rambla, Bauzá y Cía., 1928).
2. From the title of Alejo Carpentier, *La ciudad de las columnas* (Barcelona: Editorial Lumen, 1970).

Fig. 3. The new Paseo del

Prado, Havana. Photograph

courtesy of University of Miami

Library, Special Collections

Department, Coral Gables,

Florida. Darden Beller collection.

Fig. 2. *Plano de la primitiva*

Plaza de Armas de La Habana

con la iglesia parroquial y el

castillo de la Fuerza, 1691.

© M. y P. Santo Domingo, 96.

Courtesy of Archivo General

de Indias, Seville.

of the nineteenth-century entrepreneurial class but reduced in the last decades — despite the reconstruction by General Wood's administration — to a mere terreplein crossed by electric wires, Forestier created the "salon" of the twentieth-century city.[3] Under a vault of laurel trees, the *paseo* became an architectural promenade, a Caribbean *rambla*, visually articulating two main monuments, the Capitolio at one end and Morro Castle at the other, by the sea. By elevating the *paseo*, paving it, and bordering it with benches made from coral rocks (local oolithic rock containing fossils) that supported bronze streetlights, the Cuban architect Raúl Otero and Forestier gave the *paseo* a mineral character; it became an excretion of the soil, a memory of the geological origins of the island (fig. 3).

3. Carlos Venegas Fornias, *La urbanización de las murallas: dependencia y modernidad* (Havana: Editorial Letras Cubanas, 1990), 12–15. The Paseo de La Habana, first traced in 1771–1776, had its direct inspiration from the Prado in Madrid. See *El Arquitecto D. Ventura Rodríguez* (Madrid: Museo Municipal, 1983).

Forestier made three trips to Havana between 1925 and 1930 (8 December 1925 to 28 February 1926, 19 August to 15 December 1928, and 23 January to 23 March 1930). He worked quickly and intensely, surrounded by a brilliant team of young French professionals, many of them recipients of the Grand Prix de Rome, and some of the best local talent. By integrating their preliminary ideas into his own plan, he became a catalyzer for the transformation of the city. Aware of Le Corbusier's methods, he flew in an airplane above the city and its outlying region to comprehend their size and landscape. Confronting Cuba, and the strong, ambiguous relationship maintained between its towns and landscape, he expanded to metropolitan dimensions a concept he had previously developed in his private and public gardens in France, Spain, Morocco, and Argentina, namely the notion of "the science of gardens at the service of urban art."[4] In an article published in *Urbanisme* in 1952, Henri Prost, the most important French urbanist of the first half of the century, wrote about Forestier: "His secret was to compose with nature and conceive broad ideas on the land. One understood all the power behind this man when he was seen on the site itself: before imagining and designing, he looked it over, he smelled it, he saw everything, and then, in his imagination, the great lines of change or a new creation crossed the landscape."[5]

In his essay "Entre Le Nôtre et Le Corbusier" Salvador Tarragó i Cid recalls that, born in the Alps in the city of Aix-les-Bains, Jean Claude Nicolas Forestier (1861–1930) renounced his ambition to become a naval engineer to follow a career in forestry and the care of parks and gardens. Such a change of mind was not surprising given the close relationship between shipbuilding and the exploitation of forests at the time.[6] Becoming a civil servant in Paris as a young man, he soon was put in charge of the forest of Vincennes in the administration created by the engineer and landscape architect Adolphe Alphand (1817–1891), Baron Haussmann's principal collaborator in the great beautification projects of Paris. Named caretaker of the walkways of the western districts of Paris in 1898, Forestier met his first public success with the redesign of the park of Bagatelle, between 1905 and 1908. There he inaugurated a strategy for the restoration and protection of landscape "based on the comprehension of history and the rejection of pastiche."[7] Founded on a synthesis of "memory and modernity,"[8] this doctrine was to dominate his work, including his projects in Havana: "Imagining and inventing, but, in the great moments, always obeying solemn tradition."[9]

In April 1911 the committee of the 1929 Exposición Ibero-Americana de Sevilla entrusted Forestier with turning the private gardens of the Palace of San Telmo into a public park, originally the work of the French landscape architect Lecolant. Breaking with picturesque tradition, Forestier designed the new

4. Translation of the title of Bénédicte Leclerc, "La science du paysage au service de l'art urbain," *Pages-Paysages*, no. 2 (1989).

5. Henri Prost, "Hommage à Forestier," *Urbanisme*, no. 3–4 (1952), 74–75. On the exceptional career of Henri Prost (1874–1959), see André Siegfried, Louis Hautecoeur, Henry Lacoste, et al., *L'oeuvre de Henri Prost* (Paris: Académie d'Architecture, 1960); and Jean-Louis Cohen, "Henri Prost: The Career of a French Urbanist (1874–1959)," *The New City* (Modern Cities, no. 3, 1996), 106–122.

6. Salvador Tarragó i Cid, "Entre Le Nôtre et Le Corbusier," in Bénédicte Leclerc, ed., *Jean Claude Nicolas Forestier, 1861–1930: du jardin au paysage urbain* (Paris: Picard, 1994), 253–254.

7. Jean-Pierre Le Dantec, "Forestier aujourd'hui," in Leclerc, *Forestier*, 244.

8. Ibid.

9. J. C. N. Forestier, dedication to the book *Pour comprendre l'art décoratif moderne en France*, quoted in Le Dantec, "Forestier aujourd'hui," 244.

Fig. 5. J. C. N. Forestier, plan

of the Parque de María Luisa,

Seville, 1911. From Georges

Gromort, *Jardins d'Espagne*,

vol. 2 (Paris: A. Vincent & Cie,

1926), pl. 115.

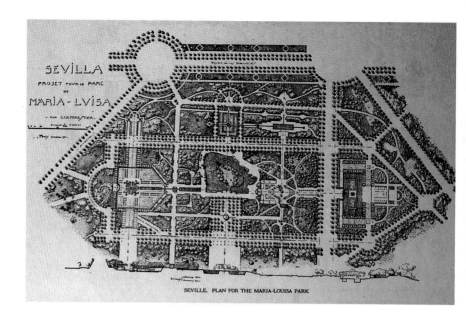

Fig. 5. J. C. N. Forestier, plan of the Parque de María Luisa, Seville, 1911. From Georges Gromort, *Jardins d'Espagne*, vol. 2 (Paris: A. Vincent & Cie, 1926), pl. 115.

Fig. 4. Parque de María Luisa, view of the environs of the Isla de los Pájaros (Island of the Birds), Seville. Photograph by the author, 1992.

Parque de María Luisa with a geometric network of paths that define a sequence of small gardens of Arabic-Andalusian inspiration (fig. 4), the most spectacular of them featuring the famous Fuente de los Leones. Moreover, as advisor to the architect of the exhibition, Aníbal González, Forestier projected the exhibition developing south along the Guadalquivir River, as a prolongation of the park. A modern reinterpretation of the Arabic art of gardens and its basic vocabulary, the Parque de María Luisa, completed in 1914, met with tremendous success and gave birth to a vital aesthetic movement that influenced the designs of many public parks and private gardens in Spain and France. For the first time in the twentieth century the Mediterranean garden was brought forth as an alternative to the prevalent picturesque model (fig. 5).

In 1915 Forestier arrived in Barcelona. He had been recommended by his friend the painter José María Sert to redesign the Montjuïc Hill in anticipation of the 1929 Exposición Internacional de Barcelona. His achievements in Parc Laribal — exemplified in the rose garden (1918) and the celebrated Gat Fountain (1916) — and his unfinished project for the Miramar terraces (1923), built over the sea, were decisive to the renaissance of the classical Mediterranean garden (figs. 6 and 7).[10] His international reputation extended further with his book *Jardins: carnet de plans et dessins* (*Gardens: A Notebook of Plans and Sketches*), published in France and the United States in the 1920s.[11] The "Garden of the Orange-Tree Climate" was exalted by his disciple and friend Rubió i Tudurí in his splendid work as director of parks and gardens of Barcelona.[12]

His park projects and his gardens, though not always completely realized, served as a laboratory for the urban works that Forestier embarked upon, as a self-taught city planner, in Morocco, Lisbon, the Paris suburban ring, Buenos

10. See Cristina Domínguez Peláez, "Los jardines en España," in Leclerc, *Forestier*, 83–98; Sonsoles Nieto Caldeiro, "La Sevilla reformada," ibid., 99–110; and Dorothée Imbert, "Tracé architectonique et poétique végétale," ibid., 69–81.

11. J. C. N. Forestier, *Jardins: carnet de plans et dessins* (Paris: Émile-Paul Frères, 1920). In English, J. C. N. Forestier, *Gardens: A Notebook of Plans and Sketches* (New York: Charles Scribner's Sons, 1928).

12. Nicolás María Rubió i Tudurí, *Del paraíso al jardín latino* (Barcelona: Tusquets, 1981).

Fig. 7. J. C. N. Forestier, gardens of Miramar at Montjuïc, Barcelona, 1919. From J. C. N. Forestier, *Gardens: A Notebook of Plans and Sketches* (New York: Charles Scribner's Sons, 1928).

Fig. 6. J. C. N. Forestier. Font del Gat, Parc Montjuïc, Barcelona, 1918. From J. C. N. Forestier, *Gardens: A Notebook of Plans and Sketches* (New York: Charles Scribner's Sons, 1928).

Aires, and finally Havana. A grand admirer of Le Nôtre, designer of the gardens of Versailles for Louis XIV, Forestier championed the cause of public parks as a fundamental element of modern, expanding cities. In 1906 he published his only theoretical work, *Grandes villes et systèmes de parcs*. Condemning the absence of long-term planning in Paris and its outskirts, and taking advantage of his contacts with American urbanists and landscape architects, he introduced Frederick Law Olmsted's (1822–1903) governing idea for developing big cities for the first time in France. "[American cities] have realized that a city plan is insufficient if it is does not include a coordinated plan that contains interior and exterior open spaces for the present and the future — one with a system of parks and parkways."[13] For Forestier the park systems developed within the City Beautiful Movement by Olmsted and his followers represented the most advanced state in the design of a modern city and was an indispensable instrument for organizing and controlling urban expansion.

In 1911 Forestier associated with Tony Garnier (1869–1948), André Bérard, Ernest Redont, Jacques-Marcel Aubertin, Donat-Alfred Agache, Henri Prost (1874–1959), Léon Jaussely (1876–1933), and Ernest Hébrard (1866–1933) to found the Société française des urbanistes (S.F.U.). Influenced by the work of Camillo Sitte (1843–1903), Raymond Unwin (1863–1940), and Eugène Hénard (1849–1923), imbued with Haussmannian rationality, and with knowledge, moreover, of the American regional and landscape theories of Daniel Burnham and of the City Beautiful Movement, these architects aimed to create an art that would reform cities, a civic art that would be a science as much as a philosophy. Up until World War Two, and with the undisclosed intention "to recuperate French imperial prestige and reestablish a reputation for success," French urbanists and architects eagerly accepted the invitation to plan the expansions and remodel the fabric of capital cities in Latin America: along with Forestier in Buenos Aires and Havana, Hébrard worked in Guayaquil (1910s), Norbert Maillart in

13. J. C. N. Forestier, *Grandes villes et systèmes de parcs* (Paris: Hachette, 1906): 14. See also Jean-François Lejeune, "La ville et le paysage: influences et projets américains," in Leclerc, *Forestier*, 173–187.

Fig. 8. J. C. N. Forestier,

project for the Avenida

Costanera, perspective view

of the Balneario, Buenos Aires,

1924. From *Proyecto orgánico*

para la urbanización del

municipio. El plano regulador

***y federal* (Buenos Aires:**

Talleres Peuser, 1925).

Montevideo (1920s), Donat-Alfred Agache in Rio de Janeiro (1930 and onward), and Maurice Rotival in Caracas, from 1938 to the 1950s.[14]

In 1924, following in the wake of other French professionals who worked in Buenos Aires (the landscape architect Charles Thays from 1880 to 1910 and the urbanist Joseph Bouvard in 1907), Forestier was invited to design an ambitious project of parks and parkways for the Argentine capital. His goal was to have all areas of the city relating to each other and to the periphery of expansion. The unrealized project for the Avenida Costanera, which would have extended along the Río de la Plata, constituted the plan's most spectacular and poetic feature. Inspired by Burnham's plans for Lake Michigan in Chicago (1894–1909) and integrating a complex circulation network, the parkway presented a brilliantly organized succession of long curves offering calculated views, public gardens, and squares bordered by pergolas hanging over the river in ways similar to those of the gardens of Montjuïc in Barcelona (fig. 8). Unfortunately, political circumstances prevented the implementation of Forestier's ambitious system of parks, but the memory remained, for it later was incorporated in the master plan of 1929 drafted by Le Corbusier.[15]

Returning now to the subject of Havana, the circumstances surrounding the new program of large public works in 1925–1930 and Forestier's participation in their design come into focus within an outline of the hundred years of urban development that preceded the administration of President Gerardo Machado (1925–1933). At the center of this development the Reparto de las Murallas (City Walls Subdivision, or ring) played a fundamental role in bringing Havana up to the metropolitan models evolved in Spain, France, and the United States.

The first "modern" urban transformations were the work of the colonial governor Miguel Tacón (1834–1838). No other colonial or republican administration, until that of President Gerardo Machado, almost a century later, carried a reform program as wide and with such decisive effects on the central area of Havana. For historian Carlos Venegas, "both moments constituted the alpha and the omega of the Reparto de las Murallas from an urbanistic and architectural point of view and they related to each other by far more than simply spatial coincidence."[16]

At the end of the eighteenth century, when the Paseo del Prado was developed, the city walls lost strategic importance and the unbuilt space constituting the military esplanade in front of them became a mere symbolic line of demarcation, more civil than military. The area, partly urban and partly rural at the time, was turned into a "knot of urban communication, of social meetings, and a point of radiation of modern urban and architectural achievements."[17] To the works of Tacón — a representative of the new class of commercial and industrial Spaniards (in large part Catalans) — the Cuban-born intendent, Claudio Martínez de Pinillos, Count of Villanueva (1782–1853), replied with his own public program supported by the Creole aristocracy, generally connected to sugarcane production:

14. David K. Underwood, "Alfred Agache, French Sociology, and Modern Urbanism in France and Brasil," *Journal of the Society of Architectural Historians* 50 (June 1991): 130–166.

15. See Sonia Berjman, "En la ciudad de Buenos Aires," in Leclerc, *Forestier*, 207–219; and also Christiane Crasemann Collins, "Urban Interchange in the Southern Core: Le Corbusier (1929) and Werner Hegemann (1931) in Argentina," *Journal of Society of Architectural Historians* 54 (June 1995): 208–227

16. Venegas, *La urbanización*, 21.

17. Ibid.

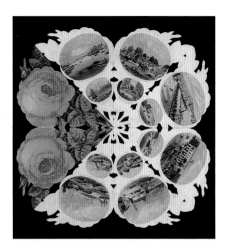

In this way the citizens could compare at their discretion the beautiful fountain of Neptune that the General ordered from Genoa in Carrara marble with the splendid Fountain of the India [or of the "Noble Havana"] placed on the Paseo de Isabel II, which is also of the same material and came from Italy. [They could also compare] the proud Tacón Market with the gracious Villanueva station; the Intendent's technical schools and hospitals with the magnificent Governor's jail, the most spacious in the Americas according to its promoter; the utility of the beautiful Paseo Militar (or de Tacón) with Fernando VII's Aqueduct, and so on. (figs. 9 and 10).[18]

Against all expectations, the new urban spaces, built by men from the Peninsula, became associated with anti-Spanish sentiment since key groups of Cubans favoring independence moved into the Reparto de las Murallas during the next thirty years. The Villanueva Railroad Station (which replaced, not without irony, the Botanical Gardens, established in 1817, bordering the Prado and the Zanja Real) as well as theaters and cafés (such as the famous Escauriza, above the sidewalk of the Louvre) and the new industrial factories, all reflected the dynamism of the Creole society "beyond the walls" facing the Spanish commercial and political oligarchy entrenched in the colonial core of the city. This situation caused the Colombian traveler Nicolás Tanco y Armero to write in 1863: "On one side they work, they earn; on the other they dissipate, they spend."[19]

Regulated not without problems and abusive speculation by engineer Mariano Carrillo de Albornoz's *Plano de Ensanche* (Expansion Plan) (1849–1850), the city inevitably grew beyond the walls, and on 8 August 1863 the walls began to be torn down. After Vienna (1858) and Barcelona (1859–1860), the new urban design for the old esplanade, approved in 1865, marked the birth of modern city planning in Havana. Two parallel streets fifteen meters wide (Monserrate and Zulueta) constituted the framework of the plan ordered by the Crown. Although the main objective of the colonial government was to take optimal advantage in the selling of lands, a large public space, a great square, and the future Parque Central, were left unbuilt at the end of Obispo and O'Reilly Streets, by the Puerta de Monserrate. This space became the core of the Havana ring. Among its most representative monuments stand the palace

18. Juan Pérez de la Riva, "Desarrollo de la población habanera," *Bohemia,* no. 46 (November 1965), 100; quoted in Venegas, *La urbanización*, 29–30.

19. Juan Pérez de la Riva, *La isla de Cuba en el siglo XIX vista por los extranjeros* (Havana: Ciencias Sociales, 1981), quoted in Venegas, *La urbanización*, 37.

Fig. 11. Lonja del Comercio
seen from the Fuente de los
Leones on the Plaza de San
Francisco, Havana, 1909.
Photograph by the author, 1994

of the Marquesa de Villalba (1872–1877); the Hotel Pasaje (1876), with the first covered gallery in the city; the Payret Theater (1877); the Jané Theater-Circus (1881); the Colón market (1891); and the Manzana de Gómez (1895). Tall arcades imposed by the Ordinances of Construction, of 1861, classic decoration and geometric order, high cornices that hid terraced roofs, and the use of iron as a structural material created a new image of Havana at the turn of the century.

Because of new immigration laws passed after the establishment of the Republic in 1902, the population of the capital grew from two hundred fifty thousand in 1900 to one-half million in 1930.[20] Architecturally the change was no less extraordinary for the city, which, having lived "under the aegis of classical antiquity," was stylistically behind the times when compared to other modern capitals.[21]

20. In 1919, 30 percent of Havana's residents were foreigners. See Roberto Segre, "Arquitectura anti-llana del siglo XX," unpublished manuscript.

21. Joaquín Weiss, *Medio siglo de arquitectura cubana* (Havana: Imprenta Universitaria, 1950), 5. Weiss recalls the existence of Italian (*L'Architettura Italiana, Edilizia Moderna*) and Spanish magazines (*Arquitectura y Construcción, Arquitectura Moderna*) in many architects' offices and clients' homes.

The first quarter of the twentieth century was a complex period. Direct American intervention — road and sanitary infrastructures, schools, clubs, hotels, hospitals — and new construction techniques (reinforced concrete) imported by major American firms, such as Purdy and Henderson, influenced the city in its entirety.[22] Private American capital contributed to develop the periphery, particularly the Vedado-Miramar-Marianao axis, as a series of garden suburbs. On the other hand, mainly the well-off Spaniards remodeled the city center. Constructed in 1908–1909 as a result of a competition by architects Tomás Mur and José Mata, the Lonja del Comercio (Stock Exchange), a building that included stores, a commercial bank, and offices, was an early symbol of the stylistic and structural revolution of the beginning of the century. With its high five-story Renaissance-style facade and beautiful terra-cotta dome crowned with a winged Mercury, the Lonja was the first non-religious structure that broke a centuries-old urban profile (fig. 11). On the east-west axis that linked the Lonja to the ring, dozens of new commercial buildings constructed in reinforced concrete, yet with plans based on colonial typologies, were built to heights beyond those legally permitted, to create "a little Wall Street"; the highest were the Banco Nacional de Cuba, the Royal Bank of Canada, the Banco Comercial de Cuba (one hundred feet), and the Banco Gómez Mena.[23]

Several historians have insisted on the importance of regional Spanish groups who imported "the representation of modernity taking place in Spain at that time: Catalan Modernism (Art Nouveau), the Neo-Baroque of Madrid, and Asturian Neo-Herrerianism."[24] Catalan Modernism found its major expression in the urban districts developed from the late nineteenth century and along the new axes, such as the Paseo del Prado, the Calzada de Reina, and the Malecón, where it was imaginatively integrated within the typology of the arcades (fig. 12).[25] The imported models were creatively adapted to local conditions and "served to identify many new social functions and established an adequate channel for applying modern construction techniques as well as the formal and spatial repertory that framed the shared life of the rich and poor classes of Havana society."[26]

Fig. 12. Catalan *modernismo* on the Prado, first decade of the twentieth century, Havana. Photograph by the author, 1994.

The first of these centers was the Palacio de la Asociación de Dependientes del Comercio (Palace of the Association of Store Clerks), by Arturo Amigó (1907), the facades of which, in a Venetian Renaissance style, concealed grandiose interiors and a spectacular glass roof.

Similarly grand were the Hotel Plaza (1909), the Hotel Inglaterra (built 1856; expanded 1891; reconstructed 1915), and the Manzana de Gómez (built 1894; expanded 1917), all with Neoclassical facades fronting the Parque Central (fig. 13). In 1905 the Centro Gallego became the owner of the Tacón Theater, or Gran Teatro Nacional, which occupied the main angle of the park and was

22. Founded in New York in 1896, Purdy and Henderson specialized in the design and calculation of large metallic structures (in New York: the Plaza Hotel, the Flatiron Building, the National City Bank, and Pennsylvania Station). The firm opened its headquarters in Havana in 1901. In 1925 it had, according to its president, L. E. Brownson, a 90 percent Cuban ownership. See *Libro del Capitolio* (Havana: P. Fernández y Cía., 1933), 116.

23. Llilian Llanes, *1898–1921: La transformación de La Habana a través de su arquitectura* (Havana: Editorial Letras Cubanas, 1993).

24. Segre, "Arquitectura antillana," section 3.4.

25. For instance, on the Paseo del Prado: the Abreu residence, the Neo-Moorish apartment building by José Toraya, and the Pérez de la Riva y Pons residence (now the Museo de la Música).

26. Segre, "Arquitectura antillana," section 3.4.

reconstructed twice after its inauguration in 1838. Four years later work on the new building began, following the design of the Belgian architect Paul Belau and under the direction of the American construction firm of Purdy and Henderson. Exploiting the Baroque repertory then in fashion in Madrid, Belau conceived "a vibrant walled box, expressive of the complexity of interior space," and he covered an undulating facade with an overflowing decoration of winged figures, tragic characters, and theater masks (fig. 14).[27] Occupying a full city block, the building included two monumental entrances. The first, to the Centro Gallego proper, featured a grand staircase, in a Neo-Baroque style, lit by a glass-roof ceiling. It led to banquet rooms, libraries, and other social spaces. The other entrance, that of the Gran Teatro Nacional (inaugurated on 22 April 1915), followed the configuration of its predecessor, the Teatro Tacón, embedded in the new structure. *Aïda*, directed by Tulio Serafín, was selected for the opening night.[28]

◀

Fig. 13. Corner tower of the

Centro Gallego, 1915, with

the Centro Asturiano, 1927, and

the Parque Central in the back-

ground, Havana. Photograph

by the author, 1994.

In contrast, the Centro Asturiano imposed a measure of severity to the civic monumentality of the area. Located on the edge of the Parque Central since 1886, the center had absorbed the historic Albisu Theater in 1914 and reconstructed it under the name of Teatro Campoamor to celebrate the memory of the greatest nineteenth-century Asturian poet.[29] On 24 October 1918 a spectacular fire destroyed the building but not the theater. Six years later, after interminable searches and an international competition, the winning project was awarded to a Spanish architect from Gijón, Manuel del Busto, who followed to the letter the strict rule of the building committee. "The exterior ornamentation will entirely conform to the purest classicism of the Spanish Renaissance style…the interior decoration will also be related to that style."[30]

The four-story Centro Asturiano, a building surrounded by arcades, opened its doors on 20 November 1927. Circular towers mark three of its corners, and a double tower with square and octagonal sections crowns the fourth angle, on the side of the Parque Central. "The Señera Torre [Solitary Tower], like a Mount Ijuju molded onto rock, [stands like] a watch tower of the remote seas behind which the Cantabric coast could be delineated."[31] A highly ornamented interior contrasts with the severe exterior of the building and reflects its many functions and complexities. A number of spaces stand out within that remarkably theatrical atmosphere, such as the stairway of honor, finished with a great stained-glass ceiling representing the arrival of Columbus and his caravels (fig. 15); the enormous *salón de fiesta* (banquet room) (two thousand square meters by fifteen meters high); the library, with furniture inspired by the Escorial; a café with tiled walls; and a billiard room, with twenty-two tables, facing San Rafael Street.

On the edge of the ring the Palacio del Gobierno Provincial (Palace of the Provincial Government), later transformed into the presidential palace, was completed in 1920 and decorated by the American firm of Tiffany and Company. The building was also the work of the Belgian Belau, this time associated with

27. Ibid.

28. Francisco Rey Alfonso, *Gran teatro de La Habana: cronología mínima 1834/1987* (Havana: Banco Nacional de Cuba, 1988).

29. *El libro del Centro Asturiano de La Habana, 1886–1927* (Havana: Centro Asturiano, 1928).

30. Ibid., 352. At the time of the fire the Centro Asturiano had 47,603 members. After it burned down, the Campoamor Theater was rebuilt several blocks west, at the corner of Industria and San José Streets.

31. Ibid., 537.

Fig. 14. Centro Gallego, detail of facade, Havana, 1915. Photograph by the author, 1994.

Cuban architect Carlos Maruri (fig. 16). Duly eclectic, the palace triumphs over the landscape; its beautiful dome, in a Baroque style and covered with colored ceramic tiles, was the highest in the city until the Capitolio was completed in 1929, after eighteen years of projects and constructions.

During the administration of President José Miguel Gómez (1909–1913), an exchange of land took place in 1910, allowing the construction of a new train station on the property of the old Arsenal[32] and the destruction of the Villanueva station on the Prado, to clear land for a new presidential palace. That project

32. The train station was designed by Kenneth Murchison in 1910 and inaugurated in 1912.

Fig. 16. Palacio Presidencial from the Avenida de los Misiones, Havana, 1920. Narciso Menocal collection.

Fig. 15. Centro Asturiano, gallery with stained-glass ceiling above the grand stair-case. From *El libro del Centro Asturiano de La Habana, 1886–1927* (Havana: Centro Asturiano, 1925).

lasted only a short time. In 1913 President Mario Menocal interrupted the work, directed until then by the architects Eugenio Rayneri y Sorrentino and Eugenio Rayneri y Piedra, who had won the 1911 competition.[33] Wishing to move the presidential palace to the Quinta de los Molinos, the new president assigned the architects Mario Romañach and Félix Cabarrocas to transform the palace on the Prado into a Palacio del Congreso. The new plans, in a French classical style, included a monumental entrance and a dome at the center of a symmetrical composition that integrated the two parliamentary hemicycles. At the end of World War One the flourishing sugar market fell and construction was interrupted. Cuba, and most especially Havana, entered into one of the blackest periods of its history. Bank insolvency and the bankruptcy of thousands of businesses were commonplace. In 1921 the economic crisis struck the construction industry and the public-works sector. Abandoned for four years, the Capitolio underwent a final injury when, in an image worthy of an Alejo Carpentier novel or of Fellini's film *8 ½*, two amusement parks, Galathea and Havana Park, were installed within its majestic carcass (fig. 17).

In this context, then, what were the reasons and who were the actors involved in the government's invitation to Forestier?

On 15 July 1925 less than two months after Gerardo Machado was elected president, the secretary-of-public-works-to-be, Doctor Carlos Miguel de Céspedes, designed an ambitious Keynesian public works program to modernize the country.[34] If the lucrative activities of the secretary — he was a

33. For a detailed history and description of the building, see the *Libro del Capitolio*. Eugenio Rayneri y Sorrentino was a professor of stereotomy at the University of Havana; his son, Eugenio Rayneri y Piedra, belonged to the new generation of architects educated in the United States (University of Notre Dame, 1904).

34. See Herminio Portell-Vila, *Nueva historia de la República de Cuba, 1898–1979* (Miami: La Moderna Poesía, 1986), 325. The initial budget, financed by the American Chase Bank, was fifty million dollars: 25 percent for the Capitolio, 10 percent for new streets and sewers, 5 percent for schools, 5 percent for hospitals, 5 percent for other public buildings, and the rest for administrative costs.

Fig. 17. Amusement park on the construction site of the Capitolio, Havana, ca. 1923. From *Libro del Capitolio* (Havana: P. Fernández y Cía., 1933). Photograph courtesy of Miami-Dade Public Library.

building and land developer since 1910—were not always irreproachable, his interest in the beautification of the city was undeniable.[35] In a letter written in 1955, but not published until 1957 in *Arquitectura*, the then former secretary wrote that in 1925 he had asked the French minister of culture to suggest "the name of an architect who could collaborate with Cuban architects in order to embellish and plan the expansion of the city of Havana."[36] The choice of Forestier was no surprise; his achievements in Paris and in other cities had assured him an uncontestable renown in both French and Cuban professional circles.

Two events fostered the proper climate for Forestier's arrival. During the 1920s publications such as the *Revista de la Sociedad Cubana de Ingenieros* and *Arquitectura*—founded in 1909 and 1917 respectively—promoted a movement in favor of civic art and urban planning. Pedro de Chacón, an engineer who would later become the chief of urban beautification in the Secretariat of Public Works, played a major role in it. In 1925, the year Forestier arrived, the architect Pedro Martínez Inclán published *La Habana actual* (Havana Today). Written between 1919 and 1922, the work was at once didactic, scientific, and political, while at the same time requisitive, implacable, and optimistic. Moreover, it was a denunciation of the general state of the city and the passivity of the government concerning issues of urban reform.[37]

Largely influenced by the United States, which he had visited on various occasions, and the Civic Art and Park Movements, with which he was familiar through books such as *The Improvement of Towns and Cities* (1901) and *Modern Civic Art* (1918) by Charles Mulford Robinson (1869–1917), Martínez Inclán promoted the beautification of the city through public art and gardens, the renovation of the Malecón, and the construction of parks and neighborhoods for the indigent and working classes.[38] His program, which he labeled as "social" and "patriotic," also promoted the nation's acquisition of unoccupied lands in order to create land reserves, the study of expansion plans, a program for construction of schools, the transformation of colonial fortresses into parks and public monuments (Atarés and El Príncipe), a great park project along the river—Gran Paseo del Oeste—and other innovations such as a plan for the preservation of monuments and historic buildings. The backbone of his scheme was the construction (directly or by expanding existing thoroughfares) of twenty-six great avenues and parkways and a dozen great squares that would ease circulation between different areas. He also proposed a system of axes and monuments coherent with the future expansion of the city. If the proposed demolition of the arcades of the Calzadas del Cerro, Belascoaín, Infanta, and Galiano seems today an insensitive concession to the needs of traffic, the plan, nevertheless, contained a number of important ideas, particularly those concerning the integration of the city with peripheral nuclei. Taking up ideas from Raúl Otero's 1905 graduation thesis and from Enrique Montoulieu (the city's head engineer and author of a project for bringing the Albear aqueduct up-to-date),

35. Céspedes was involved, among other ventures, as a major stockholder in the Compañía Urbanizadora de la Playa de Marianao and the Country Club Park.

36. J. M. B. [José María Bens], "Una carta póstuma del Dr. Carlos Miguel de Céspedes," *Arquitectura* 25 (May 1957): 256–259. The letter is dated 10 May 1955.

37. Pedro Martínez Inclán, *La Habana actual: estudio de la capital de Cuba desde el punto de vista de la arquitectura de ciudades* (Havana: P. Fernández y Cía., 1925).

38. Charles Mulford Robinson, *The Improvement of Towns and Cities* (New York and London: G. P. Putnam's Sons, 1901); *Modern Civic Art* (New York and London: G. P. Putnam's Sons, 1918).

Martínez Inclán identified the undeveloped zone to the southeast of the Castillo del Príncipe, known as the Loma de los Catalanes, as the future center of the modern city. As had been suggested by Montoulieu, Martínez Inclán proposed a great circular plaza, "bigger or at least as big as l'Étoile of Paris," as the core for a new civic center, from which a radiating system of grand avenues would link with different areas of the city, as well as with their future expansions.[39]

Forestier first stayed in Havana from 8 December 1925 to 28 February 1926.[40] Having received assurances concerning availability of funds and local personnel to fulfill his plan, he established a permanent team. He brought with him five young architects from the École des Beaux-Arts: Eugène E. Beaudoin (1893–1983), Jean Labatut (1899–1986), Louis Heitzler, Théo Levau, and the only woman in the group, the landscape architect Jeanne Sorugue. He also brought local architects and engineers into the group: Emilio Vasconcelos, Raúl Hermida, and J. I. del Alamo; the artists Manuel Vega and Diego Guevara; and also Raúl Otero.[41]

The *Plano del Proyecto de La Habana*, mostly designed between 1925 and 1926 and revised by Forestier after his second trip from 19 August to 15 December 1928, established a framework of extraordinary magnitude in twentieth-century urban history and contrasts sharply with Havana's appearance since the late nineteenth century (figs. 18 and 19). Since the beginning the plan embraced all aspects of urbanism, from a regional scope to detailed design of public furniture. In Engineer Chacón's description the plan consisted of:

> A series of boulevards, avenues, streets, and walkways that interconnecting with existing ones would facilitate interurban movement as well as expand and increase the city's activity and beauty, giving it squares, plazas, open areas, and parks for the people to enjoy. This would also improve on the decongestion of commercial districts, creating connections with the existing streets and roads that link the city with centers of agricultural and industrial population.[42]

Following an American tradition the Société française des urbanistes had made its own, the general plan covered a considerable geographic area that included peripheral areas. These were integrated with the metropolis. From this theoretical perspective, Forestier saw a need to recentralize the metropolis while preserving the colonial center. To achieve that aim, he chose to protect the

39. Martínez Inclán, *La Habana actual*, 200. See also Enrique Montoulieu y de la Torre, "El crecimiento de La Habana y su regularización," *Anales de la Academia de Ciencias de La Habana* (1923), reprinted in Felipe Préstamo, ed., *Cuba: arquitectura y urbanismo* (Miami: Ediciones Universal, 1995), 237–255.

40. On Forestier in Havana, see Roberto Segre, *Lectura crítica del entorno cubano* (Havana: Editorial Letras Cubanas, 1990), 91–111. More recent and less ideological is the essay by Heriberto Duverger, "El maestro francés del urbanismo criollo para La Habana," in Leclerc, *Forestier*, 221–240. A chronology of the works and studies can be found in Raúl Otero, "Obras de embellecimiento que proyectara J. C. N. Forestier para La Habana," *Arquitectura* 8 (September 1940): 208–212, reprinted in Segre, *Lectura crítica*, 110–111.

41. Of all Forestiers's collaborators, Eugène Beaudoin had the most important career. After Havana he made other urban plans for Cape Town, Marseilles, Monaco, Saigon, Montepellier, and a theoretical project for the reconstruction of Ispahan. A successful architect and professor, his most celebrated works were built in collaboration with Marcel Lodz and Jean Prouvé. Jean Labatut, known in Cuba as author of the monument to Martí at the center of the Plaza de la República, had a prestigious career at Princeton University, where he taught from 1928 to 1967.

42. Quoted in Emilio Roig de Leuchsenring, *La Habana de ayer, de hoy y de mañana* (Havana: Sindicato de Artes Gráficas, 1928), 99.

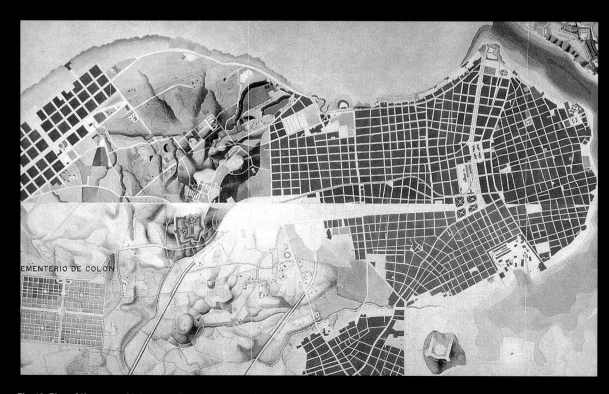

Fig. 18. Plan of Havana and its surroundings, detail, ca. 1890. From *right to left*, Morro Castle and the Cabaña Fortress; across the bay, the colonial center; the ring with El Prado, the old Villanueva train station, and the Campo de Marte; connecting from the Campo de Marte to the west, the Paseo Carlos III with the Castillo del Príncipe at its end. To the southeast of the fortress is the area where Forestier proposed the new civic center. To the left is the grid of the district of El Vedado and the Colón Cemetery. S.G.M. Courtesy Servicio Histórico Militar, Madrid.

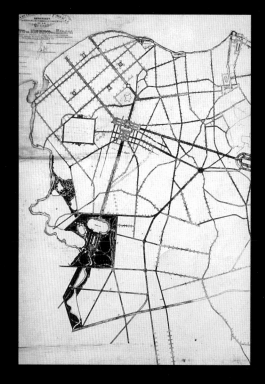

Fig. 19. J. C. N. Forestier, *Plano del Proyecto de La Habana*. Photograph of plan, Secretaría de Obras Públicas de Cuba. Courtesy of Institut Français d'Architecture, Paris, Fonds Leveau.

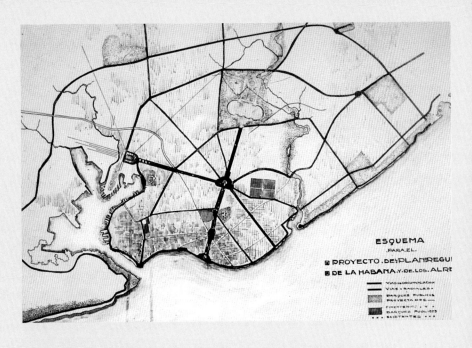

Fig. 20. J. C. N. Forestier, *Esquema para el proyecto del Plano Regulador de La Habana y de los Alrededores* (Sketch for the Project of the General Plan of Havana and Its Vicinity). Photograph of plan, Secretaría de Obras Públicas de Cuba. Courtesy of Institut Français d'Architecture, Paris, Fonds Leveau.

Fig. 21. Avenida de los Presidentes in El Vedado district (Calle G), Havana. Photograph by the author, 1994.

neighborhoods in the old colonial city from being transformed into sites for office buildings. Working at a regional scale, Forestier integrated Montoulieu's and Martínez Inclán's ideas with his own. Logically, the focus of the plan was the civic center located at the Loma de los Catalanes, but he placed it slightly north of Martínez Inclán's original location. Midway between the old city and the district of El Vedado, the proposed new center was to be articulated around the new Plaza de la República. The vast T-shaped square, featuring a central monument to José Martí, was designed on two levels connected with ramps and terraces; the plan proposed to surround it by fountains and *alamedas*, as well as by the Museums of Flora and Fauna and the Ministry of Agriculture.

From the Plaza de la República Forestier made a diagram for the modernization and expansion of the city. This mainly consisted of two perpendicular axes designed as wide parkways or *avenues-jardins*, forming a grand urban cross. The first parkway, laid across some scarcely built areas, led east to the proposed new maritime and train terminal in the Bay of Atarés. The second parkway, a sumptuous avenue one hundred and twenty meters wide, led across undeveloped land to a proposed vast park, the Gran Parque Nacional. Its central feature, a large lake, terminated the axis in the direction of the Almendares River. Other existing avenues were to be widened and planted. Three concentric rings and a system of radial and diagonal avenues and parkways, were foreseen to unite transversally the new neighborhoods, as well as the west coast of the city (Miramar) with the east side (Old Havana, La Víbora, El Cerro, and Regla).

Thus Forestier saw the city as a large garden, and far from being a mere system of radial avenues, his plan was a "proposal to take control of the landscape of the city."[43] The avenues and diagonals were always linked to larger elements, either natural or man-made. In some way one could, in talking about Forestier's Havana, paraphrase Ignasi de Solá Morales's analysis of Burnham and Bennet's Chicago Plan of 1909:

> The plan of the city as architecture is inseparable from the plan of the city as urban park…. The great process of establishing an urban dynamic… is just like the planning of a huge park in the manner of Versailles, in which certain areas are devoted to urban spaces, some monumental, some for walking around, together with smaller gardens and parks. The principles expressed by the analogies suggested by the Beaux-Arts style are taken to their limits, in such a way that the parks and gardens of the city are like a reduced section of a global concept for the unlimited metropolis, and produced according to the same principles.[44]

The design of the Gran Parque Nacional, or Bosque de Habana, fusing both the picturesque and the geometric, was the center of the scenographic system of parks and parkways integrating the Gulf of Mexico with the hinterland (fig. 20). In a grand sweeping gesture, the parks system followed upstream the scenic shores of the Almendares River to include the Gran Paseo del Río; then turned eastward toward the Colón Cemetery (transformed into a public park) and beyond, to include the Malecón, the ring, the Atarés Park, and the new avenues leading to El Cerro; finally it turned back on itself with the new ring-like parkways connecting westward back to Marianao and Miramar, beyond the Almendares. Very little of this park system was built, but Forestier's elegant

43. Duverger, "El maestro francés," in Leclerc, *Forestier*, 224.

44. Ignasi de Solá Morales, "The Beaux-Arts Garden," in Monique Mosser and Georges Teyssot, eds., *The Architecture of Western Gardens*, (Cambridge: The MIT Press, 1990), 403.

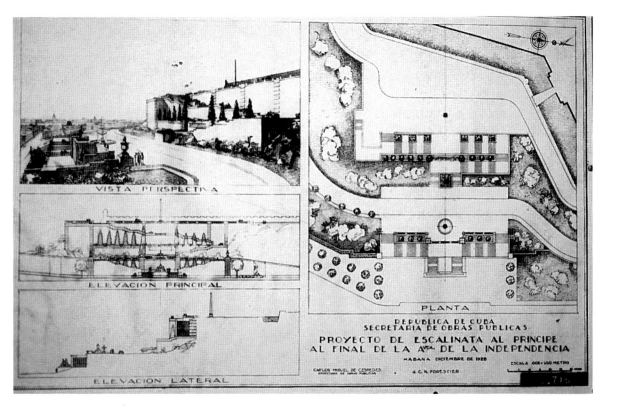

landscaping of the central promenades of El Vedado — the Avenida de los Presidentes (fig. 21) and the Avenida Paseo — or the beautiful Parque de Vento near the Pabellón de Depósitos, illustrate his intentions and ability to create a coherent, efficient, and pedestrian-friendly system of circulation encompassing the entire city.

The civic center was but one component of a larger complex integrating the Castillo del Príncipe and the university campus in Forestier's plan. As a focus to the grand perspective of the Paseo de Carlos III, he proposed to transform El Príncipe into a museum in the midst of a public park (fig. 22). A model for this design may be found in Giuseppe Poggi's approach to the Piazzale Michelangelo in Florence, with its winding drive intersecting a theatrical series of stairs leading to the top platform and its belvedere positioned over the landscape.[45] Moreover, within Forestier's own works, the design for the Barcelona neighborhood of Miramar, or the gardens of Montjuïc Hill, come to mind (cf. fig. 7).

Forestier worked on designs for the University of Havana during his first and second visits, the university being the third major structure in his *Plano del Proyecto de La Habana.* For 174 years after its founding on 5 January 1728 by the Dominicans, the Real y Pontificia Universidad de San Jerónimo de La Habana (today the University of Havana) had been housed in the Convent of Santo Domingo, behind the Palace of the Captains General.[46] A royal project

45. The Piazzale Michelangelo and the Via dei Colli were the works of Giuseppe Poggi. The projects were part of the large-scale transformations of Florence that accompanied its short status as capital of Italy (1865–1870).

46. Information on the construction of the university is very fragmented and excessively ideological. The most complete work is by Ramón de Armas, *Historia de la Universidad de La Habana, 1728–1979* (Havana: Editorial Ciencias Sociales, 1984).

to create a new university on the ring, the first stone of which was laid on 23 January 1884 near the Santo Ángel Church, had remained unfinished, an unfulfilled promise. In 1901–1902 the university was fully reorganized under the administration of the American military governor Leonard Wood and under the direction of Enrique José Varona, secretary of public instruction. It was provisionally installed on the sides of the Aróstegui Hill (then on the outskirts of the city), in the buildings of the old Pirotécnica Militar.

The secretary of public works adopted a general reconstruction plan for the university campus at the same time that its first building, the Aula Magna, was being built and subsequently decorated between 1906 and 1908 by the architect Francisco Ramírez Ovando and the painter Armando Menocal y Menocal (1863–1942). In this plan the university was conceived following the American model of an autonomous campus, an "artistic grouping of freestanding buildings,"

Fig. 25. J. C. N. Forestier, perspective of the grand parkway project (Avenida de la Ermita), seen from the university belvedere, Havana. Photograph Secretaría de Obras Públicas de Cuba. Courtesy of Institut Français d'Architecture, Paris, Fonds Leveau.

Fig. 24. J. C. N. Forestier, first project for the university campus, Havana, 1926. Photograph of plan, Secretaría de Obras Públicas de Cuba. Courtesy of Institut Français d'Architecture, Paris, Fonds Leveau.

linked to San Lázaro Street by terraced gardens.[47] In mid-1910 the architect Enrique Martínez revised and established its classical and symmetrical composition. Following that scheme he designed buildings for the departments of chemistry and physics in 1916 flanking the rectorate (finished later, in May 1921), a structure featuring a proud portico. An all but cube of light with beautiful Corinthian columns, the portico was conceived as the propylaea of an acropolis of wisdom and knowledge dominating the interior of the campus from the one side and the city from the other (fig. 23). This grouping transcended the American Academic Classicism that had inspired it and directly called forth memories of the great masters of European Neoclassicism, Karl Friedrich Schinkel in Berlin or Hans Christian and Theophilus Hansen and their Athenian works.[48] Comparison with the National Library (T. Hansen, 1885–1892), the Académie (T. Hansen, 1859–1887), or the central building of the University of Athens (C. Hansen, 1839–1889) shows the quality of the architectural and urban work of Enrique Martínez, whose vision Forestier would inherit and develop with his team as well as with such architects as Pedro Martínez Inclán.

In a schematic plan dated and signed in April 1926 (during his first visit), Forestier undertook to link the university with the sea and the Príncipe Hill through two public stairways (fig. 24). The first staircase, the one for which Emilio Heredia had proposed a landscape-type project in 1916, would have united the propylaea with San Lázaro Street below it. To the rear of the campus facing the countryside, Forestier made detailed plans for the belvedere. Beyond it would extend the proud perspective that the garden-lined Avenida de la Ermita would establish in the direction of both the Loma de los Catalanes and the new park proposed above the Príncipe Hill (fig. 25). The belvedere and the avenue were never constructed, thus leaving the connection of the rear of the university with the Paseo de Carlos III and the Avenida de los Presidentes as an unresolved urban problem.

47. Werner Hegemann and Elbert Peets, *The American Vitruvius: An Architect's Handbook of Civic Art* (1922; New York: Princeton Architectural Press, 1989), 110–111. The sale of the historic convent of Santo Domingo, unfortunately demolished, financed a large part of the plan.

48. See David Watkin and Tilman Mellinghof, *German Architecture and the Classical Ideal* (Cambridge: The MIT Press, 1987); "Neoclassical Architecture in Copenhagen and Athens," in L. Balslev Jørgensen and Demetri Porphyrios, eds. *Architectural Design Profile*, no. 66 (London, 1987).

Fig. 26. Staircase of the

University of Havana, seen prior

to the erection of two front

buildings, 1928. Photograph

Secretaría de Obras Públicas

de Cuba. Courtesy of Institut

Français d'Architecture, Paris,

Fonds Leveau.

Because of delays in the construction of the Capitolio, Secretary Céspedes decided to transfer the seat of the Sexta Conferencia Internacional Americana to the university and finish the campus's monumental entrance. In collaboration with the French team, Raúl Otero and César Guerra designed the great flight of stairs in record time. It was inaugurated in December 1927. On its summit, following Columbia University as a model, sat the statue of the *Alma Mater*, the work of Czech sculptor Mario Korbel, installed in 1919 in the middle of the campus and relocated to the entrance staircase following a suggestion of Forestier's. The sculpture, cast in bronze by the New York-based Roma Bronce Works, owes its original and unique beauty to the syncretic vision of its sculptor, who employed two models simultaneously; he took the figure of Feliciana Villalón y Wilson, a youth of sixteen years from a well-known family of Spanish origin, and put it above the body of a mulatress with a substantial figure that brought a feeling of Roman *gravitas* to the composition.[49]

The great staircase, with its geometric pavement, its eighty-eight steps, and its terraced gardens, is one of the most beautiful in the history of urban architecture (fig. 26) and deserves a place alongside Michelangelo's Roman Capitol, the parliament steps of Helsinki, or the staircase of Odessa, celebrated by Sergei Eisenstein. Perched above the square located in the angle of L Street and San Lázaro, the classically styled terraces, shaped as bastions, established a coherent relationship between Havana's colonial-type grid to the east and El Vedado's modern checkerboard style.

Forestier developed the final plan for the campus during his second visit. At the heart of it, and among old buildings standing between the rectory and the Calixto García Hospital pavilions (1915–1917), Forestier proposed a U-shaped central space bordered by freestanding buildings, again following the model of Columbia University (fig. 27).

49. On its base are bas-reliefs representing cosmography, botany, medicine, pharmacy, law, philosophy, and architecture.

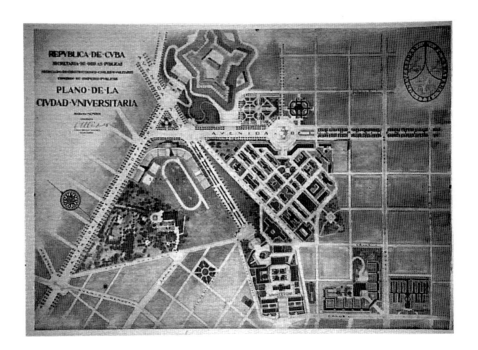

Fig. 27. J. C. N. Forestier, second project for the university campus, Havana, 1929 (partially realized). From _Album fotográfico de los actos celebrados con motivo de la toma de posesión de la presidencia de la República por el General Gerardo Machado y Morales_ (Havana: Secretaría de Obras Públicas, 1929). The Mitchell Wolfson Jr. Collection, The Wolfsonian, Miami Beach, Florida, and Genoa, Italy.

The essential elements of Forestier's plan were built in the thirties, after the re-opening of the university under Engineer Cadenas's second rectorship. Among its most beautiful features, the central garden plaza (finished in 1939) should not go unmentioned. Facing it, on axis with the rectory portico, stands the library (1938–1939) in a monumental modern style by Joaquín E. Weiss, a work that cannot but remind one of the Stockholm Concert House (Ivan Tengbom, 1920–1926); to the side, the U-shaped courtyard of the Sciences Building (1939), by Pedro Martínez Inclán, opens to the square, closed off by a majestic Corinthian colonnade in which the capitals are woven with palm trees in an architectural vision of magic realism. The Enrique José Varona Building, the buildings of the departments of philosophy and letters, and of pedagogy, by architect Luis Dauval, and the departments of commercial sciences and pharmacy (1936–1937), conceived by Pedro Martínez Inclán, should also be singled out. The latter two structures stand above a tall podium and each is finished with an Ionic colonnade; they are placed symmetrically at the foot of the monumental stair-case on the location of the former gardens and terraces of the late 1920s.

The Malecón, first proposed by the engineer Francisco de Albear (1816–1887) in his 1874 plan, was another important project. Following the tenets of the Civic Art Movement, the American engineers working in Havana during the first American military intervention (1899–1902) began to reclaim the land-scape values of the Gulf of Mexico. Their objective was threefold: to improve the sanitary conditions along a chaotic coastline, establish a major artery able to handle future traffic, and embellish the city. Until then the coastline had been neglected and no public spaces had been established on it. Only three elements structured the waterfront. First, there were the military installations, such as the _baterías_ de la Chorrera and de Santa Clara, built by Charles III after the English conquest of 1762. Secondly, there were bathhouses (_baños_ de San Rafael, de los Soldados, de la Madama). Their construction paralleled the growth of the city and the beginnings of a bourgeois way of life that trickled down to the lower classes in the last decades of the nineteenth century. These houses, generally built of wood, occupied spectacular sites along the coast.

Fig. 28. Glorieta de La Punta,

Havana, 1902. From a postcard.

Narciso Menocal collection.

Finally, there was the issue of traffic between the colonial center and the new neighborhoods of El Vedado — mostly a question of horse carriages and streetcar lines at the time. Prior to the construction of the Malecón, traffic was handled almost exclusively along the Calzada de San Lázaro, parallel to the coast, behind a row of houses facing the sea.

The first stretch of the Malecón, from the intersection of the Prado to Lealtad to the west, was constructed in 1901.[50] Although the first sketch showing a treelined *paseo* parallel to the roadway was not followed, the Ordenanzas de Construcción, of 1861, were respected to build reclaimed parcels of land, with continuous arcades on their fronts. At the eastern terminus, a circular temple, or *glorieta*, built in 1902 in memory of the students assassinated by the Spanish government on 27 November 1871, soon became one of the major focal points of social and recreational life in Havana for amorous encounters, family reunions, meetings, concerts, and political rallies (fig. 28).

Fig. 29. Monumento al Maine,

Havana, 1925. Narciso

Menocal collection.

Construction of the Malecón continued during the Tomás Estrada Palma administration, in 1902. Later, in 1914, it was decided to continue the project to the Almendares River and create two monumental plazas overlooking the sea: one was built in the small bay and beach of San Lázaro — Martínez Inclán would bitterly lament its disappearance — for the General Maceo monument (realized by the Italian sculptor Domenico Boni in 1916); the other was built for the Maine monument at the foot of the Santa Clara Battery (fig. 29).

Forestier was familiar with the first sections of the Malecón since 1918, when Manuel Tejedor, secretary of the Cuban delegation in Paris, and a group from the Cuban intelligentsia commissioned him, on behalf of President Menocal, to redesign the small park around the Punta Fortress and connect it through a new *paseo* to the Palacio Presidencial. Published in *Jardins* in 1920, the unbuilt project consisted of small interconnected gardens, conceived as a sequence of enclosed, green spaces (fig. 30). At the center of the park, near La Punta, stood a statue of Columbus, facing a series of marble steps going down into the water. Another feature was the wall memorial to the eight students killed

50. For the initial works of the Malecón, see José María Bens Arrarte, "Urbanismo y arquitectura, siglos XIX y XX," *Arquitectura*, no. 206 (1954): 486–504; "El Malecón de La Habana. Su reconstrucción actual. Datos históricos. El primer proyecto hecho en 1901," *Arquitectura*, no. 262 (1956): 34–38. Both articles are reprinted in Préstamo, ed., *Cuba*.

Fig. 31. View of the Malecón at the intersection of Paseo del Prado before demolition of Governor Tacon's jail. With photomontage of cupola of the Capitolio, Havana, ca. 1928. Narciso Menocal collection.

Fig. 30. J. C. N. Forestier, project for a park at La Punta, Havana, 1918. From J. C. N. Forestier, *Gardens: A Notebook of Plans and Sketches* (New York: Charles Scribner's Sons, 1928).

in 1871.[51] Although drawn in Paris, Forestier's plan was well-adapted to the character of the Malecón at the time, a limited waterfront promenade and drive connecting the coastline to the Paseo del Prado (fig. 31). Ten years later the requirements of modern traffic around La Punta would isolate the old fortress as a monument detached from the urban fabric, a regrettable but nevertheless necessary solution.

Although not fully built according to the plans and sketches designed during Forestier's first and second trips, the new Malecón was the climax of his method for staging urban landscape. This pedestrian and automobile promenade along the Gulf of Mexico was conceived as the metropolitan facade of the modernized city. Forestier exploited familiar elements of the Mediterranean world found in the modern promenades or *paseos marítimos* of Cádiz, Málaga, Naples, and Nice. That is to say, he conceived it as a succession of terraced viewpoints, esplanades, parks, and gardens clearly and geometrically delineated, combining enclosures from the streets, alignments of royal palms, and monuments. The Mediterranean city, more than Paris, was the model for Forestier. Carlos Miguel de Céspedes rightfully dreamed of Havana as a tropical Nice.

The master plan proposed to expand the existing Malecón west from the Maine monument to an aquarium and a General Machado Plaza, but neither was built. The idea was to continue on from that point to the Almendares River and beyond, to the developing districts of Miramar and the Country Club Park (fig. 32). Forestier's design for the Malecón had the character of a wide beachfront park with garden-like sections connected to the interior with large parks and parkways that linked in turn with a citywide park system, and most particularly with the Gran Paseo del Río. Twenty-five years were necessary to complete the works initiated in 1930 to reach the Almendares River. In the meantime the process of privatization of the waterfront in the new western suburbs of Marianao had accelerated, and the Malecón could not be continued in its public form west of the river. (However, the last section of the Malecón, from the Avenida de los Presidentes to the tunnel under the Almendares, was completed by Nicolás Arroyo y Márquez, minister of public works, in 1952–1954.)

51. Forestier, *Gardens*, 187–188.

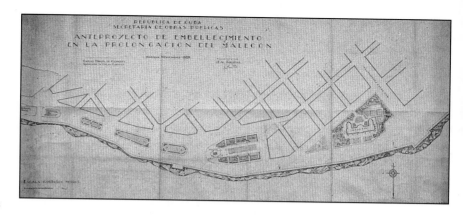

Fig. 32. J. C. N. Forestier, project of embellishment and prolongation of the Malecón between the Plaza del Maine and the Avenida de los Presidentes (Calle G), Havana, November 1928 (partially realized). Print Secretaría de Obras Públicas de Cuba. Courtesy of Institut Français d'Architecture, Paris, Fonds Leveau.

Fig. 33. J. C. N. Forestier, sketch for the Plaza del Maine, Havana, 1928. Photograph Secretaría de Obras Públicas de Cuba. Courtesy of Institut Français d'Architecture, Paris, Fonds Leveau.

Forestier designed the Plaza del Maine as an entrance to El Vedado. Circling the monument built by Moisés de Huerta and Félix Cabarrocas in 1925, and reconstructed after the October 1926 hurricane, geometric gardens were developed at the foot of the cliff dominated by the gardens of the Hotel Nacional. Now bereft of the exquisite small gardens designed by Forestier (fig. 33), and above all, without the street lamps and specially designed urban furniture, the square is nothing more than a pallid reflection of the aerial photographs from the 1930s.[52]

To the east, between the Punta Fortress and the Plaza de San Francisco, along the entrance channel to the bay, Forestier's new Avenida del Puerto (which extended the Malecón towards the bay) radically transformed the appearance of the colonial city and its relationship with the sea. Surviving portions of the walls were demolished, as was the Cárcel de Tacón (Tácon Jail) and the romantic Cortina de Valdés. A new linear esplanade along the bay, partially built on fill, created a straight edge to replace the former, more organic, walled waterfront (fig. 34).

A connection with the Palacio Presidencial was a main feature of the plan. Forestier designed the Avenida de las Misiones on axis with the palace and perpendicular to the Avenida del Puerto as a formal link with the coastline, with a central garden bordered by symmetrical ranges of royal palm trees. The Baroque design of the 1926 project, with an arcaded half-circular open space at the intersection of the Avenida del Puerto, was revised in 1929 as a downsized plaza anchored by the Punta Fortress and a monumental pier, flanked in turn by two high obelisks with sculpted reliefs illustrating scenes of Cuban history (fig. 35). Although for the 1928 Conferencia Internacional Americana President Machado insisted on the pier, or *embarcadero*, Martínez Inclán had suggested in 1919 as a grand, symbolic entrance to the city, the idea was abandoned in the end. Similarly, the large public buildings in classical Deco Modern style were not constructed, and the Avenida del Puerto never became an administrative and cultural center, as had been anticipated. In its place Forestier designed a series of promenades of royal palm trees and classical gardens. In 1939 the architect Eugenio Batista built there a serene open-air auditorium set against one of the most beautiful stage sets of the Americas, Morro Castle and the Cabaña Fortress standing on hills beyond the entrance to the bay (fig. 36). Although the park obscures the colonial city, it does engage

52. There were also three busts by Gutzon Borglum on the square, representing Americans linked to the liberation of Cuba: McKinley, Roosevelt, and Wood. See Emeterio Santovenia, *Libro conmemorativo de la inauguración de la Plaza del Maine en La Habana* (Havana: Talleres de Sindicato de Artes Gráficas, 1928).

Fig. 34. J. C. N. Forestier, perspective view of the final project for the Avenida del Puerto
and the Plaza and Avenida del
Palacio Presidencial, Havana,
1929 (partially realized).

1) Presidential Palace

2) Palace of Justice

3) American Institute of
International Law

4) Coliseum

5) Navy Headquarters

6) Army Headquarters

From *Album fotográfico de los
actos celebrados*, 1929. The
Mitchell Wolfson Jr. Collection,
The Wolfsonian, Miami Beach,
Florida, and Genoa, Italy.

the *promeneur* in the observation of the natural and artificial landscape of the city. It operates like an evocation of an expanded fortification wall and protects the spirit and scale of the colonial city while giving it a metropolitan facade. The new esplanade also aimed to improve traffic in the highly congested city center.[53] Its prolongation from the former Arsenal (which was to be transformed into a park) to the Atarés Fortress (also to be dedicated for public use) and finally to the grand square in front of a new station was unfortunately not carried out.

Another unsuccessful attempt of Forestier's team was to link visually the Plaza de Armas with the bay as it had been originally in the tradition of the Law of the Indies (1573). Related to that idea, one should mention the plan for a triumphal arch on the axis of the Avenida del Puerto, a beautiful project for the Capitanía del Puerto, by Palacios, and an even grander pier facing the Palace of the Captains General (fig. 37). Quite arguably, these projects would have supposed the demolition of the palace of the Conde de Santovenia (eighteenth century) and the isolation of the Templete, the earliest surviving Neoclassical monument in the city (1828).[54] In contrast the beautiful reform project of the square alongside the cathedral was partially realized in the 1930s; the delicate pavement and its elliptical form, designed by Forestier and inspired by Michelangelo's Capitol, was accordingly installed (fig. 38). Yet moving the fountain of the Alameda de Paula into the cathedral square was judged as too controversial and was not executed.

53. At the same time that Forestier was working in Havana, the Austrian architect Fritz Malcher (1888–1933) was hired as consultant by the secretary of public works. He developed a project for traffic reform based on one-way streets and roundabout intersections that was partially implemented from 1927 to 1928. See Fritz Malcher, "Verkehrs-Reform. Das System 'Straßenkreuzung ohne Fahrkreuzung' als Grundlage des neuen Verkehrsprojektes fur Havana, die Haupstadt von Cuba," *Der Städtbau* 24 (1929): 97–108.

54. It is a paradox that Forestier did not propose the reconstruction of the historic water moats, in the shape of a cloverleaf, that surrounded the Fuerza Castle on the square, next to the Templete. These were restored in 1959–1960.

Fig. 35. J. C. N. Forestier, project for an *embarcadero* near the Plaza de Armas and the Fuerza Castle, Havana, February 1930 (unrealized). Photograph Secretaría de Obras Públicas de Cuba. Courtesy of Institut Français d'Architecture, Paris, Fonds Leveau.

Fig. 36. Eugenio Batista, open-air auditorium on the Avenida del Puerto, Havana, 1939. Photograph Secretaría de Obras Públicas de Cuba. Author's collection.

ESTUDIO PARA LA CAPITANIA DEL PUERTO.

Fig. 37. Study for the port in front of the new Capitanía del Puerto, 1930 (unrealized). Photograph Secretaría de Obras Públicas de Cuba. Courtesy of Institut Français d'Architecture, Paris, Fonds Leveau.

Fig. 38. J. C. N. Forestier, project for the Plaza de la Catedral, 1929 (partially realized). Photograph of drawing Secretaría de Obras Públicas de Cuba. From *Album fotográfico de los actos celebrados*, 1929. The Mitchell Wolfson, Jr. Collection, The Wolfsonian, Miami Beach, Florida, and Genoa, Italy.

The last great work of the decade was the completion of the Capitolio and its gardens (fig. 39). The year he began his service as secretary of public works, Carlos Miguel de Céspedes had taken up the project again, and in December of the same year, the firm of Purdy and Henderson agreed to have the Capitolio finished for the opening of the 1928 conference. Félix Cabarrocas's plans, this time with Evelio Govantes's assistance, established the general outline for the project as we know it today. The great stairway and portico, the flanking colonnades, and the colossal pilasters on its rear facade appeared on this project. However, the French architects Heitzler and Leveau, members of Forestier's team, simplified the composition by applying those design tendencies then fashionable in Paris since the 1925 Exposition des Arts Décoratifs et Industriels Modernes. After Otero's brief second tenure as artistic director in 1926, the project passed on to José María Bens Arrarte. A year later, due to construction delays and cost overruns, Céspedes opted in favor of Eugenio Rayneri y Piedra, who returned to take control of the building fourteen years after he had started it. As technical and artistic director, Rayneri finished the titanic job (it had more than five thousand drawings) of conception, design, construction, and coordination of the numerous artists, sculptors, painters, advisors, and international suppliers.

In spite of its beautiful proportions and impressive dimensions (305 feet high and 692 feet long), the Capitolio was frequently and severely criticized because of its references to French and American models. Although the sources of inspiration may be irrefutable, one should not forget its architects' inventive capacity as much in the architecture as in its relationship with the city at large and its integration with the public spaces around it. One should also remember that it was Forestier who brought all this to fruition. According to the report submitted by Bens and Rayneri, the Havana dome was inspired by the Parisian Pantheon and followed its design. A drum, 105 feet in diameter, sustains a Corinthian peristyle, and there is a second, interior drum as well. The dome, supported on a steel structure, has a section and profile designed with Saint Peter's in Rome in mind: "The profile of [Saint Peter's] and the vigorous projecting ribs of its principal dome have also served as inspiration. The windows

and the dormers have been left out since they had no reason to exist in the capitol."[55] In the preliminary projects of Govantes y Cabarrocas, Otero, and Bens, the facets of the dome would have received a metallic covering representing large stylized palm fronds. Sadly, this was not realized (fig. 40).

The control over perspective from the 120-foot-long entrance portico with its double range of six 45-foot-high Ionic columns is closer to the view the Roman Capitol commanded prior to Mussolini's demolitions of the 1930s than to the classical relationship of axiality characteristic of the École des Beaux-Arts and the American City Beautiful Movement. In contrast to many buildings of this type, the Capitolio of Havana was not conceived to be seen frontally. In the version of the overall plan for the city designed during his second and third trips (1928 and 1930), Forestier proposed widening Teniente Rey Street as an avenue on axis with the dome and creating a plaza in front of the building (fig. 41). This project would have entailed significant demolition — specifically of the eighteenth-century convent and church of San Francisco — and fortunately was abandoned. Revealing externally the shape of the two hemicycles — hidden in the two previous projects — Rayneri lightened considerably the composition and gave it a dynamic longitudinal effect, achieving a transition between the building and the Plaza de la Fraternidad on one side and the Centro Gallego on the other. This observation is important because the general symmetry of the longitudinal facades hides an interesting asymmetry in the building's interior. The placing of the dome forward on the building allowed for a series of notable spaces and rooms on the main level — the two grand courtyards, the Salón Martí, the library, and the great Salón de los Pasos Perdidos, in particular. The latter, despite an overabundance of materials, constitutes an impressive interior space of greatness and also comfort, thanks to the climatic effect of the lateral loggias and its rear windows (fig. 42).

55. *Libro del Capitolio*, 113.

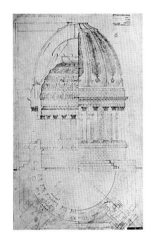

Fig. 40. Capitolio, preliminary

drawing of the cupola. From

El Libro del Capitolio, 1931.

Photograph courtesy of Miami-

Dade Public Library.

Forestier, Leveau, and Labatut subtly reinforced the architectural composition of the building with the gardens. The space in front of the building was designed as a grand square with almost no vegetation; the rear was conceived as a less formal esplanade. Four linear gardens highlighted the four corners of the Capitolio with ranges of palm trees and streetlights similar to the rostrum columns of the Roman forum. Furthermore, the two gardens on the building's longitudinal axis were designed to reduce the visual importance of its mass and diffuse the thrust of the two hemicycles that penetrated them. Forestier used small clumps of trees and relied primarily on "the royal palms that he located as close as possible to the walls of the edifice to give, through comparison of heights, an exact impression of the capitol's height."[56] A paved pathway made a rectangular frame around the building, but the two large Baroque fountains designed by Cabarrocas and dedicated to the Sea and the Earth were unfortunately not built (fig. 43). Finally, Forestier's most spectacular intervention was to eliminate the double row of trees that had lined the avenue in front of the main facade of the Capitolio. By doing so he established a monumental esplanade, a dynamic plaza, flooded with light and facing the opposite side of the avenue, which contained a long arcade with the Payret Theater, the Hotel Pasaje, and other buildings.

The ring was, therefore, the culminating achievement of Forestier and his team, and that work was carried out to completion. To compensate for a disparate assembly of styles — with nineteenth-century buildings and Neoclassical constructions standing next to the Spanish social centers, modern hotels, and the new republican emblems — the architects provided a unifying scheme on a large scale, one based on monuments.

They relocated the Fuente de la India and designed beautiful street lamps and other bronze works produced by the Darden Beller Workshops (fig. 44). There was also the lushness of vegetation: "to the rigid geometry imposed by the architectural circling frame, [Forestier] added the chromatic and formal diversity of the tropics — the linearity of the royal palm tree, the volume and spaciousness

56. Théo Leveau, "Los jardines del Capitolio," *El arquitecto* 4 (May 1929): 398, cited in Duverger, *El maestro del urbanismo criollo*, 227.

of the *ceiba* or the banyan tree; the voluptuousness of the fern or the philo-dendron."[57] With the Plaza de la Fraternidad and the new designs of the Parque Central and the Paseo del Prado, described at the beginning of this essay, the ring became one of the most beautiful urban settings of the Americas. At night the five vertically and horizontally rotating projectors installed in the summit of the Capitolio — the *centellador* — created a magical spectacle, visible from the Florida coasts, some said, with a degree of exaggeration (fig. 45).

57. Segre, "Los epígonos del modelo haussmaniano," *Quadernes/Cuadernos* 151 (March–April 1982):26. Segre also indicates that the *paseo*, sketched by Forestier with Deco-Modern forms, was in fact detailed by Otero but with Baroque forms closer to the colonial tradition.

After more than sixty years Forestier's contribution to Havana remains one of the most important moments in the urban history of Cuba. Quite often his plan has been presented in a negative light as a Haussmannian destructive project, as a retrograde plan at a time when Le Corbusier's theory was being discussed more and more.[58] Yet, Forestier's plan was not at all an imported Haussmannian concept. First, it acknowledged ideas from his Cuban predecessors and, through drawings, gave them an urban form, a comprehensible and mobilizing image. Second, it was a modern plan, inspired by American concepts of the City Beautiful and Park Movements. Such influences demonstrated a widespread awareness of issues of modernity with which Le Corbusier was also concerned: hygiene, traffic reorganization, densification of city centers, urban expansion, and open space versus enclosed urban space. The French engineer Jean-Pierre Le Dantec clearly expressed how Forestier approximated the American vision:

> For Haussmann and his successors, the city was a political center to be dominated militarily and administratively, this demand being the first condition for its development (economic, financial, hygienic, etc.). On the other hand, in the case of Forestier, who had meditated on the American example, a great city was a historical phenomenon in which the form and the quality express a culture in development. The same can be said with respect to French influence versus originality — he had an aptitude for reinventing [the past] into new forms.[59]

Forestier's heritage was thus primarily a picturesque one and, in spite of the political and social conditions of his works, fundamentally democratic. The public spaces, parks, and other embellishments that he gave Havana were well-designed, solidly built, symbolically powerful, and accessible to all citizens. They have survived many political crises, and while deteriorating rapidly due to lack

58. Such an attitude has been prevalent since 1959: see footnote 40. In absence of detailed research, everything seems to indicate that the contemporary reception of Forestier's projects and ideas in the professional circles was generally positive. On the relation between Le Corbusier and Forestier, see Salvador Tarragó i Cid, "Entre Le Nôtre et Le Corbusier," in Leclerc, *Forestier*, 260–261.

59. Le Dantec, "Forestier d'aujourd'hui," in Leclerc, *Forestier*, 243.

Fig. 45. The *centellador* on top of the Capitolio, Havana. From *Album fotográfico de los actos celebrados*, 1929. The Mitchell Wolfson Jr. Collection, The Wolfsonian, Miami Beach, Florida, and Genoa, Italy.

of care, they have endured as testimonies of a time when regimes were guided by fundamental symbols of permanence, stability, optimism, and illusion.

The crisis of 1933 and the fall of Machado cast many of Forestier's plans into oblivion. Some of his ideas, such as the civic center, lost their urban value in the Modernist period of the 1950s. Speculation made his park system obsolete. His vision, therefore, belongs more than ever to the collective memory of the city and certainly will be an inevitable reference point for Havana in the twenty-first century. A recognition of Forestier's insight with respect to the role and place of "the big city" within nature is more urgent now than ever. I would summarize it in the words of Karl Brunner, an Austrian architect and urban planner who, in Santafé de Bogotá, where he directed the department of urban planning in the 1930s, wrote in his *Manual de urbanismo*:[60]

"The final objective—the beauty of the city—depends as much on the consideration given to nature as to the architecture which must be present. The natural beauty of plants and trees and a rational architecture devoid of exoticisms and based on order give a sense of proportion to plastic urban beauty."[61] □

60. On the fascinating career of the Austrian architect and urbanist, see Carlos Morales and Mauricio Pinilla, "Karl Brunner: Architect and Urbanist," *The New City* (Foundations, no. 1, 1991): 34–39.
61. Karl Brunner, *Manual de urbanismo* 2 (Bogotá, 1938); quoted in *The New City*, 43.

Note
The original version of this article was written in French.

Fig. 1. Frédéric Miahle, *El quitrín*, lithograph, 18.5 x 27.2 cm, 1847. Author's collection.

Fig 2. Frédéric Miahle, *El día de reyes*, lithograph, 19.5 x 27.4 cm, 1847. Author's collection.

An Overriding Passion—
The Quest for a National Identity in Painting

By Narciso G. Menocal

Narciso G. Menocal is a professor of architectural history in the Department of Art History, University of Wisconsin-Madison. He has been a recipient of Buell and Guggenheim Fellowships and has published and lectured widely on Louis Sullivan and Frank Lloyd Wright. His most recent publication is *The Tobacco Industry in Cuba and Florida: Its Golden Age in Lithography and Architecture* (Miami: Cuban National Heritage, 1995).

As is well-known, mature societies are different from one another because of particular historical conditions that sometimes act upon them for centuries. Cultural development in post-colonial societies, however, is much more compressed in time than in nations with longstanding traditions. In that accelerated process art becomes useful for discovering intrinsic values, disclosing the myths that describe them, and revealing the complex whole that distinguishes a newly minted society from its mother culture. Cuban art conformed to that pattern from about the mid-1860s to about the mid-1940s, a span of eighty years one may label as its post-colonial period, a term used here in a cultural sense and not in a political one. Painting developed in three stages during that time. First it represented the physical environment, then it developed an imagery around social idiosyncrasies, and finally it made evident an abstract concept of nationality. The result was a collective portrait in which Cubans were able to recognize themselves.

Two basic themes, the identification of folk characters and the depiction of the physical environment as a poetic entity (principally the landscape), appeared in painting shortly after the mid-nineteenth century, but only after being defined by novelists and poets. As a corollary, an investigation of ways to paint tropical light and its effects on color also ensued. Those nineteenth-century discoveries were developed further in the twentieth century and became meshed with coopted European avant-garde styles. One result of that cooptation is that modern Cuban painting may appear to some as a peripheral cultural extension of European art. Yet such is not the case. In Europe establishing new definitions of form and pictorial space were major concerns, as is evident in Cubism, German Expressionism, or the *neue Sachlichkeit*— however different from each other these movements may have been and whatever their respective iconographical agendas were. In Cuban art, by contrast, establishing a national imagery through a search for the characteristic and exploring national identity were the major issues. Techniques for representing space and form in modern art, while enthusiastically received, were considered more as tools for establishing a corpus of national imagery than as a means for describing a new, abstract universe. Such a corpus would facilitate an assertion of national identity, collectively; and it would also help each person to discern how to fit within the broad spectrum of a national culture, individually. Nationalism made Cuban art *sui generis* in style and general appearance, but perhaps more interestingly, in the manner in which it should be read and interpreted.

As one last prefatory note, I wish to point out that a connoisseur of Cuban art may be surprised by the absence of several important painters from my discussion and by the little attention I pay to a number of major figures.[1] Like any other critical work on history, this one establishes its own standards concerning the importance of events and imposes its own sense of order upon them. Its purpose is to show how a major historical process took place. That process entailed the invention of an imagery illustrating the national ethos above and beyond the individual efforts of artists who attempted to create a Cuban aesthetic.[2]

Cuba was a Spanish colony through 1898. From the sixteenth to the mid-eighteenth century Havana was scarcely more than a fortified port, a protected gathering place for ships laden with goods that would sail back to Spain together as a *flota*. In spite of those conditions an intellectual life of sorts developed. Poetry was written from the early seventeenth century onward; the Dominican Order founded a university in 1728; the first newspaper was published on 24 October 1790; and a history of Havana, *Llave del Nuevo Mundo*, written circa 1752–1761 (but not published until 1830), gives evidence that a conscious "Cubanness" was evolving and that its author, José Martín Félix de Arrate, considered himself to be Cuban rather than Spanish. Conditions, however, improved drastically in the last quarter of the eighteenth century and throughout the early nineteenth. A belated Enlightenment brought with it a series of progressive measures in politics, agriculture, industry, and commerce — and Cuban culture began to evolve, first in literature. No national art existed yet. Art was mostly an imported commodity generally circumscribed to religious articles and pictures for the church and the laity and to those pieces of industrial art — silverware and the like — required by the best households.[3]

Painting began to develop in the second half of the eighteenth century with the religious art of José Nicolás de la Escalera (1734–1804), followed in the

1. Among the artists not mentioned are the following. From the nineteenth and early twentieth centuries: Francisco Javier Báez, Eliab Metcalf, Leonardo Barañano, Hippolyte Garneray, James Gay Sawkins, Guillaume-François Colson, Felipe and Augusto Chartrand, Miguel and Miguel Angel Melero, Ercole Morelli, Henri Cleenewerk, Miguel Arias, Federico Martínez, Juan Jorge Peoli, Domingo Ramos, Domingo Ravenet, Esteban Valderrama, Juan Emilio Hernández Giro, and Mariano Miguel; Armando Menocal, José Joaquín Tejada, and Leopoldo Romañach will be dealt with in one sentence. From the modern period: Enrique Riverón, Pastor Argudín, R. López Dirube, Luis Martínez Pedro, Mario Carreño, José María Mijares, Marcelo Pogolotti, Raúl Milián, Felipe Orlando, Mirta Cerra, Daniel Serra Badué, Roberto Diago, Carmelo González, Enrique Caravia, Servando Cabrera-Moreno, Sandú Darié, Palko Luckacs, Armando Maribona, Luis Martínez Pedro, and Jorge Arche. Artists who began to paint after the mid-1940s are beyond the scope of this work.

2. For surveys of Cuban art, see Loló de la Torriente, *Estudio de las artes plásticas en Cuba* (Havana: Úcar García, 1954); Guy Pérez de Cisneros, *Características de la evolución de la pintura en Cuba* (Havana: Ministerio de Educación, Dirección General de Cultura, 1959); Adelaida de Juan, *Las artes plásticas* (Havana: Instituto del Libro, 1968); Martha de Castro, *El arte en Cuba* (Miami: Ediciones Universal, 1970); Ricardo González Jane, ed., *The National Museum of Cuba: Painting* (Leningrad: Aurora Art Publishers, 1978); Cuban Foundation Collection of the Museum of Arts and Sciences, ed., *Two Centuries of Cuban Art: 1759–1959*, with an essay by Gary Russell Libby (Daytona Beach, Fla.: Museum of Arts and Sciences, 1980); Jorge Rigol, *Apuntes sobre la pintura y el grabado en Cuba* (Havana: Editorial Letras Cubanas, 1982); Ministerio de Cultura [de Cuba], ed., *Pintura española y cubana y litografías y grabados cubanos del siglo XIX (Colección del Museo Nacional de Cuba)* (Madrid: Museo del Prado/Sección del siglo XIX/Casón del Buen Retiro, 1983); and Museo Nacional de Cuba, ed., *La Habana: Salas del Museo Nacional de Cuba, Palacio de Bellas Artes* (Havana: Editorial Letras Cubanas, 1990).

3. However, one Juan Camargo is mentioned in the *acta capitular* (minutes of the Cabildo) of 7 March 1597 as painting the retable of the main parish church in Havana. Cited in De Juan, *Las artes plásticas*, 9. For further evidence of early paintings, most of which have not come down to us, see Rigol, *Apuntes*, 31–42.

early nineteenth century by the portraits of Vicente Escobar (1757–1834).[4] Neither of the two was exceptional other than by standards like those of Cuba at the time. Needless to say, a programmatic identification with a national ideal was far beyond their imagination. Nor does one find a Cuban content in the rest of the art of the period, such as the religious pictures of Giuseppe Perovani (1765–1835), a Brescian artist who lived in Havana for a short time, or the far more extensive work of Jean-Baptiste Vermay (1788–1833), a disciple of David, and the person responsible for making the profession of painting socially acceptable, inasmuch as he was French and white and not a "free man of color" like Escalera and Escobar. His local importance notwithstanding, Vermay was little more than an adequate painter; the best artist on the island only by default.

Cuban themes began to evolve when Romanticism initiated a search for a national identity, first in literature and then in painting. Two of its manifestations are relevant here: the analytical and the lyrical.

Analytical Romanticism appeared first in *Cecilia Valdés*, a novel Cirilo Villaverde finished by 1839. Notwithstanding influences from Sir Walter Scott and Alessandro Manzoni, the novel is broadly based on Victor Hugo's *Notre-Dame de Paris*.[5] Villaverde turned Havana and the many characters who inhabited it into symbols of themselves, and proved himself to be as skillful in doing it as Hugo was in portraying fifteenth-century Paris. But such definitions of a national imagery did not find their way into painting immediately. Painting itself, as a medium of expression, had to mature first, as literature already had.

Important in that respect was the work of European lithographers arriving during the second quarter of the nineteenth century, especially since they looked at Cuban subjects from a fresh perspective, with eyes that were discovering the tropics.[6] What becomes remarkable is that those artists portrayed so well the characters and sites Villaverde explored, although they had no knowledge of the novel, which was not published until 1882 (but a "primitive version," as Villaverde called it, appeared in the magazine *La Siempreviva* in 1839). Indeed, associating the novel with their work has become commonplace — a factor of

4. On the painting of this period, see Academia Nacional de Artes y Letras, ed., *Discursos pronunciados en la sesión solemne celebrada por esta corporación a la memoria del académico electo fallecido Sr. Bernardo G. Barros y Gómez, el día 12 de mayo de 1924* (Havana: Imprenta "El Siglo XX," 1924); and Corporación Nacional del Turismo, ed., *La pintura colonial en Cuba, exposición en el Capitolio Nacional* (Havana: Corporación Nacional del Turismo, 1950). On Vermay, see Francisco Calcagno, *Diccionario biográfico cubano* (New York: Imprenta y Librería de N. Ponce de León, 1878), 680–681; Emile Bellier de la Chavignerie and Louis Auvray, *Dictionnaire général des artistes de l'école française depuis l'origine des arts du dessin jusqu'à nos jours* (Paris: Librairie Renouard, 1882), 2:651; Ulrich Thieme and Felix Becker, later, Hans Vollmer, ed., *Künstler-Lexikon* (Leipzig: Verlag von Wilhelm Engelmann and Verlag von E. A. Seemann, 1907–1950), 34:261; for Escobar, see Evelio Govantes, "Vicente Escobar, uno de los precursores de la pintura en Cuba," *Cuadernos de historia habanera*, no. 13 (Havana: Municipio de La Habana, 1937): 89–100; and Arturo G. Lavín, "Familia del pintor habanero Don Vicente Escobar," *Revista de la Biblioteca Nacional*, 2nd ser., vol. 4 (April–June 1953): 154–89.

5. The parallels of Cecilia Valdés–Esmeralda, Leonardo Gamboa-Phébus, and José Dolores Pimienta-Quasimodo are almost transparent, as much as the instances of Esmeralda and Cecilia being separated from their mothers at birth, the two mothers going insane, and daughters and mothers eventually reuniting (at the end of the novel for Cecilia and just before her death for Esmeralda). Hugo's exquisite precision in describing medieval Paris found a counterpart in Villaverde's descriptions of Havana, a coffee plantation, and a sugar mill.

6. For the early development of lithography in Cuba, see Zoila Lapique, "La primera imprenta litográfica en Cuba," *Revista de la Biblioteca Nacional* (September–December, 1970): 35, 41–45; and Narciso Menocal, *The Tobacco Industry in Cuba and Florida: Its Golden Age in Lithography and Architecture* (Miami: Cuban National Heritage, 1995).

Fig. 3. Frédéric Miahle,

El zapateado, lithograph,

18.7 x 27.5 cm, 1847.

Author's collection.

no small importance in the subsequent development of themes of nationalism in art, especially in the twentieth century.

One of those lithographers was the Frenchman Frédéric Miahle (1810–1881; in Cuba, 1838–1854), who created a series of seminal images in his illustrations for *Viaje Al Rededor de la Isla de Cuba* [*sic*] (1847–1848).[7] *El quitrín* is by far the best known among them (fig. 1). It depicts three women taking the late afternoon air in a *quitrín*, a carriage typical of the island in which the coachman, a lavishly attired slave, rode on the horse. This lithograph turned out to be so popular that it became one of the standard icons of Havana, especially since Miahle placed the *quitrín* crossing in front of the Fuente de la India, an important local monument that in itself represents the city. In *El día de reyes* (The Feast of the Epiphany) he showed black members of the Abakuá secret society wearing African dress and masks and dancing in San Francisco Square on the Feast of the Epiphany, the only day of the year in which they were allowed to do so, to collect *aguinaldos* (gifts of money) on the Feast of the Kings, the magi who brought gifts to Jesus (fig. 2). The third most relevant lithograph is *El zapateado*, showing white country people enjoying the traditional dance of the *guajiros* (peasants) (fig. 3).

Beyond any aesthetic significance, *El quitrín, El día de reyes*, and *El zapateado* are important for showing the four major social classes of the 1840s: leisurely and poor whites and free blacks and slaves. It was partly out of a commingling of characters, attitudes, and modes of language of these four kinds of people that Cuban patterns of behavior evolved. In Cuba, contrary to developments in the United States and elsewhere, factors of nationality have always taken precedence over racial issues. Such a peculiarity, while not precluding racism, toned it down; enough to eventually allow for an integration to take place, at least among the popular classes. Of necessity, that integration became a stratum of nationality.

7. On Miahle, see Bellier de Chavignerie and Auvray, *Dictionnaire*, 2:84; and especially Emilio Cueto, *Miahle's Colonial Cuba* (Miami: The Historical Association of Southern Florida, 1994).

Miahle's imagery was complemented by the work of the Spanish Basque Víctor Patricio de Landaluze (1828–1889; arrived in Cuba in 1863). The twenty-six years Landaluze lived in Cuba were rife with the anti-Spanish sentiment that led to the first war of independence, from 1868–1878. Fervidly pro-Spanish, in many of his paintings and in practically all of his newspaper illustrations, Landaluze reveled in making evident his anti-Cuban opinions. Yet, attempting to be mordant and satirical in his depiction of Cuban types, Landaluze displayed an acuity of vision that fleshed out characters whom Miahle had portrayed not without a measure of classical idealization and academic detachment (fig. 4). Beyond this, he brought into painting a sensuousness and even a sexuality that are seminal to the national character and had long been present in Cuban music. Also, his best work is imbued with *choteo*, that peculiar form of humor in which Cubans seem to enjoy making light of what is perceived as someone's personal or social shortcomings, but which is also an expression of friendship, of making known to the butt of one's jest that one shares in an understanding of the problem, or even tragedy, that gave rise to the joke. Finally, while his purpose was to make use of blacks, mulattoes, and poor white peasants to portray what he saw as a typically inferior colonial life, he presented Cubans with folk types in whom they could recognize themselves, and which they subsequently transformed into national symbols, especially those he depicted in his book *Tipos y costumbres de la Isla de Cuba* (1881).[8] Hence his presenting folk characters in situations that he as a Spaniard found embarrassing was not seen by Cubans as at all malicious but as delightfully true to life and therefore as a mirror-like image of themselves.

While an identification of folk types was important to the development of a national art, the depiction of more subtle elements of the environment — of its scale, light, and color — was also required for identifying a national aesthetic. Lyrical Romanticism brought those concerns to the forefront. That mode appeared first in Cuba, seemingly all of a sudden, in the poetry of José María Heredia (1803–1839), especially in his *Oda al Niágara* (1824). A political exile, when facing the falls Heredia became anguished by a memory of palm trees and recalled a countryside not magnificently sublime but amiable and smiling and inviting in bright sunlight. In this and other poems Heredia fixed for all time an image of the countryside as a nationalistic metaphor. That trope, once translated into painting, became a recurring image in art. But before Cubans explored their landscape in painting, foreigners worked first at representing it, again, mainly in lithography.

The illustrations by the Frenchman Édouard Laplante (born 1818; in Cuba circa 1848) for Justo Germán Cantero's *Los ingenios* (1857), a book on sugar mills, are reputed to be the best work of lithography produced in Cuba (fig. 5).[9] Laplante's vision was as fresh as it was accurate and faithfully captured the rhythms, colors, and scale of the countryside. But when one compares those lithographs with equally well-rendered views of similar landscapes elsewhere, one realizes that Laplante's eye, although extraordinarily analytical, was unencumbered with nationalistic affective considerations for the Cuban countryside,

8. Víctor Patricio de Landaluze, *Tipos y costumbres de la Isla de Cuba* (Havana: Miguel de Villa, 1881); for Landaluze, see Lázara Castellanos, *Víctor Patricio Landaluze* (Havana: Editorial Letras Cubanas, 1991).

9. While the book bears an 1857 imprint, it quotes statistics of as late as 1863. *Los ingenios* was printed in stages, each at a different time, in the Litografía de Luis Marquier, the same that printed Miahle's *Viaje Al Rededor de la Isla de Cuba* in 1847–1848. Eighteen fifty-seven probably was the date the project began.

Fig. 4. Víctor Patricio de Landaluze, *Los negros curros*. From *Tipos y costumbres de la Isla de Cuba* (Havana: Miguel de Villa, 1881). Private collection, Miami, Florida.

as would be expected of a Frenchman living on the island for only a period of time. His lithographs are indeed superbly rendered and painstakingly printed, but his aesthetic intention went no further than producing topographical views of sugar mills. Nowhere does one find in them the nationalistic intensity of Heredia's poetry. His contribution, as well as Miahle's (who also did landscapes), was limited in that respect.[10]

It was through a knowledge of the Hudson River School that Cuban artists came to paint landscapes capable of evoking an emotional national identification. Cubans sensed an aesthetic and programmatic affinity in the way American artists put forth the landscape as a primordial image of America, pristine and

10. In respect to this, I do wonder if the kind of national self-identification Cubans often find in the landscapes of Laplante and Miahle may not be a result of a transference of readings from later landscape paintings by Cuban artists well acquainted with a romantic poetry rich in national rural imagery.

Fig. 5. Édouard Laplante,

Ingenio Buena-Vista, litho-

graph. From Justo Germán

Cantero, *Los ingenios* (Havana:

Litografía de Luis Marquier,

1857). Private collection.

unsullied. Also, an influence from painting to painting was easier to establish than one from lithography to painting, especially since artists moved freely between Cuba and the United States after the mid-century.

Federico Fernández Cavada (1831–1871) was one of those artists. He studied engineering in Pennsylvania and later fought in the Civil War, earning the rank of lieutenant colonel in the Union Army. He subsequently settled in Cuba, where he favored the cause of independence. As a painter he had an intimate knowledge of the Hudson River School. In *Río San Juan, Trinidad* (1865) he brought to a Cuban subject the cosmic, transcendental grandeur of nature that Frederick Edwin Church portrayed in much of his work, especially in *The Heart of the Andes* (1859), to which *Río San Juan* is compositionally close, including minute human figures that remind us of the smallness of man in comparison with the sublime. In the preceding year Fernández Cavada had painted *Paisaje cubano* (Cuban Landscape), also of the Trinidad mountain range, but in this work the central feature was two palm trees, the national symbol, the very trees that Heredia had yearned for in Niagara.

But it was Esteban Chartrand (1840–1883) who best fixed on canvas the characteristics of the Cuban landscape.[11] His knowledge of the countryside was of long standing, having been born and raised in his family's sugar mill near Matanzas. He also was conversant with American painting; he lived for long periods in New York City and was represented there by the Goupil Gallery. Eschewing the grandeur and breadth of Frederick Edwin Church or Albert Bierstadt, Chartrand approached the quieter luminism of Martin Johnson Heade (figs. 6 and 7). The sublime has no place in his amiable world, a poetical idealization of a nation seeking self-actualization. In *Paisaje* (Landscape), of 1880, Chartrand conveyed those feelings in one of his best works. It is a lyrical scene in which palm trees, a pond, and a *bohío* (hut), with two *guajiros* (peasants) in front of it were given a life of their own by the painter, who had mastered the golden transparency of light from the setting sun. Suffused in that glow, the hut, the pond, and the grove are part of a poetic whole. Moreover,

11. On Chartrand, see Raúl R. Ruiz, *Esteban Chartrand* (Havana: Editorial Letras Cubanas, 1987).

Fig. 6. Martín Johnson Heade, *Sunset on the Marshes*, **oil on canvas, 68.6 x 134.6 cm, 1867. Manoogian collection.**

Fig. 7. Esteban Chartrand, *Paisaje*, **oil on canvas, 38.5 x 64.5 cm, 1880. Photograph courtesy of Emilio Cueto.**

the human being is now a partner of the environment, not a negligible entity in the presence of greater, mightier forces. Cuba, as well as Cubans, are represented in the painting by a number of images. First, there is the landscape as an indication of the poetry and beauty of the national environment. Then, there are the *guajiros*, images of unspoiled rural nobility and virtue: synecdoches of an ideal society. As one final national symbol there is the *bohío*, the one native-Indian building type that survived as a rural dwelling. Chartrand's work embraced all these signs and meanings, equipoised now in an arcady of harmonious delight, in order to bring the landscape up to the level of a metaphor standing for nationality. In the process he transformed the rhapsodic bravura of the Hudson River School into a soft, soothing melody, like an adagio in a minor key. Such was, at the time, the poetic essence of the Cuban vernacular.

Another American influence in Chartrand's work appears in *El tren de Güines* (The Train to Güines), a painting with a train traveling across a landscape (fig. 8). Such a realization of the coming together of modern industrial technology and nature is also a nineteenth-century American theme, one that Leo Marx identified as "The machine in the garden." [12] An early use of this subject

12. Leo Marx, *The Machine in the Garden: Technology and the Pastoral Ideal in America* (London: Oxford University Press, 1964).

in art appears in George Inness's *The Lackawanna Valley*, of 1855, a painting that shows an interaction between a train and a landscape. Chartrand may well have seen this work in one of his many visits to New York.

Chartrand's perception of nature's loss of innocence through technology was an isolated incident in nineteenth-century Cuban culture. In point of fact most of his work depicts that "perfect arcady" most everyone seems to have been longing for. In poetry, for instance, it was described in *Rumores del Hórmigo*, a volume of poetry Juan Nápoles y Fajardo (1829–ca. 1862), who wrote under the pseudonym of El Cucalambé. (The book was published in 1856 and the author included in the title the name of the river that runs by his native Las Tunas.) *Rumores del Hórmigo* is a continuous sylvan paean to the beauty of the countryside and to the emotions it causes to swell in the hearts of innocent and virtuous *guajiros*. Steeped in the pastoral classical poetry of Theocritus, Virgil, and the Horace of the bucolic odes, El Cucalambé created with the *décima*—the standard form of peasant versification—an apparently simple and naive but in fact not unsophisticated vision of a perfect, idyllic, and pristinely beautiful national rural imagery. This imagery also served him to express metaphorically his longing for independence from Spain, a desire he made patent by his deep involvement in early anti-Spanish conspiracies in 1848 and then again in 1851. The lyrical content of El Cucalambé is different from that of Chartrand in that it is direct and even seemingly objective by design; the narrator is often a person different from the character reacting emotively to the landscape. Yet there is a commonality of interests between the poetry of El Cucalambé and the art of Chartrand, one that, avowedly, may be innately lyrical. In spite of their differences, their individual efforts were consecutive attempts at defining national virtue through a use of rural themes, as opposed to urban ones vitiated by European custom, and therefore by Spain.

Fig. 8. Esteban Chartrand,

***El tren de Güines*, oil on board,**

26 x 34.1 cm, date unknown.

Photograph by Sandy Levy.

Private collection, Miami, Florida.

Less than half a generation after Chartrand, Valentín Sanz Carta (1850–1898) added a new dimension to the depiction of the landscape as a national theme. A former disciple of Carlos de Haes in Madrid, Sanz Carta usually narrowed his vision to one tree, bush, clump, or at most a narrow section of landscape that he made monumental and depicted in all of its luxury (fig. 9). Thus he added a hitherto absent expression of tropical sensuality to the representation of nature. But political events soon changed the course of art. A lovely vision of the totality of nature standing for an image of the nation became psychologically unsustainable in the tense political climate of the 1880s and 1890s, which led to the last war of independence (1895–1898) and the Spanish-American War (1898). But while illusions of a placid, pastoral utopia were shattered, a desire for calm and peace became ever more evident in painters and poets.

Following that vein, José Arburu Morell (1864–1889) and Guillermo Collazo (1850–1896) depicted a domesticated nature. Their world would include the refuge of a garden or a prospect to be enjoyed from the secure vantage point of a well-appointed house interior. To emphasize the otherness of this pictorial environment in contrast with the harsh political realities of the world beyond, ladies of leisure—the people most removed from political cares according to the conventions of the day—usually dwell in these canvases, if at all. In Arburu Morell's *El jardín* (1888) a lady sits in a rattan chair in a garden, by a fountain, fanning herself, a picture he painted the year before he died at age twenty-five (fig. 10). Two years earlier, in *La siesta*, Collazo had likewise depicted a woman lounging in a chair, this time inside a room partly appointed with potted palms and a large oriental carpet, looking out onto an enclosed garden and a beach beyond (fig. 11).

Fig. 9. Valentín Sanz Carta, *Paisaje*, oil on canvas. Courtesy of Otto G. Richter Library, University of Miami, Coral Gables, Florida.

Fig. 10. José Arburu Morell, *El jardín*, oil on canvas, 36 x 24.5 cm, 1888. Courtesy of Otto G. Richter Library, University of Miami, Coral Gables, Florida.

These paintings are stylistically a world apart from the poetry of Julián del Casal (1863–1893), although the poet found affinity with them since they reflected as much of a desire for refuge from the realities of the day as his work did.[13] In a country torn apart by war and political strife, Casal had embraced in his work the exquisite aesthetics of Baudelaire, Rimbaud, and Mallarmé and described paintings of Gustave Moreau in some of his poems. More to the point at hand, he created for himself in his rooms a rarefied atmosphere of Chinese silks, Japanese screens, Moorish lamps, and Persian carpets, where the realities of the world beyond were excluded as much as the harsh tropical sunlight the poet so much disliked.

Decadence, however, had no place in painting, since artists continued to develop the theme of nature-as-symbol. But the landscape was no longer the image of

13. See his essay on Arburu Morell, in Julián del Casal, *Busto y rimas* (1893; Miami: Editorial Cubana, 1993), 119–136.

Fig. 11. Guillermo Collazo, *La siesta*, oil on canvas, 65.5 x 83.5 cm, 1886. Courtesy of Otto G. Richter Library, University of Miami, Coral Gables, Florida.

nature artists pursued; tropical light had taken its place. Arburu Morell, and even more so Collazo, expanded their experiments on chromatic brilliance. The more they followed the lead of Sanz Carta by focusing on a narrow field of vision, the more they became conscious of effects of luminosity, both on shiny surfaces of vegetation and on reflections from walls, white or otherwise. *El patio*, a picture by Collazo representing a courtyard rich with tropical plants drenched in sunlight, is possibly the best example of this trend. The work attests to Collazo's mastery over new artistic conceptions of pure, tropical color bursting with light; with reds, greens, whites, and yellows contrasting with each other, all existing in a world where there is no possibility for the chiaroscuro of foreign latitudes. With this and other pictures, Collazo, and Arburu Morell as well, all but completed the repertory for pictorial representation of national physical characteristics. In hindsight we recognize that only two steps were missing to close the cycle the landscapes of Fernández Cavada had begun a few decades earlier: an analysis of national idiosyncracy and a programmatic nationalist synthesis. Those two stages would come in the twentieth century.

Yet, after independence in 1902, painting changed little. Armando Menocal (1863–1942), José Joaquín Tejada (1867–1943), and, above all, Leopoldo Romañach (1862–1951) extended late-nineteenth-century art well into the new century, strengthening a free academicism. But as painting turned into a series of exercises of excellent and even superb academic virtuosity, literature was creating a new vision. Once independent from Spain, writers chose to confront truth instead of inventing an ideal future (as had been the goal of much of the literature of the last seventy years or so of colonial rule). Writers now transferred nationalistic values from a rural utopia to urban realities; the exoticism of Casal had died out with him.

Twentieth-century culture was heralded mostly by the novels of Miguel de Carrión (1875–1929). His two best works, *Las honradas* (1918) and *Las impuras* (1919), concern themselves with social realities of middle-class women and prostitutes living in a world dominated by men. The social criticism of Carlos Loveira (1882–1928), a self-taught railroad worker and world traveler, went beyond Carrión's, especially in *Los inmorales* (1919) and, above all, in *Juan Criollo* (1928), the story of a poor young man who, because of social constraints, finds it necessary to commit all kinds of immoralities to raise himself from servant to member of the House of Representatives. Beyond the work of Carrión and Loveira, the novels of Jesús Castellanos (1879–1912), Alfonso Hernández Catá (1885–1940), José Antonio Ramos (1885–1943), and Luis Rodríguez Embil (1879–1954) completed a picture of social reality that was far from perfect, much less utopian.

A major cultural event of this period, one that opened many avenues for expression, was the publication of the first issue of *Social* in January 1916. A monthly magazine covering literature, art, architecture, fashion, travel, and society news edited by Conrado W. Massaguer (1889–1965), *Social* was published through 1933, and again from 1935 through 1938. Elegantly printed, richly illustrated, and served by a first-rate staff that included Emilio Roig de Leuchsenring,[14] *Social* became an open forum for the avant-garde, both national and foreign; it created as well an extraordinary amalgam by bridging the gap between the haute bourgeoisie and the world of writers, thinkers, and artists. Soon the offices of *Social* became a meeting place for the intelligentsia, but since they were located on the Calzada del Cerro and therefore somewhat removed from the center of Havana, in 1923 the group began meeting for lunch at the Lafayette Hotel on Saturdays. In 1927 that group of intellectuals and artists — by far the most important in the nation — organized themselves as El grupo minorista and made known their manifesto in favor of political freedom and cultural reform, supporting "the new ideas."[15]

In that same year of 1927 the *revista de avance* [sic] was founded by Jorge Mañach, Juan Marinello, Francisco Ichazo, Alejo Carpentier, and Martí Casanovas (the latter two soon replaced by José Zacarías Tallet and Félix Lizaso). This important publication, which only lasted through 1930, was created expressly to promote the *vanguardia* in literature and the arts and supplanted *Social* as the main standard bearer of progressive thought, with some issues dedicated to one writer, as was the case on the occasion of García Lorca's visit to Havana in 1930.

Concurrently, a modern poetry had been developing since 1913 when Regino Boti (1878–1958) published *Arabescos mentales*. Subsequently Agustín Acosta (1886–1979) published *Ala* in 1915 and José Manuel Poveda (1888–1926) *Versos precursores* in 1917. In 1928 Mariano Brull (1891–1956) wrote *Poemas en menguante*, a book in which he made use of meaningless combinations of letters having an inner rhythm all to themselves. He used the collective name of *jitanjáforas* to identify these poems, which were an attempt to attain to the purely abstract realm of rhythm. More importantly for painting, a *poesía negra* also

14. Emilio Roig de Leuchsenring (1889–1964) was an outstanding scholar and historian. From 1956 on he served as official historian of the City of Havana, heading the Oficina del Historiador de la Ciudad. For Roig and his accomplishments, see Instituto de Literatura y Lingüística de la Academia de Ciencias de Cuba, ed., *Diccionario de la literatura cubana* (Havana: Editorial Letras Cubanas, 1980–1984), 2:917–921.

15. Besides Conrado Massaguer and Emilio Roig de Leuchsenring, the group comprised Eduardo Abela, José Manuel Acosta, Juan Antiga, Luis A. Baralt, Otto Bluhme, Diego Bonilla, Mariano Brull, Alejo Carpentier, José Antonio Fernández de Castro, Antonio Gattorno, Luis Gómez Wangüemert, Max Henríquez Ureña, Francisco Ichazo, Félix Lizaso, Luis López Méndez, Jorge Mañach, Armando Maribona, Juan Marinello, Guillermo Martínez Márquez, Rubén Martínez Villena, Andrés Núñez Olano, Alfredo T. Quílez, Arturo Alfonso Roselló, Octavio Seigle, Enrique Serpa, Juan José Sicre, José Zacarías Tallet, Jaime Valls, and Orosmán Viamonte. See Max Henríquez Ureña, *Panorama histórico de la literatura cubana* (Puerto Rico: Ediciones Mirador, 1963), 2:354.

came into being partly as a result of an awareness of the central role of black culture in the European avant-garde. Cuban poets suddenly took notice of their own surroundings; the Afro-Cuban culture in their midst was the original document Europeans sought. In the opinion of Jorge and Isabel Castellanos, "The aesthetic values of Afro-Cuban religions were discovered in Cuba in the 1920s and established an influence of great strength in the national poetical movement."[16] To most everyone's admission, black culture was a major discovery, and themes, rhythms, and language taken from the black vernacular became fused with rhythms and meters adopted from the new European poetry—Lorca's being by far the major influence in that respect. In 1926 Alfonso Camín published *Elogio de la negra* and in 1928 Ramón Guirao wrote *Bailadora de rumba* and José Zacarías Tallet *La rumba*. Also in 1928, Alejo Carpentier and Amadeo Roldán collaborated in the production of *La rebambaramba*, a ballet mixing themes derived from Miahle and Landaluze and avant-garde music based on black rhythms and forms. In 1930 Nicolás Guillén published *Motivos del son*, followed a year later by *Sóngoro cosongo. ¡Ecue-Yamba-O!* (1933), Carpentier's first novel, was also based on Afro-Cuban themes. This new interest in Afro-Cuban culture was, as well, part of an international movement taking place in the Hispanic world and paralleled similar events abroad, as when the Indian became central to a new vision of Mexico, the *gaucho* the symbol of Argentina, and the gypsy an important feature in the Spanish intellectual landscape. In Cuba, however, the trend became much more racially inclusive than abroad. Whites and mulattoes were indiscriminately brought forward as much as blacks to create an image of the new Cuba, a consequence of the cultural and racial integration that had already taken place among the popular classes.

Following in the wake of the poets, painters became convinced that the most important function of a new art should be to reveal newly discovered national values through methods of *vanguardia*. Given that premise, the creation of a national imagery took precedence over investigation of modern form. Thus, the intellectuality inherent in the monochrome of the early Cubists found no echo in Cuban art, which pursued its interests in the emotional, pure, vibrant, contrasting colors of its natural environment. Moreover, Cuban artists dismissed the standard subjects of the new painting — as fixed by contemporaneous European masters — and concentrated on folk characters, thus strengthening the cultural integration of painting and poetry.

The limits set by nineteenth-century art to the extent of nationalist topics were subverted in the process. Notions of Cubanness were now identified with urban themes, and when rural ones were explored, their signification was distinctively social or psychological, never lyrical or utopian, since both characteristics were now considered to be irrelevant and superficial, even maudlin. Collectively, therefore, the "Generation of 1927"—so called because the first exhibition of *arte nuevo* took place in May 1927—made much broader iconographical and iconological statements than did previous artists (fig. 12).[17] By turning to the vernacular to create works of high art, the new painters, like the new poets, embraced characters, features, and emotions they felt to be innately theirs,

16. "El valor estético de las religiones afrocubanas fue descubierto en Cuba en la década de los veinte de este siglo, influyendo entonces con gran fuerza sobre el movimiento poético nacional." Jorge and Isabel Castellanos, *Cultura afrocubana* (Miami: Ediciones Universal, 1988–1994), 4:209.

17. Iconography refers to the particular meaning of a given image; iconology is the sum total of meanings that rise from the consciousness and subconsciousness of a nation or period. See Erwin Panofsky, "Introductory," *Studies in Iconology: Humanistic Themes in the Art of the Renaissance* (New York: Oxford University Press, 1939), 3–31; as reprinted in Panofsky, *Meaning in the Visual Arts* (Garden City, N.Y.: Doubleday Anchor Books, 1955), 26–54.

Fig. 12. Eduardo Abela,

logo for the *Exhibición de*

arte nuevo. From *revista de*

avance 1 (15 April 1927).

Courtesy of Otto G. Richter

Library, University of Miami,

Coral Gables, Florida.

Fig. 13. Víctor Manuel,

Guajira cubana, mixed media

on paper, 33.6 x 26 cm,

ca. 1940. Photograph by

Sandy Levy. Private collection,

Miami, Florida.

which preceding generations had been loathe to acknowledge since they held different notions of decorum. In their enthusiasm the painters of the *vanguardia* all but exhausted the catalogue of national idiosyncracies and characteristics, representing them one by one within a span of about fifteen years.[18]

It is standard to open a discussion on the Generation of 1927 with Víctor Manuel (1897–1969), an elegant draftsman, an able colorist, and the first Cuban artist to demonstrate an interest in abstraction.[19] The work he did upon

18. On modern Cuban art, see José Gómez Sicre, *Pintura cubana de hoy* (Havana: María Luisa Gómez Mena, 1944) and "Modern Painting in Cuba," *Magazine of Art* 37 (February 1944): 51–55; Alfred H. Barr, "Modern Cuban Painters," *Bulletin of the Museum of Modern Art* 11 (April 1944): 2–14; Luis de Soto, "Esquema para una indagación estilística de la pintura moderna cubana," *Universidad de La Habana* 9 (January–June 1945): 65–138; Edmundo Desnoes, *Pintores cubanos* (Havana: Ediciones Revolución, 1962); and Juan A. Martínez, *Cuban Art and National Identity: The Vanguardia Painters, 1927–1950* (Gainesville: University Press of Florida, 1994).

19. His full name was Víctor Manuel García, but he was commonly known as Manolo García. One day, at Gattorno's studio in Paris, his Cuban friends recommended a change of name. From that day on he became Víctor Manuel. See Armando Maribona, *El arte y el amor en Montparnasse* (Mexico, D.F.: Ediciones Botas, 1950), 242–243. On Víctor Manuel, see Consejo Nacional de Cultura, Museo Nacional, ed., *Víctor Manuel: exposición retrospectiva*, with an essay by Jorge Rigol (Havana: Consejo Nacional de Cultura, Museo Nacional, 1969); Museo Cubano de Arte y Cultura, ed., *Víctor Manuel: un innovador en la pintura cubana* (Miami: Museo Cubano de Arte y Cultura, 1982); and Jorge Rigol, *Víctor Manuel* (Havana: Editorial Letras Cubanas, 1990).

his return from Paris shows a flattening of perspective, mostly derived from Gauguin. Also, he brought into a twentieth-century context conceptions of tropical color and studies on the reflection of light pursued by late-nineteenth-century Cuban artists. Color, rather than being a reality, now became an abstraction of its own reality, a depiction of an idea of what was tropical rather than a representation of factual luminosity. Furthermore, Víctor Manuel introduced into art folk characters who no longer were presented as curious specimens of picturesqueness, as had been previously the case not only in painting but also in the *teatro bufo* since the 1860s (fig. 13).

One result of the new iconographical importance of the popular classes was that painters made use of them to depict sensual and sexual subject matters they considered to be features of the national iconology and, hence, worthy of recognition. Three pictures, one by Antonio Gattorno (1904–1980), another by Eduardo Abela (1889–1965), and a third by Carlos Enríquez (1900–1957), will serve to explore the progression of this theme from allusion to a frank depiction of lust.

The understructure of Gattorno's *El río*, of 1927, was a result of influences stemming mainly from the Mexican muralists (fig. 14).[20] The important factor of the painting, however, is that Gattorno's deliberate sensuality of line and color has made two monumental female nudes harmonize with a background of a banana tree and a landscape of rounded brown hills that echo the shapes of their bodies. Tropical sensuality has made an appearance here, albeit indirectly. Gattorno makes a veiled ithyphallic suggestion in the forthcoming fruit of the banana tree and reinforces his message with the presence of a fruit vendor who walks toward the women carrying a basket of bananas; all of this taking place within the curvaceous atmosphere of the composition.

◄

Fig. 14. Antonio Gattorno, *El río*,

oil on canvas, 193 x 117 cm,

1927. Courtesy of Kohler Library,

University of Wisconsin.

In *El triunfo de la rumba*, of circa 1928, Abela, on the other hand, openly brought to painting the rhythm, excitement, and syncopation of Afro-Cuban music (fig. 15).[21] In a nervous, almost calligraphic style reminiscent of Pascin (Abela had been to Paris and Pascin had been to Havana),[22] the artist portrayed an allegorical group that rushes forth from a beach pounded by the surf. The main figure is a mulattress dressed in white, who seems to hover above ground. Behind her swirl three *bongoseros* (drum players) and two allegorical protective deities, whose wings become as one with palm fronds and banana leaves. Here Abela has recalled a standard religious iconography of saints and angels to portray the power, energy, and sensuality of the rumba, as it sways to and fro and surges forth from the sea onto the island with all the strength and self-assured presence of a conquering force demanding to become a national icon.

Raw sexuality exploded in the paintings of Carlos Enríquez, and *El rapto de las mulatas* (The Rape of the Mulattresses), of 1938, is the best example of his

20. For an early appreciation of Gattorno's work, see Ernest Hemingway, *Gattorno* (Havana: Úcar García, 1935). This catalogue, which was supervised by Gattorno, gives *El río* as the title of the painting under discussion. Subsequent catalogues, which may not have been supervised by the artist, give it as *Mujeres en el río*. I have chosen to use the earlier version of the title.

21. On Abela, see Loló de la Torriente, "El mundo ensoñado de Abela," *Revista del Instituto Nacional de Cuba* 1 (June–September 1956): 41–56; José Seoane, *Eduardo Abela cerca del cerco* (Havana: Editorial Letras Cubanas, 1986); and Museo Cubano de Arte y Cultura, ed., *Abela: Magic & Fables/Magia y Fábulas* (Miami: Museo Cubano de Arte y Cultura, 1984).

22. Jules Pascin was in Havana several times between 1915 and 1920, and he had a long stay in 1916–1917. See Yves Hemin, Guy Krogh, Klaus Perls, and Abel Rambert, *Pascin, catalogue raisonné: peintures, aquarelles, pastels, dessins* (Paris: Éditions Abel Rambert, 1984), 116–123, 130–132, 142, 145, 149, 152, 156, 159, 162, 169, 173–176, 178–180, 182, 398.

Fig. 15. Eduardo Abela, *El triunfo de la rumba*, oil on canvas, 65 x 54 cm, ca. 1928. Courtesy of Kohler Library, University of Wisconsin.

style (fig. 16).[23] In it he depicted two couples, each one on a horse and each consisting of a barebreasted mulattress and a white *guajiro* who is also a highwayman, as suggested by the bandoliers slung over his chest. The *bandolero*, the white-peasant-turned-highwayman, had long been a symbol of maleness, of the *macho* who lives on his cunning, courage, and fortitude. His lust is part of his legend. Tales of his sexual prowess precede him and most women give themselves openly to him, although he will indulge in rape if he so desires. The mulattress is his symbolic counterpart. Beautiful and boastful of her looks, her appetites are best served by assertive, impetuous debauchery.

In *El rapto de las mulatas* the man to the far right holds one of the women fast against him. His eyes are concealed under the brim of his hat, but one senses that he is looking lustfully at her breasts, which she pulls up by bringing her shoulders back while looking at him, clearly proud of her body. In the

23. On Carlos Enríquez, see Félix Pita Rodríguez, *Carlos Enríquez* (Havana: Editorial Lex, 1957); and Museo Cubano de Arte y Cultura, ed., *Carlos Enríquez* (Miami: Museo Cubano de Arte y Cultura, 1986). Carlos Enríquez wrote three novels: *Tilín García* (Havana: La Verónica, 1939), and two others, published posthumously, *La feria de Guaicanama* (Havana: Ministerio de Educación, Dirección General de Cultura, 1960) and *La vuelta de Chencho*. The latter was published, along with *Tilín García*, in Carlos Enríquez, *Dos novelas*, with an introduction by Félix Pita Rodríguez (Havana: Editorial Arte y Literatura, 1975).

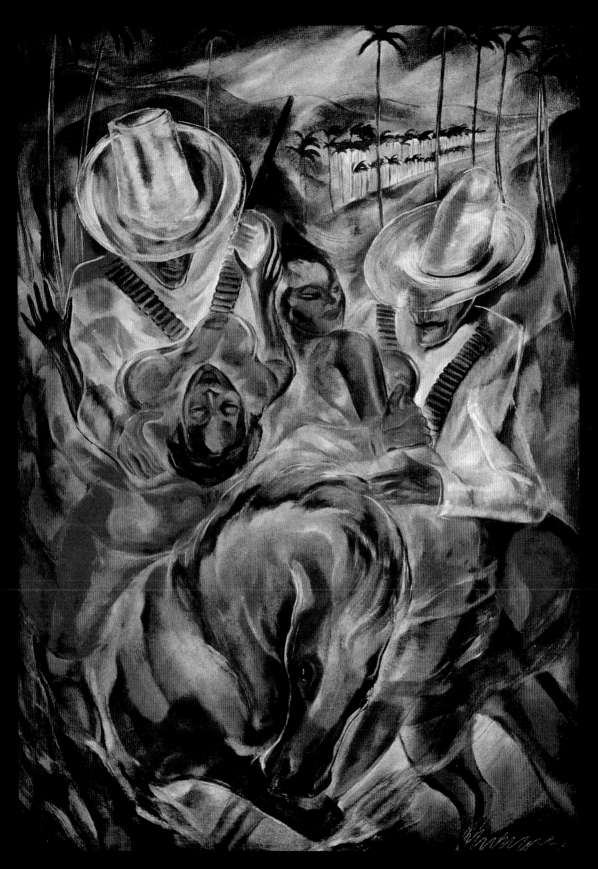

Fig. 16. Carlos Enríquez, *El rapto de las mulatas*, oil on canvas, 162.5 x 114.5 cm., 1938. Photograph courtesy of Emilio Cueto.

Fig. 17. Fidelio Ponce,

Adoración, **oil on board,**

90.4 x 118.75 cm, 1938.

Photograph by Sandy Levy.

Private collection,

Miami, Florida.

meantime the *guajiro* on the left has already mounted the other woman, who arches her back under him and offers him her breasts as a gift. To make the imagery complete, Enríquez shows the couples riding unbridled wild horses — images of raw animal lust that he painted in a fiery, almost demonic, red. To strengthen his iconography, Enríquez worked in his peculiar style of frenzied juxtapositions and superpositions of reds and blues, yellows and greens, blacks and browns, and purples and greys. They slide into each other and swirl and twist to become either transparent planes of color, translucent surfaces glowing with inner fire, or masses of sumptuously erotic substance, all in combinations that make the wildest dreams of Franz Marc (whose work Enríquez may have seen during his European sojourn of 1930–1934) seem subdued and tame by comparison.

In less than a decade Gattorno, Abela, and Carlos Enríquez shattered most notions of bourgeois decorum, celebrating joy, sensuality, and lust. Concurrently, Fidelio Ponce (1895–1949) worked from the other side of the spectrum: that of what he considered to be the worst remaining aspects of the Spanish heritage, traits that in his opinion were still ever-present and dominating within certain circles.[24] His was a world of religious hypocrisy; of grief and fear and sorrow; of dried up, pious, ignorant old women; and of people dying of tuberculosis. Ponce never turned to the avant-garde; he created his art by himself out of elements and pieces he chose from sixteenth- and seventeenth-century Spanish painting, the period of history whose influence he seems to have wanted to exorcise out of the national experience (fig. 17). In his paintings figures reminiscent of those of El Greco inhabit a desolate landscape permeated by the white of the paintings of Zurbarán (never the joyful white of the young

24. On Ponce, see Maruja Rodríguez López, "Esquema para un estudio de Ponce," *Revista Cubana* 31 (July–December 1957): 83–95; and Juan Sánchez, *Fidelio Ponce* (Havana: Editorial Letras Cubanas, 1985).

Goya), where Baroque clouds have turned into an all-pervasive dirty-white primeval muck expressed through an extraordinarily thick impasto, and where relief is offered only by an occasional strand of sickly green, deathly grey, or ominous brown.

Among the manifold aspects of the national collective psyche being represented at the time, innate nobility and innocence also called out for recognition. Rural themes furnished the required imagery; the *guajiro* became an iconographical entity standing for redemptive qualities unattainable in the corrupt quagmire of cities Carrión, Loveira, and others had depicted in their novels. The *guajiro* was meant to make the viewer recall his lost innocence and supposedly make him long to retrieve it, although knowing all along that such a desire was no longer possible to fulfill. This moralizing function does not imply that the *guajiro* was seen as a hero. On the contrary, these paintings are mostly anecdotal, created in the hope that a desire for goodness might result from contemplating images of the charming simplicity of the rural life. One such instance would consider, for example, that having a family picture taken was a grand, important event, as Arístides Fernández (1904–1934) described it in *La familia se retrata* (The Family Has Its Picture Taken). The generosity of the *guajiro*, even when living in extreme poverty, was to be revealed also. Lorenzo Romero Arciaga picked up the subject and represented it through the ritual of offering a cup of coffee as a sign of welcome in *La taza de café* (The Cup of Coffee), of circa 1940 (fig. 18). Furthermore, in *Jugadores de dominó*, 1942, Abela made evident the nobility of the type in the calm monumentality in which he depicted a group of *guajiros,* even if they are engaged in something as commonplace as a game of dominoes (fig. 19). The imagery of the new rural themes, therefore, lacked the universality typical of nineteenth-century examples in which nature had stood as an emblem of a culture to be attained, and the *guajiro* had been but another element within a lyrical, all-encompassing, utopian landscape. The collective discourse of modern artists and avant-garde intellectuals was much too complex to reach consensus, especially since different currents seemed at cross-purposes, either extolling, denouncing, or merely making evident as many aspects as possible of the national idiosyncrasy. The *Weltanschauung* was too confusing; too much was being revealed too fast and too richly. Competing with diverse images, each one as culturally important as the next, the subject of the *guajiro* was, if not a call for collective moral improvement, at least a respite looking back at mythical origins that, ironically enough, never existed.

Fig. 18. Lorenzo Romero Arciaga, *La taza de café*, oil on board, 97.3 x 123 cm, ca. 1940. Museum of Arts and Sciences, Daytona Beach, Florida, Cuban Foundation Collection.

A theme parallel to innocence was that of *tener confianza*, a typical form of spontaneously open behavior that allows one to call a new acquaintance *mi hermano* (my brother) and any person of the opposite sex *mi querercito* (my little darling) with no aforethought or intention of disrespect. *Confianza* was more conspicuously evident among the urban working class, a social category untainted by the reticence of the haute bourgeoisie. Instinctively, people seemed to realize that the main virtue of *confianza* resided in its capacity for diffusing many of the tensions of living in close proximity to each other, a condition that could lead to abrasiveness at times. So deeply ingrained was *confianza* in popular neighborhoods that people who did not practice it, who "gave themselves airs," while not ostracized, were certainly the butt of everyone's *choteo* behind their backs. *Estampas de San Cristóbal*, of 1926, a book by Jorge Mañach, is a good introduction to the subject. Ostensibly a collection of vignettes of popular life in Havana, it is in fact a sociological document of the first order, describing a rich variety of urban human types interacting with each other. A series of paintings by Cundo Bermúdez (born 1914) correspond

with the text of Mañach not by reason of a direct influence but because of a cultural affinity, as had been the case with Miahle and Villaverde.

Barbería (Barbershop), a painting from 1942 by Cundo, appears to be influenced by Picasso's so-called Neoclassical period, especially in the monumentality of the figures.[25] But as usual when analyzing Cuban art, stylistic filiation is of less interest than iconological content; formal issues here are but a point of departure for delving into the national ethos (fig. 20). An important feature in this painting is that, contrary to standard practice, the barber is sitting down while giving a customer a haircut. He sits on a *taburete*, a cheap chair made out of wood and rawhide. The use of a *taburete* is a sign that this barbershop is in a popular neighborhood, the kind that doubles as a poor man's club, where men come after work to talk or read a newspaper far more often than for a haircut or a shave. Cundo's barbershop is a microcosm where *confianza* is a

25. I follow the standard Cuban convention — one that is totally arbitrary — of calling some artists by their first names, others, by their last names, and yet some others by their first and last names. Hence, for instance, it is always Cundo, Mariano, and Amelia, never Bermúdez, Rodríguez, or Peláez. Portocarrero, on the other hand, is always Portocarrero, or at times "Porto," but never René. Equally, Wifredo Lam is always called Lam, yet Carlos Enríquez is known always as Carlos Enríquez, never as Carlos or Enríquez.

Fig. 20. Cundo Bermúdez,

Barbería, oil on canvas,

63.4 x 53.4 cm, 1942.

The Museum of Modern Art,

New York. Inter-American

Fund. Photograph © 1996

The Museum of Modern Art,

New York.

result of each person being like every other. He represented this condition not only by showing the barber sitting down like his customer but, even more tellingly, by giving each the same face. The two men stand as portraits of the same archetype. As extensions of each other they trust one another implicitly, in the goodness of complete *confianza*.

It could be argued that such trusting behavior may be found among people of a similar class in many parts of the world, and undoubtedly this is so, but *Barbería* is specifically a representation of Cuban *confianza* because the iconography is fully Cuban. For instance, Cundo gave the men features that could be taken for those of a typically white middle-class Cuban with poor immigrant Spanish parents. By contrast, Orozco or Rivera would have probably painted a Mexican scene and given them Indian features. Cundo's barbershop is also telling. It has the flavor of a room in an old colonial palace, the kind that original owners had abandoned generations earlier and perhaps turned into a *solar*, or tenement house. The exaggerated Baroque-like ornamentation of the chair, the pattern of the tile floor, and the classical monumentality of the cabinet in the background, with two barberpoles on top that look like fat columns, speak to a colonial grandeur that anywhere else would be inconsistent with a

Fig. 21. Carlos Enríquez, *Muerte de Martí*, oil on board, 41.9 x 37.5 cm, 1934. Photograph by Sandy Levy.

Private collection, Miami, Florida.

barbershop, much less one where a Devil-may-care barber sits down to work on a *taburete* with his guitar next to him. The painting, then, tells a tale of informality, of friendships that are made quickly and last forever, and of a trust in one's fellow man based on a deeply rooted notion of social and cultural equality. Such is the camaraderie of *confianza*.

Inasmuch as *vanguardia* painters sought their subjects in daily life, the traditional grandiloquence of history painting remained outside their interests. Nevertheless, historical subjects did crop up here and there. In 1934 Carlos Enríquez made use of his characteristic fiery style to paint one of the best examples of the genre. His *Muerte de Martí* (Death of Martí) is a splendid portrayal of the manic essence of a heroic death (fig. 21).

It would indeed be hard to overemphasize that the artists of the Generation of 1927 discovered the multifariousness of Cuban culture. By so doing, their work established the second stage in the process of expressing the national iconology. *Confianza*, sensuality, lust, *machismo*, Afro-Cuban music, the nobility of the *guajiro*, the consequences of exaggerated views on religion, the easygoing ways of the middle class, and even occasionally, the national sagas were but a few of the many themes painters explored. Without fear of exhausting the list, one could add as well contrasts between rich and poor, the allegorical qualities of the local flora and fauna, the importance of Afro-Cuban religions, and the ubiquitous presence of the blue of sea and sky. Although it only lasted for about fifteen years, the Generation of 1927 left a splendid legacy: it solidified the position of Cuban modern art, nationally and internationally; it investigated a considerable number of solutions to formal and compositional problems; and it created a body of work of substantial quality. But perhaps its outstanding contribution — establishing the second stage in the development of the national iconology — hinged on its analytical acumen, one that was as collective as it was spontaneous. Likewise, the enthusiasm it shared with poets in a mutual intent to reveal the scope of national culture had also certainly been important to its success.

After such an extraordinary collective feat of analysis, a synthesis was in order, or at least a series of them. Mariano Rodríguez (born 1912), René Portocarrero (1912–1985), Amelia Peláez (1896–1968), and Wifredo Lam (1902–1982), with no thought whatsoever of consensus — other than that furnished by a strong *Zeitgeist* — proceeded to shape the third and last stage in the unfolding of a national iconology. They set for themselves, individually, the task to represent in pictures that which was transcendentally Cuban. Yet to accomplish their work all they had was the standard immanent medium of form and color. Of necessity, their artistry was to provoke an empathetic response from the viewer, or at least his recognition of an evocation.

The collective title of *Gallo pintado* (Painted Rooster) given by Mariano to a number of his paintings is telling. The reality of artifice is acknowledged and thus the irreality of painting is made evident. These are not roosters but images of roosters, abstractions that appear to be concrete whatever the circumstances, even if two of them are engaged in a cockfight (fig. 22). From such a position the artist was then able to consider the rooster as a symbol of whatever he wanted it to be. Mariano chose to concentrate on the idea of a rich polychromy that stood for the entire chromatic experience of the physical environment. But unlike Collazo, who depicted in the nineteenth century what he saw as the reality of tropical light, Mariano considered only the idea of it, and arbitrarily transferred that conception to the plumage of a rooster. That

Fig. 22. Mariano Rodríguez,

Pelea de gallos, oil on canvas,

63.3 x 73.4 cm, 1942. Private

collection, Miami, Florida.

Fig. 23. A *medio punto*.

Photograph by Cathy Leff, 1994.

▶

Fig. 24. René Portocarrero,

Interior del Cerro,

watercolor on paper,

55.4 x 35.2 cm, 1943. Private

collection, Miami, Florida.

representation was to him an abstraction as well, an image that looked like a fact. Thus Mariano brought a Platonic paradox to Cuban iconology. A gorgeously tropical entity was made to convey a meaning approaching an absolute abstraction, an ideality.

Portocarrero also transformed his knowledge of Cuba into a chromatic synthesis, and while not attempting to define an essence, he did evoke it. In his work both the iconological and aesthetic significance of color surpassed any importance the iconographical content might have, even though that content ran practically the full gamut of the Cuban repertory, from colonial interiors to landscapes to images of *santería*. Portocarrero's color is of a special quality, for it is based on the experience of seeing sunlight going through *medios puntos de colores*. A *medio punto* consists of a geometrical pattern of fairly large pieces of colored glass, predominantly blue, red, yellow, and green, with occasional transparent pieces, inserted in the semicircular area of an arched doorway in a colonial building (fig. 23). As an architectural device *medios puntos* softened the harshness of tropical light while allowing it to filter into rooms. *Medios puntos* make an extraordinarily rich statement in the stately interiors of colonial palaces, especially if there are several doors in a row; richer yet is the velvety geometric patterns of color that light going through the *medios puntos* makes on the marble floors. That visual experience allows for an exquisitely intimate understanding of the chromatic essence of what is usually meant by "tropical." [26] Moreover, inasmuch as that understanding can only take place in colonial buildings that evoke strong empathetic responses to tradition and

26. In spite of obvious differences in style, scale, and historical context, the experience is similar to coming to an understanding of the chromatic essence of the Gothic when seeing light coming through a stained-glass window in a medieval building.

PORTOCARRERO
1943

history, it is not surprising that Portocarrero availed himself of that experience and turned it into the nationalist cornerstone of his art. It is easy to see in a painting like *Interior del Cerro* (1943) how Portocarrero based his work on the *medio punto* (fig. 24). The entire surface, including the girl, the chairs, the plant stand, and the doors beyond, is painted to recall stained glass — or its reflection. However, a landscape like his *El diablito rojo* (The Red Small Devil) (1944), to choose an example at random, makes one realize why Portocarrero retained the same chromatic values throughout his life (fig. 25). Time and again he was bringing to his art what he had learned from *medios puntos* as an embodiment of the essence of tropical light and color. Thanks to that lesson, his chromatic symbolism of nationality became far more reflective of the Cuban essence than even the large number of national subjects he painted.

So far all Cuban iconography had been based on clearly recognizable representations of people, animals, plants, objects, and the environment, whether urban or rural. An imagery everyone could easily understand was a quintessential requirement of a nationalist iconography; otherwise art could not fulfill its didactic and even propagandistic purposes. The representation of the Cuban iconology, or of aspects of it, placed such limitations on composition.

Amelia Peláez's extraordinary contribution was to show how an abstract imagery could be used to present an all-encompassing view of Cuban culture instead of

Fig. 26. Amelia Peláez,

Marpacífico, oil on canvas,

73.4 x 94.93 cm, 1936. Private

collection, Miami, Florida.

Fig. 27. Amelia Peláez,

Naturaleza muerta,

oil on canvas, 66 x 100.5 cm,

1946. Photograph by

Sandy Levy. Private

collection, Miami, Florida.

only selected aspects of it. Yet she always kept her work well within the boundaries of a sensuously organic Cuban aesthetic and never allowed her sense of composition to digress into the intellectualism that is so often a characteristic of abstraction.[27] A former disciple of Alexandra Exter in Paris, Amelia would usually begin a painting with a rigorously geometric structure that would stand as a basis for the composition and bring order to it. Upon this she would superimpose a winding black Baroque line that reminds one of colonial ironwork. Bursting with energy, that line sways in undulations, bends back upon itself, and then moves on, sweeping across the canvas with a cadence Amelia seems to have extracted out of the essence that also gave birth to the nineteenth-century *contradanza*. Beyond this, she would paint a background of vibrant, primary colors that she took directly out of a *medio punto*, or of her idea of the primordial one. Finally, as her Cuban signature, she would add a central feature of tropical fish — still fresh from the day's catch — or fruit just purchased from a vendor who had come to her door or perhaps a flower, more often than not a hibiscus she had just picked in her garden and monumentalized on her canvas, an imagery she began to develop shortly after her return from her Paris sojourn (1927–1934) (figs. 26 and 27).

Strong and bold in her painting, but shy and gentle in her everyday life, Amelia's synthesis of the Cuban experience was as personal as it was introspective. Perhaps recalling her uncle, the poet Julián del Casal, she created a refuge for herself and her mother and sisters in a house in La Víbora, an early-twentieth-century suburb of Havana. There, houses rendered in the Neo-Baroque style

27. On Amelia, see mainly José Gómez Sicre, "Amelia Peláez: Modern Baroque," *Americas* 6 (December 1954): 12–17; Loló de la Torriente, "Ambiente y estética de Amelia Peláez," *Cuadernos Americanos* 27 (1968): 236–243; Museo Cubano de Arte y Cultura, ed., *Amelia Peláez, 1896–1968: Una Retrospectiva/A Retrospective*, with an essay by Giulio V. Blanc (Miami: Museo Cubano de Arte y Cultura, 1988); and Alejandro G. Alonso, *Amelia Peláez* (Havana: Editorial Letras Cubanas, 1988).

of the day still partook of an ample colonial scale, and generally opened to enclosed private gardens and patios laid out in the tradition of those painted by Arburu Morell and Guillermo Collazo in the late nineteenth century. The lushness of her garden, which she tended herself, as well as the experience of light going through a *medio punto*, and a realization that the Baroque quality of the decorative ironwork in her windows matched the sensuousness of tropical fruit, fish, and flowers, and that their color, in turn, was also that of the *medio punto*, were things that Amelia came to understand and enjoy every day without having to leave her house, a microcosm representing for her the entire Cuban experience. All of this, and nothing more, she proceeded to synthesize on her canvases. Amelia — in the opinion of Alfred Barr, founding director of the Museum of Modern Art of New York — "helped to bring Latin American art into the twentieth century."[28]

But still another synthesis was to take place. During the century that spans from the lithographs of Miahle to the early Afro-Cuban pictures of Wifredo Lam, black culture was frequently described by artists, often with intimate knowledge. None, however, penetrated its essence. An observer gets the impression that those artists were outsiders looking in, even if they shared in the beliefs of *santería* and *mayombe*, the two principal religious systems Africans brought with them, and which many whites subsequently adopted. Lam was different from the rest. His work touched upon the essence of black hagiography.[29]

Lam gained consciousness of his Cubanness — at least as an artist — when he returned from Europe at the outbreak of World War Two. Once he reimmersed himself in the Afro-Cuban religious practices of his youth, he matured into the artist he was meant to be. His painting of a *Cuarto fambá* (1947), a room with symbolic markings used for religious practices, is a landmark within that process of reacquaintance (fig. 28). His previous work in Paris, and being befriended there by Picasso and André Breton, had been means to hone his skills for his life's work; his experience in Paris had been similar to that of a gifted student who attends an outstanding school with superb teachers (fig. 29). As is standard with Cuban artists, foreign influences provided him with a set of discrete features that he pieced together as the infrastructure upon which he constructed his art. Another Cuban characteristic of Lam was that the iconography he discovered was far more important than any stylistic filiation his work might show.

Lam transcended his Cubanness while making use of Afro-Cuban subjects; his depiction of black lore portrays emotions that are felt universally.[30] There is a hermetic quality to his work that goes far beyond a direct depiction of images of *santería* and *mayombe*. Nowhere in his pictures does one find an image that anyone could recognize as any of the saints of the Catholic Church blacks of the diaspora associated with African deities, a standard iconography of other painters who treated the subject. The power of his imagery lies in being allusive,

28. Quoted in Geraldine P. Biller, *Latin American Women Artists, 1915–1995* (Milwaukee, Wis.: Milwaukee Art Museum, 1995), 103.

29. On Lam, see Fernando Ortiz, *Wifredo Lam y su obra vista a través de los significados críticos* (Havana: Ministerio de Educación, 1950); Edmundo Desnoes, *Lam: azul y negro* (Havana: Cuadernos de la Casa de las Américas, 1963); Alain Jouffroy, *Lam* (Paris: Georges Fall, 1972); Gérard Xuriguéra, *Wifredo Lam* (Paris: Éditions Filipacchi, 1974); Sebastià Gasch, *Wifredo Lam a París* (Barcelona: Ediciones Polígrafa, 1976); Max-Pol Fouchet, *Wifredo Lam* (Barcelona: Ediciones Polígrafa, 1976); Museo Nacional Centro de Arte Reina Sofía, ed., *Wifredo Lam* (Madrid: Museo Nacional Centro de Arte Reina Sofía, 1992); and Dominique Tonneau-Ryckelynck, *Wifredo Lam, oeuvre gravé et lithographié: catalogue raisonné* (Gravelines: Éditions Musée de Gravelines, ca. 1992).

30. The person who has best studied this aspect of Lam is Gerardo Mosquera, "Modernidad y africanía: Wifredo Lam en su isla," in Museo Nacional Centro de Arte Reina Sofía, ed. *Wifredo Lam*, 21–41.

Fig. 28. Wifredo Lam,

Cuarto fambá, oil on canvas,

64.6 x 81 cm, 1947. Private

collection, Miami, Florida.

Fig. 29. Wifredo Lam,

La Lettre, gouache on paper,

99.1 x 67.9 cm, 1938.

Photograph by Teresa Harb

Diehl. Private collection,

Miami, Florida.

and in its capacity to convey a meaning of transcendence. Afro-Cuban beliefs, however, do not include an idea of a supreme transcendent being beyond Olofi and Olordumare, respectively the father and mother of heaven and earth.[31] Through allusions to the *orishas*, or African deities, Lam forces us to sense awe, reverence, and deep fear; we are standing face to face with aspects of supernatural power, each more magical and mysterious than the next.

Lam's religious purposes imparted strong surreal qualities to his work. In his canvases women become birds, birds become plants, and anthropomorphic beasts have four legs that end in hands (fig. 30). These stand side by side with strange and often frighteningly anthropomorphic, gynecomorphic, or androgynous figures of his own creation. While some of these figures have a ground to stand on, most hover and fly in an oneiric landscape, one without even a reference to a horizon line, even if they might have a teleological signification. The light in which they exist is also different from that which most Cuban artists loved to capture. Lam's world is suffused with the strange light of dreams and the colors it engenders (fig. 31).[32] There are further puzzles to his iconography. In some of his works breasts and testicles metamorphose themselves into meanings that seem to be other than sexual, for each cancels the other as much as they complement each other. And such may be the case as well when the attributes of a beast comprise a moon crescent that itself may be part of a face and a cloven hoof that hangs from a limp, ribbon-like limb. The signification of a horned bird that issues out of, but remains attached to, a mother's neck is equally difficult to read. One can go no further than saying that these figures

31. See Rómulo Lachatañeré, *El sistema religioso de los afrocubanos* (Havana: Editorial de Ciencias Sociales, 1992), especially 100–102.

32. Through his work the chiaroscuro — the quintessential light of ambiguity — made its appearance again in Cuban art, especially in his later graphic work, which recalls bright colors seen under a cold, overcast sky, as is so often the case in Paris.

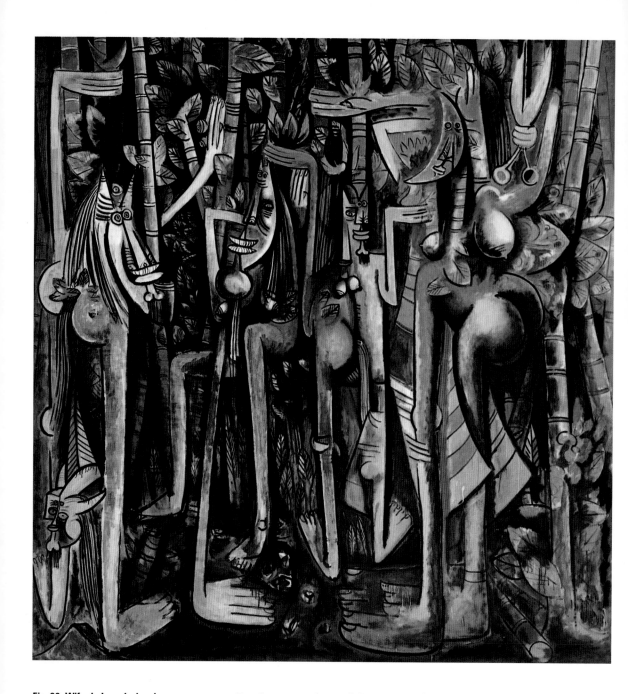

Fig. 30. Wifredo Lam, *La jungla*, gouache on paper mounted on canvas, 239.4 x 229.9 cm, 1943. The Museum of Modern Art, New York. Inter-American Fund. Photograph © 1996 The Museum of Modern Art, New York.

represent Lam's private view of the universal truth; a truth, however, that he could no more than intuit, and therefore presented to us as an adumbration, as a metaphor at best. It may also be possible that what we perceive as a riddle is nothing more than a result of the ineffable character of the universal. When we face Lam's work — as is standard when we encounter the sublime — it regales us with the fulfillment of knowing that we have recognized the existence of the universal beyond what is nothing more than a pictograph of a man's intimation of the supernatural.

The culmination that Lam and Amelia represent was matched and even surpassed in literature by José Lezama Lima (1910–1976), a hermetic poet for whom it was standard to enclose a metaphor within another metaphor to reach still a third, which in turn conveyed an intimation of the transcendent.

Lezama was also the person who brought together El grupo de Orígenes, a group of poets and intellectuals with parallel interests whose main venue was *Orígenes*, a journal Lezama published from 1944 through 1956, reputedly the most important literary periodical in the Hispanic world at the time. A sign that El grupo de Orígenes exhausted the expression of the tangible within the collective Cuban experience in literature, as much as Portocarrero, Amelia, and Lam had done in art, was their search for metaphors and adumbrations probing into far deeper layers of the Cuban experience than those hitherto explored. One of their interests — as made evident in the journal's issue of winter 1948 — was an exploration by María Zambrano of the characteristics of "prenatal Cuba," a literary image meant to signify that aspects of nationality were of such a particular intimacy that they could be compared to genetic characteristics, albeit almost mystical in nature.

Lezama completed the group's search for the origins and nature of transcendence in his most representative works, his two novels: *Paradiso* (1966) and *Oppiano Licario* (1977, posthumous), on which he worked most of his life, especially *Paradiso*. The novels take place mostly in Havana and comprise a unified whole with scores of characters, each with a different personality and a limited range of capabilities, urges, and aspirations, but each representing an aspect of the archetypal man. With the help of that device the reader is taken up a pyramid of ever-ascending layers of the human experience to embrace the final transcendence in the last chapter of *Oppiano Licario*. Once the summit of awareness is reached, the reader understands that all the sundry and seemingly disparate events covered in the two novels were but severally perceived material, emotional, and intellectual clues to the existence of a final truth, and that those separate facts, feelings, entities, and thoughts were part of a collective whole, and also, mysteriously related to each other. In point of fact, while Lezama's style has often been called Baroque, the structure of his novels recalls the manner in which in a Gothic cathedral seemingly unrelated elements of architecture, sculpture, and painting combine themselves together into a whole that in the end expresses transcendence.

Lezama's universal synthesis closed a chapter in Cuban literary history that Heredia's lyricism and Villaverde's analysis had opened in the nineteenth century. Similarly, Amelia and Lam, by attempting to encompass the whole of the Cuban experience in their paintings, completed the task begun by Fernández Cavada and Chartrand. Thus, there is an elegant symmetry to the stages of the Cuban process of self-identification through art and literature.

In art that process began with a prefatory period running from the 1830s to the early 1860s, dominated by French lithographers. Then came the first truly Cuban painting from the 1860s through the first quarter of the twentieth century. In that stage artists explored many of the bucolic themes defined by Romantic poetry from the 1820s through the late 1850s. Concurrently, folk characters that Villaverde had described in *Cecilia Valdés* were identified pictorially by Landaluze; another interest of the times was an exploration of the characteristics of tropical light. The second stage came with the Generation of 1927. Artists of that period expanded on the discoveries of their predecessors and added their own extraordinary contributions during the approximately fifteen years of the *vanguardia*, laying bare most of the characteristics of the national ethos. Finally, in the third period, running from the late 1930s to the mid-1940s, new artists created syntheses that stood for the entire national experience. Like the plot in Lezema's novels, the development of a national art was an ascending process: the first stage investigated physical characteristics of the environment; the second depicted the social idiosyncracies of the nation; and the third embraced the entire culture in abstraction. All of this had taken place in a compressed period of around eighty years. By 1947, at the time the APEC—Agrupación de Pintores y Escultores Cubanos — became incorporated "to establish a Cuban sense of plasticity," the aim, in fact, had been fully accomplished.[33] All subsequent art could find a base on the iconology discovered roughly between 1865 and 1945, as much as, for instance, Renoir made use of French themes set in place in the seventeenth and eighteenth centuries.

The development of a Cuban national art brings some thoughts to mind. First, one encounters an extraordinarily rich production in a country that at the turn of the nineteenth century could boast of no better painters than Escalera, Escobar, or Vermay. Secondly, one finds a close symbiotic relationship between society and the physical environment. The quality of light on the island is very important in that respect. Its effect on hills and valleys, on palm fronds and fruit and flowers, on the color it gives to the sea, on how it reflects from surfaces of buildings, and on the way it makes human skin glow brings an important measure of joy and insouciance to the quality of life.[34] It promotes *confianza* and laughter, *choteo* and camaraderie. Without that particular light the physical environment would be meaningless; and without the physical environment the zest for life wilts. Thirdly, Cuban sensuality must be taken into account. The intellectual rigor made evident by the quality of literature and art is always concealed under an exploding sensuality. It appears under many guises, whether in the pervading light of Chartrand, the reflections of sunlight on the vegetation of Sanz Carta or Collazo, or in the languor of a figure by Arburu Morell. Later, it is evident on the faces of Víctor Manuel's characters, the hills of a background of a painting by Gattorno, a mulattress representing *El triunfo de la rumba*, or more directly, in the work of Carlos Enríquez. Even Ponce, the most ascetic of Cuban painters, brought a measure of sensuality to the lines and rhythms of figures that dwell in a world purposefully anti-Cuban — grey and sad and dense. Sensuality appears as well in the plumage of Mariano's roosters, Portocarrero's chromatic synthesis, and above all, the paintings of Amelia. There it all but explodes joyfully in the intensity of her colors, the lushness of her fruit and flowers, and the musicality of her Baroque line, which responds to a rhythm that is neither Spanish nor African because it is typically Cuban. With Lam the cycle of national self-identification in the arts came round. His work is surreal, oneirical, and transcendent. While many of his figures are forcefully sexual, the sensuality of his art, especially in the later work, is subsumed under the characteristics of his personal landscape, in which the Cuban physical environment is in scant evidence. Such a personal — as opposed to collective — notion of sensuality is a further indication of his position at the close of the cycle of national self-identification, with some characteristics beginning to move away from a century-old norm. Finally, one notices idealization as a strong constituent

33. Needless to say — and as is widely known — Mariano, Portocarrero, Amelia, Lam, as well as the earlier painters, continued working for years; some are still doing so. The APEC, as an institution, lasted until 1950. Its members were Amelia Peláez, Víctor Manuel, Fidelio Ponce, Carlos Enríquez, Wifredo Lam, Mario Carreño, René Portocarrero, Mariano Rodríguez, Luis Martínez Pedro, Cundo Bermúdez, Felipe Orlando, Roberto Diago, Julio Girona, and Osvaldo Gutiérrez. See Castro, *El arte*, 58.

34. These facts have often been noted by travelers. One of the best examples of such statements is that of the Swedish novelist Fredrika Bremer (1801–1865), who, in 1851, writing to her sister, noted time and again how enthralled she was by the quality of Cuban light. See Fredrika Bremer, *The Homes of the New World: Impressions of America* (1853; New York: Negro Universities Press, 1968), 2:252-420.

Fig. 31. Wifredo Lam,

Visible/Invisible, color

etching, 37 x 47.3 cm, 1971.

Author's collection.

of the national iconology. Perforce this kind of imagery needs to be allegorical mulattresses, Amelia's hibiscuses, or Lam's *orishas*.

In retrospect, one realizes the obvious, namely that the process we have surveyed bears the twofold mark of a post-colonial development: it was passionately self-conscious and it took place in a fairly short period of time. Its success is likewise evident. It is made patent by the many ways literature and art portrayed the national idiosyncracy; and even closer to the subject at hand, by the quality of the paintings. □

Note

I wish to thank my colleagues Gail Geiger and Steve Orso and my student Paul Stoller for their suggestions on this paper, but most especially I wish to acknowledge my debt of gratitude to my late teacher, Eugenio Batista, who many years ago taught me how to look at Cuban art. I also acknowledge the help of William Bunce, Emilio Cueto, Thomas Gombar, and Lesbia O. Varona, who helped me to obtain illustrations. Mr. Richard Manoogian kindly allowed me to reproduce his superb *Sunset on the Marshes*, by Martin Johnson Heade. The Museum of Arts and Sciences, Daytona Beach, Florida, and the Museum of Modern Art, New York, also provided illustrations. To the wonderful people who opened their home and their collection to me, I can only say *¡muchísmas gracias!*

Fig. 1. Amelia Peláez in her studio, ca. 1945. Photograph by José Gómez Sicre. Courtesy of Carmen Peláez.

Estrada Palma 261
Still Life with Dream about Amelia Peláez

By Juan Antonio Molina

Translated by Narciso G. Menocal and Renato E. Perez

Introduction by Helen L. Kohen

Juan Antonio Molina is an art historian and a curator at the Fototeca de Cuba, Havana. His articles have been published in European and Latin American journals.

Helen L. Kohen is an art historian and former art critic of *The Miami Herald*. She has written and lectured extensively on art and architecture.

Fig. 3. Amelia Peláez,

La pianista, oil on canvas,

79 x 73 cm, 1944. Photograph

by Cathy Leff, 1994.

Introduction

Note: My remarks about the work of Amelia Peláez (fig. 1), her family house, and her life are based on personal responses to the many works I have seen and studied as an art historian and critic. In addition, I visited the Peláez house at Estrada Palma 261, La Víbora, in Havana, Cuba, in February 1988, and interviewed the artist's two surviving sisters then living there. But mostly I owe what I know of Amelia to the published work of my late colleague Giulio V. Blanc, specifically, "The Secret Garden of Amelia Peláez," from the catalogue accompanying the exhibition Amelia Peláez 1896–1968: Una Retrospectiva/A Retrospective *at the Cuban Museum of Arts and Culture, Miami, Florida, 1988.*

It is certain that a Cuba-of-the-Imagination exists inside as well as outside Cuba (fig. 2). It is what Juan Antonio Molina, a Cuban national living in Cuba, exalts in this fantastical and uncommon "Estrada Palma 261: Still Life with Dream about Amelia Peláez," a surreal and loving tribute that came of a visit to the painter's home and studio.

It is understood that such fantasies are real, that they are the likely results of playing tourist in the precincts of Amelia (1896–1968), an artist of such force that her personal world inspires poetic ramblings (fig. 3). The house is both an encircling cosmos of the art and life of Amelia and a microcosm of the Cuba of her day (fig. 4). It casts a spell even on the precise intellect of Molina, a curator, historian, and poet who obviously could not resist the impulse to create a vision of a tropical Xanadu where direct description would have been welcome, even expected. Has he crafted a piece too strange to include in an academic publication on the art and architecture of Cuba?

I think not. Amelia's paintings beg for just that kind of looking and dreaming. What you see in them, even in illustrations, is self-evident. Peláez made art of the design features of her home environment (fig. 5). She created an aesthetic from Havana's elaborate iron grilles, its stained-glass windows and fanlights, the intricate patterns of its tiled floors, its Baroque versions of classical columns and entablatures, the lacy curves of its wicker furniture, its ubiquitous still lifes — bowls of lush fruit, platters of tropical fish, hibiscus picked in her garden. She ordered a paradisal system, a whole voluptuous out-of-this-world universe from what was literally at her right hand (fig. 6).

Molina clearly understands the relationship between Amelia's work, her life experience, and the family home, a single-tiered wedding cake of a Havana house. Carmen, a surviving sister, still lives there, in ten rooms built by her father in 1912 (fig. 7). Now a kind of museum/shrine to Amelia, arguably the

Fig. 2. Peláez house, mother's bedroom with photos of friends and relatives and view of dining room. Photograph by Eduardo Luis Rodríguez, 1995.

Fig. 4. Peláez house, *la saleta*. Photograph by Tetsuo Fukaya, 1994.

Fig. 5. Peláez house, dining room. Painting, Amelia Peláez, *Florero*, oil on canvas, 116.5 x 89 cm, 1943. Photograph by Eduardo Luis Rodríguez, 1995.

Fig. 6. Peláez house, dining room. Painting, Amelia Peláez, *Retrato de Sofía Otero*, oil on canvas, 1957. Photograph by Helen L. Kohen, 1988. Courtesy of The Art Museum at Florida International University, Miami, Florida.

most Cuban of artists, whose work injects the essence of Cuba into the grander scheme of International Modernism, the very existence of the suburban villa seems to have startled Molina. "I even thought that Amelia didn't have a house," he writes, "that she had always lived inside a painting" (fig. 8).

In fact, her paintings are interiors, as seen from outside, beyond the fancy wrought-iron grilles that barely manage to keep public and private separate. What is seen through such airy structure is an illusion after all. And it is ghostly talk he hears too, when the paintings appear to conjure up long-gone intellectual discussions over "identity." Painter and painted alternate identities in the coolness of the high-ceilinged Peláez house (fig. 9). They are merely different species of house flowers, recognizable for blooming from within, living fully, inside.

Fig. 8. Peláez house, library.

Painting, Amelia Peláez,

La pianista, oil on canvas,

79 x 73 cm, 1944. Photograph

by Cathy Leff, 1994.

Fig. 7. Amelia Peláez,

Maternidad, oil on canvas,

76 x 61 cm, 1947. Photograph

by Helen L. Kohen, 1988.

Courtesy of The Art Museum

at Florida International

University, Miami, Florida.

Even so, had Peláez a true choice, she might have preferred a grander, more public art life than shy reticence and circumstance allowed her. Born the fifth of eleven children to a cultivated couple ambitious for them, Amelia was early encouraged in her painting. In 1916, a year after the family moved from Yaguajay, a small town in the north of Cuba, she was enrolled at the conservative but thorough Academia de San Alejandro in Havana, where she studied under Leopoldo Romañach (1862–1951), who painted two portraits of her (fig. 10).

After graduation, Amelia traveled to New York to spend half a year at the Art Students League, and in 1926, then accompanied by the Cuban ethnologist Lydia Cabrera (1899–1991), she left for Paris. There she studied art and observed it in the museums, trying out new influences as she became acquainted with the work of the most important new artists. The Russian Constructivist Alexandra Exter (1882–1949) became her teacher and friend (fig. 11). After seven years, in the spring of 1933, Amelia succeeded in winning good reviews for her first solo exhibition in Europe, at the Galerie Zak. The critics nonetheless noted the private nature of her art and how it was turned in, away from common, human experience (fig. 12). In the next year, following a showing at the Salon des Indépendants, the artist returned home to Cuba. The sugar boom of the 1920s that had supported her life as an expatriate in Europe had at last ended.

Back home at thirty-eight in her mother's house, Amelia remained there for the rest of her life, living out of her time in everything but her art. Her daily routine, aside from the art activity, was that of a colonial maiden lady, retiring and reserved. In contrast, she wished her paintings, and later, her ceramics, to live on the outside. She wanted them seen in museums and on gallery walls and in the homes of collectors, so she continued to take part in exhibitions from New York's Museum of Modern Art to venues all over Europe and Latin America. If her bibliography and exhibition history appear modest by today's standards, it is because fame came to her at the rate celebrity traveled on its own. She never spent her talent seeking it.

"Inside" remains the key word in the life of that cloistered, albeit sophisticated, and well-traveled Cuban artist. Molina is keenly aware of the allusions in Amelia's

Fig. 9. Peláez house, view of dining room from the hall. Paintings, Amelia Peláez, *left, Retrato de Sofía Otero,* oil on canvas, 1957; *center, Florero*, oil on canvas, 116.5 x 89 cm, 1943; *right, Maternidad,* oil on canvas, 76 x 61 cm, 1947. Photograph by Helen L. Kohen, 1988. Courtesy of The Art Museum at Florida International University, Miami, Florida.

Fig. 10. Leopoldo Romañach, portraits of Amelia. *Above*, at age 20, oil on canvas, 1916; *below*, at age 28, oil on canvas, 1924. Photograph by Cathy Leff, 1994.

paintings, and once inside the house itself, speaks of views issuing from inside broken mirrors, of trains chugging Magritte-like through the heart of the house to the outside, of the horse "between one's legs...forbidden to swim with the girl," of the secrets, the code words, and the squelched directions Amelia's art took that she, in real life, could not follow.

Though there are moments in Molina's musings when he comes down to earth, sighting the house as the crown in a domestic neighborhood, where, for a moment, "I smell a faint odor of onions," the poetic idioms soon return.

Fig. 12. Peláez house, hallway.
Painting, Amelia Peláez,
Naturaleza muerta con piña
y mameyes, oil on canvas,
103 x 100 cm, 1967. Photograph
by Tetsuo Fukaya, 1994.

Fig. 11. Alexandra Exter, title
unknown, gouache,
1925. This was a gift from
Exter to Amelia. Photograph
by Cathy Leff, 1994.

Continued exposure to the Peláez house yields a sense that either the house or the visitor is in the "wrong dimension." It is true. The house tilts back into another time, when people were smaller, their gestures more ordered, their movements less random than ours. The house in La Víbora is a doll house, still furnished with its original little-girl beds, its mix of low proportioned furniture and high art. Visitors feel they are dwelling in a dimension outside scale and texture.

Taking inspiration from her surroundings and combining that with what she learned from the Old Masters and, more significantly, what she absorbed of the art of the best of this century — Picasso, Braque, and Matisse — Amelia created a signature art. Standing in the long center hall of the house, in full view of the formal arrangements of stiff and casual furniture, a model for her own syncretic art emerges.

The way the furnishings fit together, the 1950s modern bookshelves with the European chairs and chests, how they each "go native" in the tropical light, become metaphors of the Amelia style, providing clues to her singular arrangement of mid-century rhythms — new with old, line with curve, blocks of clean, simple form with lush, emotional color (fig. 13). The work transcends each and all of its sources, entering a realm both richly Baroque and sharply Cubist. Molina takes off from there in his "Still Life with Dream," pressing his illumination upon us, providing yet another view of the house in La Víbora and its beloved occupant. □

Still Life with Dream about Amelia Peláez

the train entered thundering through the narrow door of the living room (fig. 14). It sabotaged the coffee that rested delicately in its cup. It stirred up the whole interior as it gamboled down the empty hallway. And as it was going out, leaving behind a trail of smoke and grit in bedrooms that prepared themselves for the intimacy of a siesta, the house was no longer the unknown dwelling on the riverbank, with its back turned, but not rudely so, to a sugar cane plantation and a country trail that remained useless in their absurd sfumatto. Suddenly, the horse dreamt up in the humid morning disappeared from between one's legs. And it was no longer the house in neverland, where the horse was always the well-endowed pony forbidden to swim with the girl by the soft shore lapped by the bluish-green water. She continued to live under the rocking chairs and the beds, atop wardrobes and windows (fig. 15). Ahead was the last door through which the train escaped, dethroned and sad.

Before 1986 seldom had I ventured beyond the periphery of El Vedado, which I looked upon as the exact frontiers of the world. La Víbora resounded in my mind like an echo, incalculably distant and, in a way, dangerous. Through one of those twists of fate, what once was a neighborhood favored by the bourgeoisie and certain intellectuals, a symbol of the city's first major expansion in the twentieth century and a fertile land for experiments of colonial Neoclassicism and later of Eclecticism, had become a peripheral space, disconnected from the city, far from commercial and cultural centers, gradually losing its otherwise questionable exclusivity. Its style was no longer a cause for its prestige. The only things La Víbora contributed to my scale of values were the well-deserved reputation of its rock musicians and the never-waning beauty of its women. Therefore, its only attraction was its offer of adventure. And since I was never the adventurous type, by the time I was over twenty I was not yet familiar with that neighborhood — other than having occasionally passed through it.

It was while looking at Amelia Peláez's paintings at the Museo Nacional that I felt compelled to walk the streets of El Cerro and La Víbora, to walk wide-eyed into the houses of Old Havana, and to breathe with renewed vigor the city's beguiling atmosphere. Beyond style and form, Amelia's paintings revealed to me an environment that was the hallmark as well as cause and consequence of a way of life (fig. 16). If such a revelation had anything to do with the topic of discussions on "identity" that used to pop up at every intellectual gathering at the time, then I was willing to "identify myself" with an environment of which I had been a parasitic consumer for two decades.

it was a house like all others in the city, yet different from all others. It had two white columns, two single columns with an Ionic air (fig. 17). Two columns rising from the sea propped up the entire house—the boat-house, the cloud-house, the frieze-house, the island-house. Two columns like two groans such as the tide makes when it withdraws at dawn. An angel is shipwrecked in the living room. His laughter is like ephemeral crystal dust. He arrives at the shores of the house transformed into a fish. And the party begins (fig. 18).

the fish: its shape, its renunciation eternal. The fish: its trapeze eyes, its rhombus fin—its radiance, its trail made of refractions and wily bubbles. It takes a dance step and leaves a mark in the lady's heart. It woos her,

Fig. 14. Peláez house, hallway viewed from garden to front door. Painting on right wall, Amelia Peláez, *Florero*, oil on canvas, 116.5 x 89 cm, 1943. Photograph by Eduardo Luis Rodríguez, 1995.

Fig. 13. Peláez house, library. Photograph by Eduardo Luis Rodríguez, 1995.

invites her to leap, to lose herself in that black hole which the fish's limpid and ephemeral wake has become—a door into another space and another time. A frontier suddenly multiplies in the wood of the furniture, shining like a mirrored surface. The party stops. The waltz, suspended like a cascade of postcards, spills its notes among motionless feet.

I expected Amelia's house to be yellow, like one of her paintings. I even thought that Amelia didn't have a house, that she had always lived inside a painting. It seemed to me ridiculous and profane to take a bus to Amelia's house. Because no one takes a bus to go to a semi-abstract landscape, to a still

Fig. 15. Peláez house, view under the table in the living room. Photograph by Richard Weston, 1995.

life, or to a colonnaded interior. Can you imagine riding a route 37 bus through a maze of a collage some call Havana one afternoon in March 1986? Can you think of anything more incongruous than a Hungarian-made bus and a bunch of yellow flowers in a neighborhood with the inexplicable name of La Víbora [The Viper]?

That's why I felt strange taking a bus the first time I visited the house at Estrada Palma 261. The sun — it should have been spring, but here it's nothing more than the beginning of summer — crushed the city against the hot earth and enveloped it in a fume that dissolved perspective and fragmented objects and people. Everything was volatile and unstable, almost immaterial. Going through the lower section of El Vedado it seemed as if the bus were flanked by walls that blocked the view of the sea or kept me from wondering what lay beyond the nearest corner. I was afraid of going nowhere. Of making a senseless, aimless trip in a city that was like a carousel inside a kaleidoscope. I had experienced all of that before, but I didn't remember the details.

> the angel, sleepless, sings, showing off himself solicitously. In front of the mirror the woman smashes the landscape with a sudden blow. Right now the angel's proximity is her only shield. Meanwhile, beyond, the smoke of a passing ship draws a parabola of coal. With this gesture the flow of dawn begins. The woman runs to her tempera colors; she wants to save all of that glass in her memoirs. The angel, dressed as a rubber plant, rushes through the arboreal night like fire. Naked, he lacerates the inner fist. Tied to the lattice gate, he defends the commotion the pupil enjoys. It was the final bet, the autumnal loss. No one saw him leave, riding a white horse, barely kissing the ashes with his trail. There was no halo

Fig. 17. Peláez house. Photograph
by Richard Weston, 1995.

Fig. 18. Peláez house, view of
hall from dining room. Painting,
Amelia Peláez, *Hermanas*, ca.
1967. Photograph by Eduardo
Luis Rodríguez, 1995.

*in the stalking that was about to begin—jealously. Dawn arrived like a
soft-textured chalice.*

When the bus reaches the more-or-less huge Jesús del Monte Boulevard, I
recognize walls built of dust and smoke, the smell of rancid urine in lascivious
corners of porticoes, and the carnival of noises that lays bare the display
windows of aging stores. In a while we shall turn a little more to the south
and then, from up high, we shall see the sea, which from that angle is like a
suggestion of blue. The landscape makes unexpected movements and assumes
fragile poses. I begin to ascend and descend alternatively, going through passageways, sensing a hospitable architecture. Everything is so domestic that I
think I smell a faint odor of onions (fig. 19).

That afternoon I learned what poinsettias looked like. I saw them in a garden
in La Víbora, and I also saw geraniums and bougainvillea. I saw white ironwork
gates and porches with checkered tiles glowing in the shade. One felt like lying
there, feeling the coolness of the tiled floor through one's bare feet. Then I
thought that Amelia had no studio. That she painted thus, lying on the floor.
And that's why nothing in her paintings is like what we see when we are standing
up but like what we picture from the floor — tables, landscapes, fruit, curtains,
windows, wicker furniture. Why have a studio when one can lie down on the
porch and from below paint the sea, the linen tablecloths, or the piano keys?
Paint light and shadow, the breeze and freshness, the scents that visit this
house at this time of the evening.

*on the table lies the silverware, undecipherable. Meanwhile, the bells
announce the zigzag, the prancing of winged trivia. In the garden conversation rings, barely touching its own image. The hues of hibiscuses*

Fig. 20. Peláez house, garden.

Photograph by Eduardo Luis

Rodríguez, 1995.

and begonias, of ferns and lilies, of carnations and cacti shape the tiny rainbow that dominates over the vertical, itself dominated by the dust, which is nothing but time on the lookout (fig. 20). *And there are other colors that are unknown so far. Wings never before seen, eyes not open before this discovery, beyond the smoke of a toy-like city, between the orchard and that airy vanity table that is the mirror* (fig. 21). *Greenish-yellow. Like this fan on the wall imitating the evening, secure against gusts of wind, dancing on the hallucinated moss, seeking—for God knows how many years—the light precisely now discovered. But she didn't know when it was that she chatted with bewildered fish, domestic fish placing their warm eggs under the fan. This refuge grows for indistinct lovers, preserving this corner of the city, which remains marvelously intact.*

I don't remember what streets I rode through. I do remember my astonishment at finding the bright white house. My steps toward the iron gate were timid. It looked like an embroidery [hovering] in midair. [I became aware of] the tranquility of the palm trees. When I stepped over the threshold I entered the world of pure sensations. I felt — or rather intuited — marble, crystal, wood, ceramics. I saw myself in a mirror, but I had become once more an astonished shadow drinking a glass of custard apple juice. I remember the conversation between the two women, but the words escaped me (fig. 22). At the end of the corridor there was a spot of blinding light. It seemed as if I were walking toward the end of the world (fig. 23).

And what can one say about a house? Amelia Peláez lived and died in this house. It was built in 1912. There were few houses in that neighborhood at the time. Many similar houses rise there now. Houses that seem to talk among themselves, connected by an invisible dialogue — with colonial furniture. Boys run from one sidewalk to the next, taking the house with them in a jolly confusion. In that same way Amelia took the house with her to many places. She took it to Paris and London, New York and Mexico. In Venice she placed it in the middle

of Saint Mark's Square and went inside it to dream, facing the quadriga sustained by the shit of millennial pigeons.

And what can you say to a house? Say, "Hello house, I come from Havana. I've ridden through tortuous streets where the sun filters through like a hot sword. I came, puppet-like, hanging from the door of a bus. Let me browse for a while. I promise you that once I leave I'll forget everything. Everything except that spot of light at the end of the corridor, where the flower-bedecked garden glows in humid tranquility. Everything except that canvas on the easel, waiting for the hand that will never again touch it." The persistent odor of oil paint overpowers the environment.

> *the woman sitting on the rocking chair rocks the breeze* (fig. 24). *She hums a song while she rocks, almost hovering above a bird's drowsiness. The bird dreams about the woman, but she does not exist. She is only the dream of the bird, which smiles. On a cloud in the woman's dream, a streetcar floats by. Its groaning motion almost awakens the bird. It holds the bird for five seconds above the newly painted gate. Then it releases it gently over the rails, that smell like hot metal. The umbrellas watch in amazement and make comments. The rocking chair stops rocking. For an instant—five seconds—the bird prepares to fly away over the aerials of the neighborhood. But the woman undrapes a white and bountiful breast and feeds the bird so it can continue to dream about her being supple on the moist grass.*

I touched the swinging half-door, as if I could make it real with my hands, as if I could take it with me into outer space. But my fingers lacked the necessary magic. I was there only to see — and to remember. Some visits are made to recall a life that does not exist, someone else's past. And yet, how familiar was the opalescent crystal, the voluptuous wood. Memory makes use of such tricks to resist us. And it has buttresses of concrete appearance that vanish when we attempt to give them a place, an owner, a space they don't need. This house seemed to me to be just that. Particularly when I began to feel that I could go

Fig. 24. Peláez house, mother's bedroom. Photograph by Eduardo Luis Rodríguez, 1995.

◀

Fig. 23. Peláez house, hallway from front door. Painting, Amelia Peláez, *Vaso con flores*, watercolor, 1952. Photograph by Richard Weston, 1995.

through walls. That one of us (the house or me) was in the wrong dimension. I was terrified by the thought that I might be but a dream of the house, a fleeting part of its memory (fig. 25). It was like living a Bradbury story, in which my existence always depended on being thought of and remembered by an entity whose reality escaped my control, and which furthermore endangered my very reality. Beyond metaphysics, this is an allegory of the mutation experienced by cultural objects once they have been displaced. They begin to have an existence

Fig. 25. Peláez house, view of the garden. Photograph by Eduardo Luis Rodríguez, 1995.

Fig. 26. Amelia Peláez,

ceramics. Photograph by

Richard Weston, 1995.

of their own, disconnected from collective consciousness (fig. 26). I was an excrescence within that fragment of history, which took care only of the physical attributes, as if tangible things were the most important, as if life and death were not something beyond matter, persisting in the spirituality of gesture and not in the consistency of its outcome.

> *night is intuited in her mouth* (fig. 27). *The smile is full of sharp stars. All tides flow therein with their frothy texture. They flow into her yawn through unknown channels. Everyone leaves, perhaps because the limelights have been turned off. The ocean's echo is too much for their weak souls. The surface of the sea is too vast for their timid steps. They trust their eyes too much. They're not ready for the immense blackness of the fish's mouth. Their ears praise the waltz, but they're needed in twos, at least. Only she dared, fearless. But prophets don't choose their solitude. It is revelation that opens a chasm between the chosen ones and the crowd. She moves forward, but no one sees her. She speaks, but no one hears her. Only the fish borrows her tears. Hypocritical, it fuses her into an embrace. The house is empty. Like a cadaver that has been embalmed* (fig. 28).

"I come from Havana," I said, not knowing who had spoken for me, or with whom, because I was back on the sidewalk. The visit was over. Rather, the unvisit, because my passage through the house had been like an escape. My brief stay had not been a meeting but a dispersion. One second has gone by and I'm again walking through the clean streets of La Víbora. A century ago there were

Fig. 27. Amelia Peláez, *Figura femenina*, oil on canvas, 1944. Photograph by Cathy Leff, 1994.

empty lots here, vegetation, open fields from which you could see the lights of Morro Castle marking the entrance to the harbor. The city then leaned over the sea, as if lapping it up. I begin to walk and think about this city, which becomes ever more thirsty, ever less visitable, where every contact hides a loss, where every stroll is labyrinthic, where every entrance could be an exit. The number 37 bus stop awaits me — a Hungarian bus full of yellow flowers in the middle of a still life with melons. □

Fig. 28. Peláez house, dining room. Paintings, Amelia Peláez, *left to right*: *Composición*, oil on canvas, 77 x 102 cm, 1949; *Naturaleza muerta*, oil on canvas, 66 x 100.5 cm, 1946; *Marpacífico*, tempera on board, 76 x 102 cm, 1963. Photograph by Cathy Leff, 1994.

Fig. 1. Enrique Riverón, 1989. Photograph by Ramón Guerrero.

Enrique Riverón on the Cuban *Vanguardia*: An Interview

By Giulio V. Blanc

Giulio V. Blanc was an art historian who published extensively on Cuban painting. One of his many contributions to the field is his catalogue *Amelia Peláez,1896–1968: Una Retrospectiva/ A Retrospective* (Miami: Museo Cubano de Arte y Cultura, 1988). Mr. Blanc died while this issue of *The Journal* was in preparation.

Enrique Riverón was one of the few artists of the Cuban *vanguardia* to work with abstraction and non-representational imagery (fig. 1). By the 1930s he had come to an understanding of an international modernism different from the nationalistic, representational trends of Cuban art of the period (fig. 2).

Riverón had a provincial childhood. He was born 31 January 1901 on a farm in the outskirts of La Fe, a small town near Cienfuegos, in the south of Santa Clara province. The family soon moved to Cienfuegos, where he lived until 1918, at which time he went to Havana to work in a bank; during his spare time he studied painting with the academic artist Aurelio Melero at a private school. His early work, drawings and caricatures of popular types, was brought to the attention of Conrado W. Massaguer, who included Riverón in the exhibition he organized for the first Salón de Humoristas in 1921.

From 1924 to 1926 Riverón traveled in Europe with a grant from the City of Cienfuegos. He studied painting at the Academia de Bellas Artes de San Fernando in Madrid and published drawings and caricatures in *Buen Humor* and *La Libertad* at the same time he was collaborating with *Social, Diario de la Marina,* and *Chic* in Havana. He subsequently moved to Paris, where he enrolled at La Grande Chaumière and La Colarosse, met Picasso through the Mexican poet Alfonso Reyes, and became a member of the Montparnasse group of Cuban artists. He also traveled in Belgium, Holland, and Italy and ended his European sojourn in 1926 with an exhibition at the Association Paris-Amérique Latine. Back in Havana he exhibited at the Asociación de Pintores y Escultores in 1927.

Beginning in the 1930s, after his initial phase, he developed an extensive body of collages, paintings, and sculptures. Through his travels, he came to understand — and live — the modernist idiom and his painting style evolved through the years, always expressing his own forms and spatial rhythms.

Some myths color Riverón's life, mainly that he worked for a living for only a brief period, married the proverbial wealthy American beauty, and never sold much of his work. The truth, however, is different. Riverón is an intensely private artist who expresses in his paintings and sculptures the dictates of his drive. He evolved a pictorial sense inspired in the images of what at the time was the "new art," full of the idealism of the early years of the century.

Photographs courtesy of Enrique Riverón except where noted.

Only in his collages, from the 1930s on, did he fully embrace the absurdity, chance, and nihilism of Dada and Surrealism. Combining printed images with fabrics, found materials, and paint, he excelled in the art of collage. While familiar with the work of Kurt Schwitters and Max Ernst, Riverón evolved his own

Fig. 2. Enrique Riverón,

Abstraction, tempera on

paper, 9 x 12", 1934.

compositional sense, one that, in ways, was different from the nationalist mainstream of Cuban art, since Riverón lived in the United States for most of his professional life.

In the 1950s he painted works in an Abstract Expressionist style, broadening the palette of his earlier work and embracing a larger scale. By the 1960s he had changed to a minimalist, reductive, abstract mode of flat color planes, using acrylic paints. He made sculptures during all these periods; the welded-steel works of the 1960s, for instance, relate to his hard-edged abstractions while other pieces are dimensional collages. Eventually, he merged his late paintings and sculptures into very serious, almost theoretical, three-dimensional works. Now, in his nineties, he sometimes remembers lucidly special moments in his life, but his mind tends to wander and his eyes stare at a picture for a long time.

Enrique Riverón lives today on placid Española Drive in Coconut Grove, Florida. His wife and companion in his travels, Noella Wibble, a tall no-nonsense woman whom he married in 1931, was always at his side.[1]

GB: Why did you move to Miami?

ER: Nice atmosphere to work, all year sunlight, just look at those plants. I became very involved with the Miami Museum of Modern Art in the 1960s. I was also a founder of GALA (Grupo de Artistas Latino Americanos) that existed here. The artists were José María Mijares, Baruh Salinas, McAllister Kelly, Rafael Soriano, Osvaldo Gutiérrez, and myself.

GB: Tell us about your early years in Cuba.

ER: I studied at the Academia Villate in Havana in 1918 under the notable academic master Aurelio Melero. I did caricatures for the magazines *Bohemia* and

---

1. She died in February 1993.

Fig. 3. Enrique Riverón, cover

of *Confetti*, 12 May 1921.

Confetti (fig. 3). I had many friends among the artists, especially among those who were humorists and caricaturists like myself. It was the idea of the humorist Conrado Massaguer to have dinners [and hold exhibitions]. We all got together there among friends. We called them the Salones de Humoristas. The first one was in 1921. These were more than humorous at this and later dates (fig. 4). Writers such as Alejo Carpentier and Guillermo Martínez Márquez were at our banquets. Two artists you don't hear much about these days also participated: Armando Maribona and Jaime Valls. I did caricatures of Presidents Alfredo Zayas and José Miguel Gómez for the newspapers.

GB: Why did you move to Europe?

ER: A lot of the young Cuban artists were going to Paris in the 1920s. We went to learn new things. There was only so much you could learn in Cuba. They were still very academic. However, we knew what was going on in Mexico, Paris, and New York, and we wanted to see it. I sailed for Spain on the *Orulla*.

GB: What did you do in Spain?

ER: I continued my studies at the Academia de San Fernando for a year. I sent drawings back to the *Diario de la Marina* and *Social* in Havana, and I did drawings for such Spanish magazines and newspapers as *Buen Humor* and *La Libertad* (fig. 5).

GB: Who were your friends in Madrid?

ER: Sirio, a Cuban cartoonist, helped me a lot. Other friends were the writers Gómez de la Serna and Angel Lázaro. We would get together in restaurants and cafés such as El Gato Negro, on Príncipe. There were paintings there by Gutiérrez de la Solana. The writers had long discussions among themselves.

GB: You left Madrid in 1925.

ER: I loved Madrid, it was a good time to be there, but I had [been in Europe with] a grant from the City of Cienfuegos that said I had to go to Paris.

GB: When did you go to Paris?

ER: At the end of 1925. I studied for a while at La Grande Chaumière and La Colarosse. I met Picasso, who told me to forget the academy. There were other Latin American artists and writers, and we would get together at La Rotonde and Le Dôme (fig. 6). We called ourselves the Grupo de Montparnasse and spent a lot of time at these cafés. I lived with other Latin American artists at the Hôtel du Maine near the railroad station.

GB: Did you meet the artists and characters of the period?

ER: Yes, Man Ray and José de Creeft, but my favorite was Kiki de Montparnasse. Man Ray took some famous photographs of her. She was his lover but she later switched to Foujita. She was really beautiful and sexy, all the artists wanted to have her as a model. I did a painting of her in 1946 from memory (fig. 7). I could never forget her eyes. I knew Josephine Baker later in Argentina. I got an orchestra for her. [Argentine orchestras could not play her music, so Riverón assembled three Cuban musicians in Buenos Aires to play for her. She hired them on the spot.]

GB: Weren't there a lot of Cubans in Paris?

ER: Yes, Víctor Manuel, Antonio Gattorno, who became a good friend of Ernest Hemingway, and Eduardo Abela were there (fig. 8). He was the first one of us to meet Kiki, also Armando Maribona was in Paris, too. He wrote a book on the Paris years, *El arte y el amor en Montparnasse: Paris, 1923–1930*. Here it is. I wish somebody would reprint it. It is all about our living there. It is fiction but everyone is in it. Look at the illustrations by another Cuban, Enrique Caravia. He really captured the atmosphere. Here is Kiki and an artist going crazy because there were so many different styles.

GB: Are you mentioned in this book?

ER: Yes, Maribona was a friend of mine so he put me in it. See, look at this: "Bonilla, Gattorno, Sicre, Mantilla, and Riverón would also go to La Crémière, getting personal with its hilarious *garçon*, Alfred, who confused orders to make a joke and knew a lot of droll and piquant stories."[2]

GB: What exactly was La Crémière?

ER: It was a cheap café, a place to eat. See, he says it was on the Boul. Miche [Boulevard Saint-Michel], on the left bank with many artists, students, and writers: "a whole picturesque and heterogeneous clientele who asked for their food in a loud voice and made dinnertime a lot of fun. Sometimes a strolling musician or a poet or somebody who sang or did magic tricks came by."[3]

2. Armando Maribona, *El arte y el amor en Montparnasse: Paris, 1923–1930* (Mexico City: Ediciones Botas, 1950), 217.
3. Ibid., 216.

Fig. 9. Drawing from *Enrique Riverón 16 May to 30 May, 1926*, exhibition catalogue (Paris: Association Paris-Amérique Latine, 1926). Ruth and Richard Shack collection, Miami, Florida.

Fig. 10. Enrique Riverón, advertisement for Jabón Candado (Candado soap), ca. 1922.

GB: So the Grupo de Montparnasse really lived it up?

ER: Yes, Maribona writes about one particular Christmas Eve that was a costume party: "Egas dressed up like Don Juan Tenorio with a beard and painted moustache and on his shoulders the *capa madrileña* of Riverón. He improvised to look like a Chinaman."[4]

GB: Is it true you were there when Víctor Manuel, who is considered the founder of modern Cuban painting, changed his name?

ER: Yes, we forced him to change it from Manolo García since that was too common. We baptized him with champagne.

GB: You exhibited in Paris, didn't you?

4. Ibid., 232.

ER: Yes, at the Association Paris-Amérique Latine on the Boulevard de la Madeleine. I have the catalogue (fig. 9). It was in May of 1926. The introduction is by the Mexican writer Alfonso Reyes, who was with us at the time.

GB: I see your style changed to Art Deco. Lets talk about your style in this period.

ER: In the 1920s and early 1930s I did a lot of folkloric drawings such as *Avocados* and *Market Place*. These are some of the ones I exhibited in the Paris show. I had already done Art Deco for *La Nación* and *Plus ultra*. In Chile I did some illustrations for *Últimas noticias*. I also did some covers and drawings.

GB: You had an exhibition right after you got back to Havana. Do you think you can be considered a pioneer of Cuban Modernism? You showed at the Asociación de Pintores y Escultores in Havana in February 1927 with Parisian sketches and those of Caribbean life. You picked up on the theme of cultural nationalism that was popular at the time (fig. 10). Actually, many of the shows of the Modernists occurred some time later.

ER: All of that was in the air. I had an exhibition at the Lyceum, the women's club that showed so many Cuban artists, in 1936.

GB: You didn't stay very long in Havana. What made you move to New York City?

ER: I first went to New York in 1928. I later returned there in 1931. In 1938 I went to Hollywood and worked for Walt Disney for four months on *Snow White* and *Ferdinand the Bull*.

Fig. 11. Enrique Riverón,

untitled drawing, ink on paper,

8 1/2 x 11", ca. 1937.

GB: You showed *Form and Abstraction* at the American Congress Gallery in Hollywood. Is this when you begin to use abstraction?

ER: It was earlier in the 1930s.

GB: These abstract drawings remind me a bit of Jean Arp and even Mondrian. They are such an elegant combination of line and curve, so simple yet perfectly balanced.

ER: I began to do abstract work in Paris. It has always appealed to me. Over there are abstract works from the 1930s. I like the combination of curves and lines, also the contrast of colors, although most of the drawings are in black and white (fig. 11).

GB: Lets get back to New York. You always talk about Alma Reed. Who was she?

ER: An American woman who loved Mexico and was a close friend of José Clemente Orozco in New York. She got him a lot of commissions. She also liked Cubans and gave me a show in February of 1936 (fig. 12). She also showed Fidelio Ponce in 1938. She gave great parties. All the Latin American artists were there: Orozco, Tamayo, Siqueiros, Julia Codesida from Peru, also Jean Xeceron.

GB: So what else did you do in New York besides going to parties?

ER: I did cartoons and advertising for *The New Yorker*, *Life*, *Look*, and *Modern Screen* (fig. 13).

GB: Was the reaction to your Delphic Studios show good? I have here a review by your friend the Cuban writer Jorge Mañach: "Riverón still shows a certain air of improvisation, a certain graceful levity which are the result of his first stage as a humorist and satiric artist. These two characteristics persist in spite of the artist's attempt to substantiate a sense of dramatism in his profiles. The

Fig. 12. Enrique Riverón, *2,000,000*, collage, 9 x 11", 1936.

Fig. 14. Enrique Riverón, *El maraquero* (The Maracas Vendor), pencil on paper, 1935.

Cuban tropical theme charged with Afro-Cuban reminiscences is presented here, still indecisive between the folkloric accent and that grave and poetic orientation that contemporary Mexican art has been imposing as a norm on Latin American painting" (fig. 14).[5]

ER: Yes, there was a lot of interest. Alfonso Reyes, the Mexican writer living in Paris, did the little catalogue. Here is a copy of it.

GB: We see a great deal of abstract works from the 1930s. These paintings and works are a balance of curve, straight line, and color contrast. Did you know that you and Amelia Peláez seem to have pioneered abstraction in Cuba?

5. César Trasobares, *Riverón, 1925–1950 Paris/La Habana/New York* (Miami: Lowe Art Museum/ University of Miami, Coral Gables, 1980), n.p.

Fig. 15. Enrique Riverón, *Color Abstraction*, pastel and ink on paper, 14 x 11", 1938.

Fig. 16. Enrique Riverón, *Unforgettable Things*, collage, 22 x 14", 1944.

Fig. 17. Enrique Riverón, *Veteris Vestigia Flammae*, oil and collage on canvas, 18 x 24", 1939. Photograph by Sandy Levy. Craig Robins collection.

ER: I have always been interested in abstraction. Some of the early works are experiments, but I have continued to use this style until now. It has evolved. People suddenly seem to like it very much (fig. 15).

GB: And the collages? Some of them, the ones from the 1940s, make reference to World War Two. They are very moving and even painful in their depictions of the consequences of war.

ER: I took pieces of wood, pictures from magazines, newspapers, paint, also objects. Collage is something else I continue to work with (fig. 16).

GB: César Trasobares quotes you in his retrospective catalogue: "My interest is in forms, color, and the purest of organization in obtaining from the plastic its greatest quintessence."[6] Has this affected your entire oeuvre?

ER: Yes, it has, very much so (fig. 17).

GB: During the 1940s and 1950s you lived in Wichita, Kansas, with your wife, Noella, who had an ice business there, and also your daughter Patricia. You moved from Abstract Expressionism to hard-edge abstraction.

ER: I felt strongly about abstraction, but I didn't stop doing figurative paintings and drawings, Afro-Cuban especially (fig. 18).

GB: You have a lot of painted metal sculpture. Your garden is filled with it.

6. Ibid.

Fig. 18. Enrique Riverón,

Fiesta Ñáñiga, oil on canvas,

40 x 30", 1957.

ER: I have always done sculpture, but these are from the 1950s. A lot of it is made with junk. My interest in this comes from the forms and colors of my paintings and nature (fig. 19).

GB: Thank you very much for your time.

ER: Come and visit very soon! □

Note

This interview was put together from notes, conversations, and interviews conducted by the author from the late 1970s to 1995. I am grateful to Enrique Riverón, the late Noella Riverón, and their daughter Patricia Lee, who gave me access to the Riverón archives and volunteered so much of their time; to librarians Esperanza B. de Varona and Lesbia O. Varona of the Cuban Collection of the Otto G. Richter Library of the University of Miami, Coral Gables, Florida; to artists Pablo Cano and Juan-Sí; and to my father, Lodovico Blanc.

Fig. 19. Riverón standing next to one of his sculptures, Miami, ca. 1975. Photograph by Miguel Cubiles.

Fig. 2. José Antonio Mendigutía, Francisco Argüelles residence, Marianao, Havana, 1927. Photograph by Richard Weston, 1995.

(Address: Quinta Avenida 2201 corner to 22, Miramar, Marianao.)

The Architectural Avant-Garde: From Art Deco to Modern Regionalism

By Eduardo Luis Rodríguez

Translated by John Beusterien and Narciso G. Menocal

Eduardo Luis Rodríguez is a practicing architect and historian. He is the author of *Guía de arquitectura: La Habana colonial (1519–1898)* (Seville: Junta de Andalucía, 1993) and the forthcoming *La Habana: arquitectura del siglo XX*. He has written numerous articles on Cuba and is presently the director of the magazine *Arquitectura-Cuba*. In 1995 he was a Maria Elena Cassiet Fellow at the John Carter Brown Library, and in 1996 he received a Guggenheim Fellowship.

While through the eighteenth century artistic ideas arrived late from Spain and stylistic currents lagged behind those in countries more economically and culturally developed, new styles reached Cuba much faster in the nineteenth and twentieth centuries as an anxiety for modernity pervaded the island mainly from the 1850s on. Circumstantial facts, such as the improvement of communications and the increase in cultural exchange since the establishment of the Republic in 1902, accelerated the assimilation of European and American styles. A general desire, a common hope, and a purpose shared by an important sector of the enlightened bourgeoisie to be part of the avant-garde — and to place Cuba on a par with the more culturally advanced countries — were also part of the equation. Examples of such desire in other fields were the introduction of the railway in 1837; the typewriter by approximately 1880; the telephone in 1881; public electric lighting in 1889; movies in 1897 (a little more than a year after the first exhibition by the Lumière brothers); and the automobile in 1898. However, modernity meant many things to many people. Cuban critics and journalists of the first decades of the twentieth century used the concept ambiguously, and even contradictorily. "Modernity" came to mean more the probable fact that one was "fashionable" than some sort of conceptual meaning or definite artistic program. Hence it is possible to find the word "modern" increasingly associated with the wishes of the city to modernize itself. Around 1883 we find the term referring to the buildings along the Calzada del Monte, as they neared the Reparto de las Murallas: "What we said about the old part of the city does not apply to this one, just finished at all cost, as a product of a more enlightened age. This is Modern Havana" (cf. Venegas, fig. 38, this issue).[1] Some forty-six years later the term was applied to the premier exponent of Cuban Eclecticism: "Leonardo Morales, the first who planned and constructed a building in a modern style in Havana" (cf. Lobo and Lapique, figs. 35, 36, and 37, this issue).[2]

The idea of modernity was more frequently used in reference to Art Nouveau. The assimilation of this new style in Cuba around 1905 has been interpreted, and even overstated on occasions, as a conscious rejection of the colonial architecture immediately preceding it — as a setting forth of a plan of action with defined goals.[3] In reality Art Nouveau was simply but another stylistic alternative

---

1. *Directorio criticón de La Habana* (1883), 63; quoted in Carlos Venegas Fornias, *La urbanización de las murallas: dependencia y modernidad* (Havana: Editorial Letras Cubanas, 1990), 77.

2. *El Arquitecto* (January–February 1929): 11.

3. Regarding this, see Joaquín Weiss, "Art Nouveau: la rama cubana," *Cuba* (September 1965): 62; and Vivien Acosta, "De Europa a Cuba: Art Nouveau," *Universidad de La Habana* 193 (January–March 1969): 45.

at the beginning of the century. It is doubtful that the few professionals and builders who worked in that style had any other purpose in mind than to pursue originality on the design of facades. There were three means by which Art Nouveau was introduced in Cuba: the 1905 Paris Exhibition, European journals with information on the style, and, most importantly, a strong Catalan immigration with knowledge of how to design and construct the new forms. Mario Rotllant, a Catalan immigrant, is repeatedly cited as the precursor of modernity in Cuba. "He has broken old molds with incredible tenacity and initiated the modernization of our beautiful city," reported *El Fígaro* in 1913.[4] It was really some years later, and due to the arrival of rationalist ideas and the conflict between tradition and modernity, that the word "modern" acquired a conceptual meaning.

The European architectural avant-garde was introduced through many vehicles, professional journals being one of them. After 1925 the *Revista del Colegio de Arquitectos de La Habana* and *El Arquitecto* introduced several modern currents that had taken place shortly before in Europe, broadcasted the new concepts and their corresponding polemics, and entered into a healthy debate. *El Arquitecto* published the first article about the new style in 1926. In it one finds a clear reference to the ideal posed by Le Corbusier in *Towards a New Architecture*: "Other quite beautiful forms of which we think about daily constitute the true architecture of the present moment, and they have the suggestive modernity that spurs our spirits. They are those that we can call dynamic architecture: the great transatlantic ships with gracious and energetic curves, the formidable battleships, the gigantic locomotives, the airplanes."[5]

Fig. 1. Cover of *Arte y Decoración, Revista Mensual Ilustrada* 1, August 1931.

However, save for some exceptions, new works and theoretical formulations did not correspond with the radical aesthetic of the machine but with Art Deco, a movement that had reached a large diffusion in the Paris Exposition Internationale des Arts Décoratifs et Industriels Modernes, of 1925. Because of its profuse ornamentation and frequent references to classicism, the new style was easier to understand by Cuban architects and clients than the harsh, abstract forms of Le Corbusier's mechanization. Cuban professionals who visited the exhibition returned home overflowing with ideas and images. In contrast with the ephemeral and limited development of Art Nouveau, Art Deco expanded quickly throughout the island and played a significant role in forging a unique urban expression — and there lies its importance. If the use of Art Deco was in general acritical, it is undeniable that the style became the alternative for young architects to replace the worn-out forms of Eclecticism then in fashion. Moreover, Art Deco offered a more up-to-date approach to design and decorative freedom. It was a sign of "modernism."

Another factor that influenced the acceptance of the new style was the end of the economic boom of the late teens and early 1920 when the affluence due to the high price of sugar during World War One had allowed for the construction of a number of palatial residences, notably in El Vedado. Now, at the end of the 1920s and during the 1930s, with a weak economy, Art Deco forms became more desirable. They were less expensive to produce than the earlier classical ones; their typical applied ornamentation could be reproduced with relative ease in art studios and foundries; and the new forms were highly appropriate for architectural themes requiring an expression of modernity, such as social

4. *El Fígaro* (25 May and 1 June 1913): 272.
5. Leopoldo Torres Balbás, "Las nuevas formas en la arquitectura," *El Arquitecto* (May 1926): 35.

clubs and movie theaters. Also, the lectures and writings of Alberto Camacho and Joaquín Weiss and the extraordinary graphic designs of Conrado W. Massaguer, published in *Social* and *Carteles*, gave a definitive impulse to the new stylistic current. Furthermore, architectural journals supported the new ideas, and their covers often offered strong contrasts of form and content (fig. 1).

Concerning the development of the style, a more-or-less-pure Art Deco of French extraction, mostly used in middle-class residential design, appeared first, in 1927, and grew during the 1930s, until it was replaced by the influence from the United States. A parallel trend, an Art Deco strongly related to Eclecticism, was favored for buildings with a more urban presence but was abandoned shortly after the beginning of the decade.

The first Art Deco work in Havana was the Francisco Argüelles residence, designed by José Antonio Mendigutía in 1927 as a result of a private competition (fig. 2). The house expresses its debt to the Galleries Lafayette Pavilion at the 1925 Paris Exhibition with no inhibition. As in the French example, its composition was based on a central tower flanked by *terrazas* (porches). In the interior a relatively sober ornamentation concentrated on the stylized capitals of the pilasters, the ironwork, the windows made by Ballesteros y Compañía, and in the furnishings executed by the firm of Merás y Rico. Above the main doorway a relief by Juan José Sicre alluded to the conflict between the new style and the classicism it opposed. A desire to turn each building into a *Gesamtkunstwerk* was a characteristic of the new style.

Other houses followed in a similar vein. The María Biosca residence, of 1928, by the firm of Maruri y Weiss, featured capitals with stylized tropical vegetation. The José Manuel Coroalles residence, of 1935, was designed in a "luxurious Modernist style," according to a statement its architect, Armando Puentes, made in his petition for a building permit. However, the best example in the nation of residential Art Deco is the Manuel López Chávez house, of 1932, a design in which the architect, Esteban Rodríguez Castells, achieved an integration of all design details, from landscaping to floor patterns and from furnishings to lighting (fig. 3).

The second trend, Art Deco with historicist references, was a logical consequence of the persistence of Eclecticism and of the versatility of the new style
to integrate itself with other precedents in a peaceful harmonious coexistence.
The most significant work in this sense, and also the first, is the residence of
Juan Pedro Baró and Catalina Lasa, constructed in 1927 (fig. 4). Evelio Govantes
and Félix Cabarrocas, the well-known Eclectic architects, first designed a project in a Neocolonial style with a large central courtyard surrounded by galleries. The owners, who lived in Paris most of the year, presumably preferred
the exoticism of the avant-garde to the nationalist tradition. A second project
featured Italian Renaissance facades with details from the Palazzo Strozzi and
Art Deco interiors with Egyptian references. Despite this hybrid solution, or
perhaps because of it, the result is extraordinary. The success of the building
was a result of a combination of circumstances. Important among them were
the vision of the architects, the materials utilized, and the participation of the
French designer René Lalique, who later would design the tomb for the Baró-
Lasa family, one of the most opulent in the Cristóbal Colón Cemetery (cf. Aruca,
figs. 15, 16, and 17, this issue).

Another example of this second trend of Art Deco is the Hospital Municipal
de Maternidad América Arias, by Govantes y Cabarrocas (1930) (fig. 5). For
this building they inverted the pattern they had used in the Baró residence:
the exterior is Art Deco but the main rotunda inside is strongly classical (fig. 6).
A final example is the Ignacio del Valle residence, with Renaissance facades
and interior Art Deco details, by Horacio Navarrete, of 1935.

Art Deco was easily adapted to preexisting structures, a quality that contrasted
with the ideas of a more radically rationalist avant-garde. Such was the case of

Fig. 5. Evelio Govantes and Félix Cabarrocas, Hospital Municipal de Maternidad América Arias, Havana, 1930. Photograph by the author, 1994. (Address: G between 9 and 11, Vedado.)

Fig. 6. Evelio Govantes and Félix Cabarrocas, Hospital Municipal de Maternidad América Arias, view from the central rotonda. Photograph by the author, 1994.

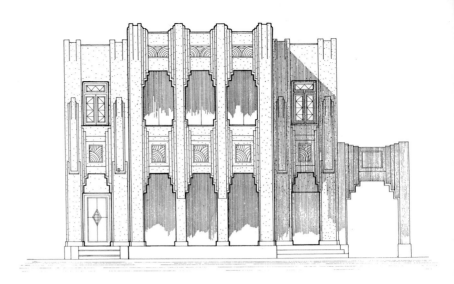

additions to a house that Angel de Zárraga had designed for Julio Tarafa in 1933. Originally one story, it was enlarged in 1938 to include a second floor by another architect, Juan M. Lagomasino, who respected the previous design in every way (fig. 7). The same strategy was followed by Morales y Compañía when they added a story to the Romagosa Pavilion of the Clínica de Dependientes years after José Ricardo Martínez constructed the original building in 1938 (figs. 8 and 9). Such flexibility saved one of the best examples of Art Deco. The Romagosa Pavilion still expresses on the outside the rotunda of its extraordinary two-story-high vestibule, one in which columns, windows, and floors establish angular patterns typical of the style.

The central library of the University of Havana, executed by Joaquín Weiss in 1937, is perhaps the most notable example of how Art Deco was integrated into a previously constructed environment (fig. 10). In spite of the long time it took to build the campus (construction began in 1905), the buildings of the university maintain an unusual coherence and harmony among them, since they were conceived partly in a sober Neoclassicism of impressive presence. It was therefore difficult to design a new building in a modern style in the center of the campus, especially when the main facade was directly across from the Hellenistic portal of the rectory. The first project for the library, a Historicist design, halfway resolved the adaptation of the new building to its environment, but it did not respond to the taste of the day. A second project, one totally modern, was rejected by the architect upon recognizing the violent contrast it would provoke. The final project assumed forms and details of the style that, in Weiss's judgment, would fully satisfy the requirements of integration of a current style within the campus. The building was constructed in an Art Deco style with classicist influence, with a monumental colonnade in perfect harmony with the surrounding structures.

The full acceptance of Art Deco by architects and investors by the early 1930s stimulated its unprecedented diffusion — fine examples proliferated in various architectural themes throughout the country. Among buildings worth mentioning are a restaurant that Mario Colli and Manuel Bahamonde constructed on the Quinta Avenida in Miramar as early as 1929 (later altered and today quite transformed); the Miramar Swimming Club (fig. 11), one of the first social institutions in a modern mode, designed by César Sotelo in 1930; the swimming

left,
Fig. 8. José Ricardo Martínez,
Romagosa Pavilion, Clínica de
Dependientes, Havana, 1938.
Photograph by the author, 1994.
(Address: Calzada de Diez de
Octubre, Santos Suárez.)

right,
Fig. 9. José Ricardo Martínez,
Romagosa Pavilion, Clínica de
Dependientes, interior view of
the rotunda, Havana, 1938.
Photograph by the author, 1994.

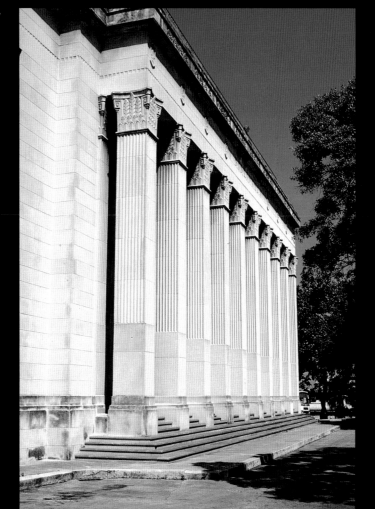

Fig. 10. Joaquín Weiss,
central library of the University
of Havana, 1937. Photograph
by the author, 1994.

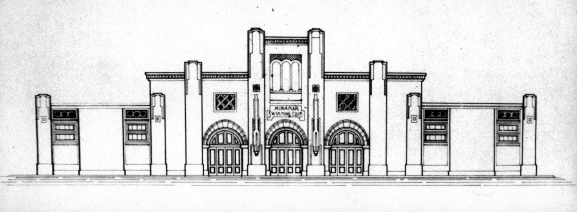

Fig. 11. César Sotelo, Miramar Swimming Club, Miramar, Marianao, Havana, 1930 (demolished). Author's collection. (Address: 1 Avenida between 8 and 10, Miramar, Marianao.)

Fig. 12. Honorato Colete, swimming club building of the Casino Español, 1937. Author's collection. (Address: Marianao Beach, Havana.)

Fig. 13. Raúl Otero, Cuban pavilion, Chicago World's Fair, 1933. Author's collection.

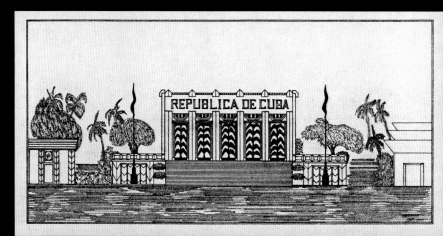

Fig. 14. Cristóbal Díaz and Rafael de Cárdenas, El País Building, Havana, 1941. Photograph by the author, 1994. (Address: Reina 158 between San Nicolás and Rayo.)

club of the Casino Español (fig. 12), a work constructed in 1937 by Honorato Colete, who also executed the Francisco Abella house in 1930; and the Cuban pavilion for the 1933 World's Fair in Chicago, by Raúl Otero (fig. 13). In downtown Havana the headquarters of the newspaper *El País* (fig. 14), with its large glass surfaces, introduced a strong note of modernity among its eclectic and colonial neighbors. Built in 1941 by Cristóbal Díaz and Rafael de Cárdenas, its waiting room features a large relief that extends across its walls (fig. 15). Its author, the Spanish painter, sculptor, and ceramicist Cándido Alvarez Moreno (born in 1908), worked with typical Art Deco motifs. One finds on it, for example, a muscular workman standing for the virtue of work and honesty thanks to the various modes of modern transportation—a theme quite appropriate for a newspaper.

Yet Art Deco was not as fully realized stylistically in residential work as in public buildings. While ornamentation with arrows, repeating panels, stairs, and

Fig. 15. Cándido Alvarez

Moreno, detail of relief in

El País Building. Photograph

by the author, 1994.

Fig. 16. Emilio Azcue, his resi-

dence, Havana, 1934–1937.

Photograph by Richard Weston,

1995. (Address: San Rafael

1165 between Masón and

Basarrate, Vedado.)

zigzag details abound in small and mid-range houses in traditional parts of the city (fig. 16), with the exception of the Baró-Lasa residence, none of the great mansions constructed in the period chose a Deco aesthetic. The opposite occurred with apartment buildings, where the new mode was undoubtedly favored. Aside from apartments, movie theaters also adopted the Deco style; their facades somehow matched the advanced technology contained within. The Teatro Fausto (fig. 17), built in 1938 by Saturnino Parajón — winner of the National College of Architects Gold Medal in 1941 — may be added to other relevant examples, such as the Moderno, finished in 1930 by Ernesto López Rovirosa, and the Florencia, designed and built by Max Borges del Junco in 1938, and later radically altered.

A movie theater, the Teatro Lutgardita, finished circa 1932, exemplifies a controversial aspect of regionalism and national identity of the Deco reality not only in Cuba but also in Latin America. Generally in Cuba Art Deco was assumed to be like a foreign language that could be used and even adapted to local circumstances. Nevertheless, in the Lutgardita a notable effort was made to bring the new style nearer to native American tradition. When the firm of Govantes y Cabarrocas received the commission to design the theater, they made a decidedly nationalistic decision to employ indigenous references, but since Cuba lacked adequate pre–Columbian art as inspiration, they ended up making use of Mayan forms. The result is spectacular. Even today it is overwhelming despite the poor condition of the theater and the alterations that it has suffered. Arcades on the two fronts of a corner building harmonize with the Neocolonial architecture of the Lutgardita Subdivision, also by the same architects. While the diagonally shaped main entrance features some Art Deco details, it is mostly the ornamentation on the floors, ceilings, and roofs that makes the design unique.

Once inside the auditorium it seems as if one were in a moonlit night, with moving clouds and twinkling stars playing on the ceiling as in an "atmospheric" movie theater, all created by a special installation.[6] Enclosing the space, the

6. The so-called "atmospheric" movie theater was created by the North American John Eberson some years earlier and consisted of decorating the interior of the building in a way that would imitate a ceiling open to the sky. The general tendency was to design it with Spanish details, most particularly, Sevillian. The Eberson archives are located in The Mitchell Wolfson Jr. Collection, The Wolfsonian, Miami Beach, Florida.

Fig. 17. Saturnino Parajón, Teatro Fausto, Havana, 1938. Photograph by the author, 1994.

(Address: Prado 201 corner to Colón.)

Fig. 18. Evelio Govantes and Félix Cabarrocas, Teatro Lutgardita, general view of the orchestra section and stage, Boyeros, ca. 1932. Photograph by the author, 1994. (Address: Calzada de Bejucal 30901 corner to Castellón, Boyeros.)

Fig. 19. Evelio Govantes and Félix Cabarrocas, Teatro Lutgardita, view from the balcony, Boyeros, ca. 1932. Photograph by the author, 1994.

stage curtain is decorated with themes from the circular rock of Tikal, and the lateral columns supporting the proscenium reproduce the chronological stele of Quiriguá, in Guatemala, at a full scale. These motifs are continued by two temples, placed on both sides of the stage to cover up ventilation ducts. The one to the right was inspired by the Palace of the Governor at Uxmal and the one to the left by the Temple of the Tigers in Chichén-Itzá, including the columns shaped as feathered serpents (fig. 18). These pieces were executed by Cabarrocas, also a sculptor, and the molds were destroyed to make reproduction impossible. On the far end of the room in the balcony, a tapestry decorated with Mayan details muffles sounds. On the side walls two murals by Fernando Tarazona represent Central American landscapes (fig. 19).[7] Paradoxically, the architects found inspiration for their achievement not in Mexico but in Seville, in the pavilion that the Mexican architect Manuel Amábilis constructed for the 1929 World's Fair, which both Govantes and Cabarrocas had attended as architects of the Neocolonial Cuban pavilion.

The majority of Art Deco buildings constructed in the 1930s only had an influence on the immediate vicinity in which they were located because of their small size and relative isolation, but there are exceptions to the rule. The classic trilogy made up by the Bacardí (1930), López Serrano (1932), and Rodríguez Vázquez (1941) Buildings is the obvious one.

The Barcardí Building is perhaps the most famous example of Art Deco in Cuba (figs. 20 and 21). It was a result of a closed contest in which several of the most important figures of the time participated. The winning project, by Esteban Rodríguez Castells, Rafael Fernández Ruenes, and José Menéndez, featured facades with Renaissance details. What happened next exemplifies both the desire for modernity of the times and the importance of foreign influences. Shortly after the contest, the architects traveled to Paris. Amazed by the new architecture they found there, upon their return to Havana they completely changed the ornamentation of the building, yet retained the original relation of

7. For the Teatro Lutgardita, see Evelio Govantes, "Un ensayo en arte maya: el Teatro Lutgardita, en Rancho Boyeros," *Arquitectura y artes decorativas* (August–September 1932).

Fig. 21. Bacardí Building,

facade detail, Havana, 1930.

Photograph by Cathy Leff, 1992.

Fig. 22. Bacardí Building, exhi-

bition hall, Havana, 1930.

Photograph by the author, 1994.

Fig. 20. Esteban Rodríguez Castells, Rafael Fernández Ruenes, and José Menéndez, Bacardí Building,

Havana, 1930. Photograph by the author, 1994. (Address: Monserrate 261 between Empedrado and San

Juan de Dios.)

Fig. 24. Ricardo Mira and Miguel
Rosich, López Serrano Building,
vestibule, Havana, 1932.
Photograph by the author, 1994.

volumes. Thus the Barcardí Building was transformed into the most salient Art Deco example in Cuban architecture. This transformation for turning their headquarters into a corporate symbol was approved no doubt by the executives of the rum-producing firm. The building presents most characteristics of the style: emphasis on verticality, applied terra-cotta ornamentation on the facade, a ziggurat profile, a new sense of color, and a tower made unique by the finishing touch of a finial in the shape of a bat, the symbol of the firm. The vestibule, the exhibition hall (fig. 22), and the mezzanine bar — the latter with bathroom doors decorated with palm trees that add a tropical touch to a decidedly French design — are notable for their composition and richness of materials. The original elevators doors, with designs of radiant suns, were substituted by others, which, while more efficient, are certainly less of an artistic achievement.

The López Serrano apartment building was conceived as a symbol of the progress of the city by its owner and its architects, Ricardo Mira and Miguel Rosich. The tenants saw it as an image of comfort, hygiene, and luxury. Its central location, its projected height, and the quick construction of the structure guaranteed a sense of novelty and spectacularity from the start. Moreover, it was advertised as the most modern. The general shape of the building suggests a strong North American influence, especially from Harvey Wiley Corbett, whose buildings in New York are notable for their successively receding upper-level stories.

Fig. 25. Fernando Martínez
Campos and Pascual de Rojas,
Rodríguez Vázquez Building,
Havana, 1941. Photograph by
the author, 1994. (Address:
Galiano 257 between Neptuno
and Concordia.)

Fig. 25. Fernando Martínez Campos and Pascual de Rojas, Rodríguez Vázquez Building, Havana, 1941. Photograph by the author, 1994. (Address: Galiano 257 between Neptuno and Concordia.)

While the 1916 New York building code demanded a stepped design for high buildings, for the ventilation and illumination of streets, such regulations did not apply in Havana — a New York model imbued the building with a highly desirable appearance of modernity. A severe exterior and protruding volumes produce strong contrasts of light and shade on the building (fig. 23). The facades are strongly vertical, with a finish that establishes an unmistakable urban mark. Ornamentation and modern details are concentrated on openings, walls, floors, and the flower stands at the doorways at the base of the building. A radial design on the vestibule floor emphasizes direction of movement (fig. 24) and a beautiful stylized metal relief represents a human figure in fast motion below a clock, a synthesis symbolizing the speed of the times.

The other building in Havana with a significant North American influence is the Rodríguez Vázquez, also known as the Cine América (America Theater), designed by Fernando Martínez Campos and Pascual de Rojas in 1939 and finished two years later (fig. 25). In the *memoria descriptiva* of the project (a description required to obtain a building permit), the architects explained their intentions: "With respect to the exterior of this building, we have selected a modern architectural style, simply highlighting the vertical lines on the upper part in contrast to the emphasized horizontal line of the awning that extends across the entire main facade, which, linked to the movement of the masses

Fig. 27. Cine América,

Rodríguez Vázquez Building,

vestibule, 1941. Photograph

by the author, 1994.

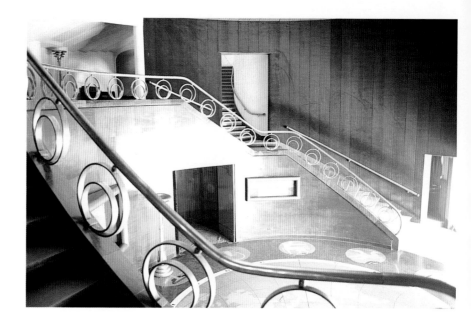

Fig. 26. Cine América,

Rodríguez Vázquez Building,

ladies' waiting room,

1941. Photograph by the

author, 1994.

of different planes, will create a desired modern effect." And further, on the details of the interior, they wrote: "The main lobby, foyer, and other waiting rooms will be soberly decorated within a schema of modernism."[8]

The building consists of an apartment tower and two ground-floor theaters (one of them previously on the site). References to North American models, such as the project for the Rockefeller Center in New York by Harvey Wiley Corbett as well as the realized design by Raymond Hood, are clear. The interior of the main theater — the América — is similar to New York's Radio City Music Hall; other details appear to be taken literally from what is considered to be one of the best North American modern movie theaters, the Paramount in Oakland, California, designed by Timothy Pflueger in 1929 — its open oval at the upper halls and the series of exotic ballerinas in relief on the wall of the gentleman's waiting room were transplanted to Havana.[9] While originality may not have been a concern of the architects, they seemed to have been moved by a challenge to achieve an agreeable presence in a unified design in which everything was correctly and coherently designed, from the exterior to the smallest interior detail. They not only achieved this but they came to happy, even creative, solutions, especially in the ladies' waiting room (fig. 26), a work of exquisite taste; in the hallways of the apartments; and in the vestibule of the new movie theater, in which a floor inlaid with a large map of the Americas surrounded by the signs of the zodiac is an allusion to the destiny of progress of the continent as well as to the theater's name (fig. 27).

Despite a few late examples, Art Deco lost popularity after the early 1940s. Yet, its short-lived glory of a decade left important footprints in Havana. While French and North American influences are undeniable, the principal architects of the style — Esteban Rodríguez Castells, Govantes y Cabarrocas, Mira y Rosich, Joaquín Weiss, and Emilio Vasconcelos, among others — designed buildings brilliantly at times, and their frequent use of royal palm tree motifs makes their Cuban origins obvious. Even more importantly, those architects, without wishing

8. The quotation from the *memoria descriptiva*, National Archives of Cuba.

9. See Barbara Capitman, Michael D. Kinerk, and Dennis Wilhelm, *Rediscovering Art Deco: U.S.A.* (New York: Viking Studio Books, 1994), 188–191.

Fig. 29. Angel López Valladares, Salomón Kalmanowitz residence, Marianao, Havana, 1936. Photograph by the author, 1994. (Address: Calle 28 Nº 4517 between 26 and 45, Alturas de Miramar.)

Fig. 28. Pedro Martínez Inclán, Clemente Inclán residence, Miramar, Marianao, Havana, 1930. Photograph by the author, 1994. (Address: Calle 8 Nº 314 between 3 and 5 Avenidas, Miramar.)

to be absolutely original, saw themselves as modern designers working in a special stylistic environment of high quality, a trait evident as well in secondary works by lesser-known architects who also left their imprint on the city.

The looming importance of Cuban Art Deco suggests that characterizing the style as a moment of transition between Eclecticism and Rationalism is an understatement. While some Art Deco works are close to the modern movement because of their scant ornamentation and formal composition, the majority of designs respond to conceptual criteria and ornamental intentions that, without a doubt, grant Art Deco its own signature (figs. 28 and 29).

Parallel to Art Deco, other tendencies derived from it. At the beginning of the 1940s Modern Classicism appeared, a type of classical-monumental rebirth with its origins in France (the Trocadero Group, Paris, 1937) and above all, Italy, where it became the official style of the 1942 Rome World's Fair. The image was now almost exclusively one of sober repetition of columns with no bases or capitals, especially around the main porticoes of buildings. In Cuba the main proponent of this style was José Pérez Benitoa, who completed the Military Hospital in 1940 and the Plaza Finlay in 1944. The latter consists of a grouping of four buildings surrounding a rotunda, at the center of which stands a 32-meter-high obelisk that serves both as a lighthouse for airplanes and pays homage to the scientist Carlos J. Finlay. Its frieze was the work of sculptors Navarro and Lombardo (fig. 30).

Streamline Moderne, a trend frequently included within the Art Deco movement because of its use of Deco details, had a greater diffusion and importance than the classicizing mode. Its origins are significantly different from those of its French predecessor because of its emphasis on horizontal planes. It also differs from the striking verticality of Art Deco in that angularity is rejected in favor of curved lines and rounded corners. Such shapes invade not only Streamline Moderne buildings but also objects produced industrially.[10] If Art Deco could be called a typically French product, Streamline Moderne is North American.

10. See Martin Grief, *Modern Depression: The Thirties Style in America* (New York: Universe Books, 1975).

Fig. 30. José Pérez Benitoa, Plaza Finlay, Marianao, 1944. Photograph by the author, 1994. (Address: Avenida 31 and Calle 100, Marianao.)

Fig. 31. Rafael de Cárdenas, Hilda Sarrá residence, Havana, 1934. Photograph by the author, 1994. (Address: 2 Nº 11 corner to 19, Vedado.)

It is a clear result of the Depression, stemming from market imperatives and from the necessity to generalize a use of products across ever wider sectors. It also responded to a then current desire for innovation and freshness and had, as well, a symbolic side of nautical associations.[11] The tendency brought with it new materials, too, among these, glass blocks. Interest in technology and efficiency was another of its characteristics. For this reason we see the repeated use of this trend in factories and centers of production. Perhaps its most important imagery had to do with its fascination for speed, which paradoxically caused it to represent static objects as moving ones. Even buildings that were decorated exclusively with three parallel horizontal lines on the corners evoked a wake left in water, or air having just streamed by an object.

11. One should note an influence of the architecture of Miami Beach on Cuban Streamline Moderne.

As was the case with previous styles, Streamline Moderne was assumed to be something originating in another country but capable of being coopted by, and adapted to, local conditions. As soon as this adaptability was realized, it undoubtedly became an important factor to advance more radical movements. Some works serve as examples: the Hilda Sarrá house, by Rafael de Cárdenas, of 1934, with a winding, continuous stairway (figs. 31 and 32); the surgical unit of the Clínica la Benéfica, completed circa 1942 by José Antonio Vila (fig. 33); the Hospital de Maternidad Obrera (fig. 34), executed in 1940 by Emilio de Soto and recipient of the National College of Architects Gold Medal (the structure contains a mural by Enrique García Cabrera in homage to mothers in which a novelty appears, the image of a black man) (fig. 35); the building on L and 25 by José Fontán and Manuel Rivero, of 1941, with doorways that seem inspired by spaceships from the Flash Gordon comic strips (fig. 36); and the Canada Dry bottling plant by Walter M. Cory, of 1946, in which the original design carried a model of the earth above the entrance representing the universalistic aspirations of the company and the style of its headquarters (fig. 37).

The Solimar Building, by Manuel Copado, of 1944 (fig. 38), announced a more advanced modernity that would culminate at the end of the decade with works of such significance as the Hospital Clínico Quirúrgico, finished in 1948 by Max Borges Jr., or the architect's own home, finished two years later. The list ends with the Radiocentro Building, of 1947, a work of the firm of Junco, Gastón y Domínguez, and above all, the work that became the most paradigmatic of that period, the José Noval residence, by Mario Romañach and Silverio Bosch, of 1949 (fig. 39).

Shortly thereafter, a young generation of architects headed by Romañach himself, Frank Martínez (fig. 40), Nicolás Quintana (fig. 41), Emilio del Junco, Ricardo Porro, Max Borges Jr., and Manuel Gutiérrez (fig. 42), among others, led a radical revolution in architectural forms and thought. This change would make the 1950s a period of rich creativity with various movements reaching unprecedented peaks. Among these trends stands Modern Regionalism, which originally integrated the most advanced Rationalism with local traditions and culminated with the extraordinary Escuelas Nacionales de Artes (National Schools of Arts), a project of five schools designed by Ricardo Porro,

Fig. 35. Enrique García Cabrera, mural, Hospital de Maternidad Obrera, Marianao, Havana, 1940. Photograph by the author, 1994.

Fig. 34. Emilio de Soto, Hospital de Maternidad Obrera, Marianao, Havana, 1940. Photograph by Richard Weston, 1995. (Address: Avenida 31 Nº 8409 between 84 and 86, Marianao.)

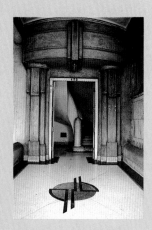

Fig. 36. José Fontán and Manuel Rivero, L and 25 Building, detail of a doorway, Vedado, Havana, 1941. Photograph by the author, 1994. (Address: L corner to 25, Vedado.)

Fig. 37. Walter M. Cory, Canada Dry bottling plant, Havana, 1946. Photograph by Richard Weston, 1995. (Address: Infanta corner to Amenidad, Cerro.)

Fig. 38. Manuel Copado,
Solimar Building, Havana,
1944. Photograph by Richard
Weston, 1995. (Address:
Soledad 205 between San
Lázaro and Ánimas.)

▲

Fig. 40. Frank Martínez, Eloísa
Lezama Lima residence, view
of the patio, Havana, 1959.
Photograph courtesy of Frank
Martínez. (Address: 45 Nº 855
between 26 and Santa Ana,
Nuevo Vedado.)

Fig. 39. Mario Romañach and Silverio Bosch, José Noval residence, Marianao, Havana, 1949. Author's

Vittorio Garatti, and Roberto Gottardi and partially built between 1961–1965 (fig. 43). Such a creative explosion was due to many factors — among them the pedagogic work and design of Eugenio Batista. But, without a doubt, the root of this explosion lies in the discreet but fundamental evolution produced by Art Deco. □

Fig. 43. Ricardo Porro, main courtyard of the Escuela Nacional de Artes Plásticas (National School of Fine Arts) at the Country Club de La Habana, Marianao, 1961–1965. Photograph by the author, 1994.

Fig. 1, Francisco Centurión, San Carlos Institute, Key West, Florida, 1924. Photograph of restored building by Margarita A. Khuly, AIA, ca. 1990.

Cuba Connections:
Key West—Tampa—Miami, 1870 to 1945

By Paula Harper

Dr. Paula Harper is associate professor of modern art history at the University of Miami, Coral Gables, Florida. She is the author of a book on Honoré Daumier, co-author of a critical biography of Camille Pissarro, and has also published numerous articles and catalogue essays on twentieth-century art.

A pattern of connections between Cuba and South Florida began to form more than one hundred years ago, based on projects and needs that remain central to the relationship: industry and commerce, political and economic migrations, travel and tourism. Elements of the pattern can be seen in architecture and advertising of the era, made visible in the public buildings designed by Cuban architects for South Florida and in cigar and travel advertising by both Cuban and Anglo-American illustrators. In contrast to the private arts of personal revelation, these public arts communicated and strengthened the popular perceptions of each community and its identity.

Cubans had begun their exodus to Key West at the outbreak of the Ten Years' War (1868–1878), the first round of the struggle for independence from Spain that ended in victory in 1898. At the beginning of the war, thousands of Cubans fled northward, establishing exile communities in the United States that became active in supporting the independence movement. Many émigrés from the Havana elite moved to New York. In contrast, Key West attracted Cubans with middle- and working-class backgrounds.[1]

These Cubans were put to work in the cigar industry organized in Key West by Don Vicente Martínez Ybor (1818–1896). Martínez Ybor, although Spanish by birth, supported the cause of separation from Spain and fled Cuba in 1869 to escape a warrant for his arrest. He quickly reestablished himself in Key West, employing hundreds of workers in his factory, producing the same brand of cigars he had made famous in Havana, El Príncipe de Gales (Prince of Wales). Martínez Ybor understood his male market and appealed to them with handsome cigar box labels and bands featuring a portrait of the future Edward VII of Great Britain, a famous smoker, bon vivant, and man of distinction. By the mid-1870s Key West had forty-five cigar factories, of varying sizes, employing about fourteen hundred workers, who were turning out twenty-five million cigars a year. The industry was buoyed by low United States tariffs on the importation of tobacco leaf and by the cheap émigré labor pool.[2] By 1873 Cubans in Key West were the majority of the population.[3] In 1875 Key West, then the

---

1. Gerald E. Poyo, "Key West and the Cuban Ten Years' War," *Florida Historical Quarterly* 57 (January 1979): 289.
2. Miguel A. Bretos, *Cuba and Florida: Exploration of a Historic Connection, 1539–1991*, exhibition catalogue (Miami: Historical Association of Southern Florida, 1991), 62.
3. U. S. Bureau of the Census figures, quoted by Poyo, "Key West," 290.

second largest city in Florida, elected a Cuban mayor, Carlos Manuel de Céspedes (1840–1915), son and namesake of the 1868 leader of the rebellion against Spain.[4]

The San Carlos Institute in Key West, one of the examples of Cuban architecture in South Florida, is a monument to the community identity of the Cuban cigar workers who settled there in reaction to changing political and economic realities at home. Through all incarnations it remained devoted to its initial political and social goals: promotion of Cuban cultural values, preservation of the Spanish language, and support of democratic ideals.

The first San Carlos Institute, a small wooden structure on Anne Street, was founded in 1871. It was named La Sociedad de Recreo e Instrucción San Carlos after Havana's Seminario de San Carlos, noted for academic excellence and support of independence from Spain among its graduates, and in honor of Carlos Manuel de Céspedes Sr. (1819–1874). A second and larger structure was built on Fleming Street in 1874, funded by contributions from the cigar workers whose children were educated there. When it burned to the ground in the great fire of 1886 that destroyed much of Key West, the Cuban community purchased a lot fronting Duval Street and rebuilt its beloved San Carlos again in the heart of Key West. The new building was a three-story Victorian timber structure; its only tropical feature was an arcade spanning the sidewalk at ground level. When José Martí came to Key West at the invitation of the cigar workers in 1891, during his eloquent efforts to unify Cuban exiles in the fight for independence from Spain, it was this building that he visited.

Another disaster struck the San Carlos in 1919 when a hurricane leveled the already dilapidated structure. Once more, a successful campaign was mounted to rebuild it, resulting in the fifth incarnation of the San Carlos Institute, which reopened in 1924. This is the building that now stands on Duval Street, recently and lovingly restored (fig. 1).[5]

The 1924 San Carlos Institute was built with the help of the government of Cuba. In June 1919 (before the September hurricane that sealed the fate of the old building) the president of Cuba, Mario García-Menocal, signed the San Carlos Act. Along with a grant of up to one hundred thousand *pesos*, it specified that a "stone building suitable to house the club, the school and the offices of the Cuban consulate be erected, provided that the San Carlos corporation relinquish title to the Cuban government."[6] In 1923 President Alfredo Zayas's administration in Havana commissioned a Cuban architect, Francisco Centurión y Maceo, a graduate of the University of Havana, to design the building. Centurión was well connected in government circles and had been commissioned to build the Cuban pavilion at the 1915 Panama-Pacific International Exposition in San Francisco (fig. 2). For Key West he designed a more restrained version of the Cuban Baroque, inspired by public buildings in Havana like the Palace of the Captains General. The San Carlos Institute echoed this building in the treatment of the pilasters and window surrounds, and in the three bays of the

---

4   Bretos, *Cuba*, 69–72; Francisco Xavier de Santa Cruz, *Historia de familias cubanas* (Havana: Editorial Hércules, 1942), 3:120.

5.   The architectural firm of Rodríguez-Khuly-Quiroga was chosen by the State of Florida (which had allocated one million dollars in the form of a general revenue grant in 1986) to carry out the restoration. A statewide effort to raise additional funds was led by Rafael A. Peñalver Jr., a Miami attorney. The six-year project was completed by architects Jorge and Margarita Khuly.

6.   Bretos, *Cuba*, 107.

Fig. 3. C. Freixa, Villa Paula,
Miami, 1925–1926. Historical
Association of South Florida,
The Miami News Collection .

facade. But Centurión more probably drew his inspiration from a type of public architecture in Havana rather than from any single structure. His version of the European Baroque retained its undulations, complex pediments and cornices, and multiplications of engaged columns, with the addition of a Mediterranean touch of ornamental wrought iron. This style properly projected the symbolic function of the building, connecting it to the history and traditions of Cuba and ultimately to the intimate ties of Cuba with European civilization. At a time when civilization in South Florida was fairly rudimentary, the splendor of the San Carlos Institute can hardly have failed to make its point.[7]

But already the San Carlos had begun to change from a working institution to a symbolic one; by 1924 the tobacco industry had largely moved from Key West to Tampa and had begun to decline even there. When the handsome restoration of the San Carlos Institute opened on 3 January 1992, it was described in its official literature as a "showcase of Cuban history and architecture that enshrines the ideals and aspirations of the Cuban people." It had become a museum and a memorial to the community of Cuban workers that José Martí visited when the building was still a meeting place and not yet a monument.

One other historic public building designed and built by Cubans to represent their country stands in South Florida. The Villa Paula, built between 1925 and 1926 to house the first Cuban consulate, in Miami, was "totally Cuban in purpose, design, materials, style and workmanship" (fig. 3).[8] Miami's first official connection with Cuba was initiated a decade earlier when consular agent Miguel Caballero set up an office at the request of a group of Dade County

7   Cuban consul Domingo Milord Vázquez inaugurated the facility on 10 October 1924. The son of a cigar manufacturer, he moved with his family to Key West at age four and attended the San Carlos Institute as a child. The consulate remained in operation until January 1961, when the United States broke relations with Cuba.

8.   Miguel A. Bretos, "A Cuban Suburban Mansion in Miami's Little Haiti," *Cuban Heritage* (Summer 1987): 38.

lumber merchants who traded with Cuba. In the 1910s Miami was still a small town surrounded by scrub and swamp, but after World War One it grew quickly. In 1925 the business-oriented administration of Gerardo Machado in Havana realized Miami's potential commercial importance and decided to upgrade Cuba's official presence to a full-fledged consulate. Machado ordered the Pensacola consulate closed and its consul, Jorge Ponce, to Miami to oversee construction, by Cuban workmen and artisans, of the new consulate's offices and residence, in what was then an undeveloped area along North Miami Avenue.[9] Ponce remained until July 1926 when his successor arrived, Domingo Milord y Vázquez, who had previously served in Key West. The elegant new consulate was named for his wife, Paula.

The style of the Villa Paula, like that of the San Carlos Institute, sent a message about the cosmopolitan civilization enjoyed by Cuba in contrast to the relatively provincial tastes of Miami. The structure, designed by the Havana architect C. Freixa, was a Neoclassical villa showing French influence in its delicacy of scale and refinement of detail. This style, cradled in the École des Beaux-Arts of Paris, had influenced architects from the nineteenth century onwards and shaped buildings in many important cities, including New York and Havana. The Villa Paula was a miniaturization of the style, similar to many upper-middle-class homes in residential areas of Havana built during the prosperous first decades of the twentieth century. A one-story building with eighteen-foot ceilings, its rooms open on each side of a long central hallway that runs from front to back. The hallway, parlors, and dining room are still graced with the original carved and gilded chandeliers, the floors are of Cuban hydraulic tile,[10] and the tall doors are Cuban mahogany topped with hinged transoms. A delicate pavilion stands in the walled back garden. The pavilion repeats the design of the villa's front portico, with a balustraded roof, dentillated cornice, and supporting corner piers flanked by Corinthian columns. The symbolic presence of Cuba in Miami, as projected by the elegant architecture of its consulate, was relatively brief. Although the building survived the devastating hurricane of 1926, the Depression hit Cuba severely and the Miami consulate was closed in 1930.

9. The Villa Paula is now in the crowded section of Miami called Little Haiti, at 5811 North Miami Avenue, and houses the offices of a Haitian physician, Dr. Lucien Albert.

10. Hydraulic tiles are thin square slabs of pressed tinted cement, twenty centimeters to a side, often carrying a pattern of different colors. The system was invented in the nineteenth century and was used extensively in Europe as well as in some important buildings in the United States, such as the Federal Capitol and the old State, War and Navy Building (presently the Executive Office Building). Hydraulic tile is the standard material for floors in Cuba.

A distant and surprising echo of this Cuban adaptation of the Neoclassical style is seen in a rare photograph of a group of houses built for Cuban workers in the cigar-manufacturing community of Ybor City in Tampa (fig. 4). The houses, seen in a pre-1911 postcard, are similar to many surviving today in working-class neighborhoods in Havana. They retain the basic image of the Neoclassical villas enjoyed by the more prosperous classes but simplify the porticoes, columns, and cornices. The Ybor City architect, if any, is unknown; the structures were most probably designed and erected by local building contractors.

The story of Ybor City as an instance of a planned "company town," perhaps influenced by the example of George M. Pullman's planned industrial community outside of Chicago and various southern mill towns, again features Don Vicente Martínez Ybor of Havana and Key West in a leading role.[11] In 1884 Martínez Ybor and another cigar tycoon, Ignacio Sánchez y Haya, took a trip to Tampa at the urging of a young Spanish entrepreneur and engineer, Gavino Gutiérrez. The two cigar makers were eager to expand their industry, which was impossible in Key West because of the lack of a fresh water supply, the absence of land transport (the railroad came only in 1912), and their militant and sometimes mercurial Cuban labor force. Strikes and work stoppages were commonplace. From the viewpoint of their employers, the ease with which workers could move back and forth between Key West and Cuba, only ninety miles away, made it more difficult to control them. Tampa offered Henry B. Plant's system of steamships and railroads (extended that very year from Jacksonville to Tampa) and an important advantage: the "city fathers pledged to aid [underwrite] capital should labor agitation threaten investment, using the police if necessary."[12]

In 1885 Martínez Ybor and his Cuban business associate, Eduardo Manrara, began to purchase land northeast of downtown Tampa — at that time a sleepy, southern coastal town, cleared from the mud and scrub, plagued by alligators and insects. Beginning with 40 acres they continued to buy until 111 acres were consolidated. Gavino Gutiérrez, trained as a civil engineer, was hired to plat the area in a grid of numbered streets and avenues (Ybor City remains the only part of Tampa where the streets are designated numerically) and to oversee the design and construction of the factory and the houses of the workers (fig. 5).[13] Martínez Ybor also hired a local building contractor and architect, C.E. Purcell, to erect a two-story factory building on Seventh Avenue between Twelfth and Fifteenth Streets, plus fifty small wooden houses as homes for workers.[14]

To persuade workers and other manufacturers to settle in this uninviting wilderness, Don Vicente offered workers inexpensive homes on an easy-payment plan and offered fellow cigar tycoons free ten-year leases on land and new factories built to their specifications. In return these firms guaranteed to manufacture a quota of cigars and furnish a fixed number of workers who would rent, or preferably buy, houses from their benefactors.[15] The strategy worked.

Fig. 5. Ybor City. Early workers' houses located on 17th Avenue between 15th and 16th Streets, photograph ca. 1960. University of South Florida, Campus Library, Special Collections Department, Tampa, Florida.

11. Gary R. Mormino and George E. Pozzetta, *The Immigrant World of Ybor City* (Urbana: University of Illinois Press, 1987), 65.

12. Ibid., 64.

13. Jesse L. Keene, "Gavino Gutiérrez and His Contributions to Tampa," *Florida Historical Quarterly* 36 (July 1957): 39.

14. José Rivero Muñiz, "The Ybor City Story 1885–1954," a translation by Eustasio Fernández and Henry Beltrán of "Los cubanos en Tampa," *Revista Bimestre Cubana* 74 (1958): 5–40, at the Otto G. Richter Library, University of Miami, Coral Gables, Florida.

15. Mormino and Pozzetta, *The Immigrant*, 67.

About two hundred Cuban cigar workers had arrived by May 1886, via the tri-weekly steamship service to Key West and Havana, to live and work in what was then described as half mining camp and half frontier fort surrounded by palmetto scrubland, swamps, and pineflats. "Inhabitants had to wear goggles to keep the gnats out of their eyes."[16] The workers from Havana, used to urban life, suffered most. Don Vicente tried to keep them happy with bonuses and parties in addition to the lure of owning their own homes. Ironically, because of a strike by Cuban workers protesting the hiring of a Spanish bookkeeper, the first cigar produced in Ybor City was not rolled at the Martínez Ybor factory — a three-story building with room for eight hundred workers — but at the factory of his friend and competitor, Ignacio Sánchez y Haya. A cigar box label documents the fact that the Sánchez y Haya factory was "No. 1, Tampa, Fla." (fig. 6).

Cigar box labels are now recognized as precious examples in the history of advertising art. The Sánchez y Haya label is an example of the chromolithography developed first in Cuba during the mid-nineteenth century in response to the demands of tobacco merchandising. Lithography shops quickly sprang up in Ybor City to service the new industry, drawing on established skills, formats, and subject matter. The Sánchez y Haya label incorporates the gold embossing developed in the early 1890s and is executed in delicate tints and shadings of color. It shows a young woman, "La Flor de Sánchez y Haya," dark haired, feminine, and modest. She has flowers in her hair, a cameo at her throat, and ruffles around her shoulders — the perfect model of a lovely *señorita*, chaste and maidenly. The practice of selling cigars with pictures of idealized women was common and designed to appeal to the special interests of the tobacco smoker, in this case a presumably gentlemanly and conservative one, with an admiration for the Latin tradition. The style of the image — realistic and detailed in drawing, tone, and color — is also appropriately traditional.

Tampa flourished with the arrival of the cigar industry. By 1900 Tampa approached Key West in population (15,839 to 17,114) and exceeded it in numbers of factories (129 to 92). Five years later the population had swelled to 30,000, including over 10,000 foreign residents, mostly from Cuba, Spain, and Italy.[17]

Each group within the close-knit immigrant community eventually built its own social club and mutual-aid society, reminiscent of the purpose of the San Carlos Institute in Key West. Following the Spanish-American War and Cuban independence, the Cubans in Ybor City founded El Círculo Cubano (Cuban Circle) and raised money to erect their splendid clubhouse, a monumental four-story Beaux-Arts edifice completed in 1918 when membership numbered eight thousand (fig. 7).[18] The Cuban Circle building perfectly fulfills its function as public architecture. In style and size it projects importance, solidity, and tradition; it materializes a desirable image of the political and social solidarity and stability of the Cuban community in Ybor City.

Like the architecture of public buildings, the style of advertising sends a specific message to a targeted audience. The chromolithographs produced in the golden age of the cigar box label, from about 1890 to 1920, are, for the most part, old-fashioned rather than modern, drawing on the tradition of nineteenth-

16. Ibid.

17. Statistics from Mormino and Pozzetta and Rivero Muñiz.

18. Only 165 members remain. The cantina and a small medical clinic continue to operate while funds are raised for restoration of the building.

Fig. 7. Clubhouse of El Círculo

Cubano, Ybor City, completed

1918, photograph ca. 1960.

University of South Florida,

Campus Library, Tampa,

Florida. Tony Pizzo Collection.

Fig. 8. Cigar box label, TA-CU,

for Tampa-Cuba Cigar Company.

University of South Florida,

Campus Library, Special

Collections Department,

Tampa, Florida.

century Academic Realism with Victorian-Baroque embellishments.[19] The imagery as well as the style establishes continuity with the past, evoking nostalgic visions of the old country — Europe, Spain, the tranquil Cuban countryside with tobacco plantations, palm trees, and busy workers. A sampling of the cigar box labels from the Tampa factories indicates the range of types.

TA-CU is an unusual logo-like image that shows the mapped peninsula of Florida almost touching Cuba on a tobacco leaf background, the close connection reinforced by the "TAmpa-CUba" brand name (fig. 8). Another combination name, Ricaroma, accompanies a romantic twosome (fig. 9). A handsome Latin, his manliness enriched by his cigar, embraces a buxom young woman who seems spellbound by its aroma. Freud admitted that sometimes a "cigar is only a cigar," but in this case the sexual symbolism seems intended. The Florida Widow is an idealized portrait of a beautiful Latin lady, surrounded by decorative borders and scenes of Cuba and tobacco plantations (fig. 10). The reference is to those Cuban women who were "widowed" because their husbands were in Florida making money in the cigar industry.

Henry B. Plant's Tampa Bay Hotel, a "Moorish palace" splendidly appointed and filled with European furnishings, appears in the label for Tampa Life (fig. 11). This image includes scenes of golf, tennis, and swimming and seems as much an advertisement for tourism as it is for cigars.

In the history of advertising art, "luxury goods such as wine and tobacco were the products on which the greatest ingenuity in advertising and presentation of goods was lavished."[20] Tourism is not a commodity like tobacco but it is

19. Joe Davidson, *The Art of the Cigar Box Label* (Secaucus, N.J.: Wellfleet Press, 1989), 10.
20. Renata V. Shaw, "19th Century Tobacco Label Art," *The Quarterly Journal of the Library of Congress* 28 (April 1971): 77.

Fig. 9. Cigar box label,

Ricaroma, for Tampa-Cuba

Cigar Company. University of

South Florida, Campus Library,

Special Collections Department,

Tampa, Florida.

Fig. 10. Cigar box label, The

Florida Widow. New York

Public Library, Rare Books

Division, Arents Collection.

certainly a luxury, and the advertising associated with it is ingenious. In striking contrast to the cigar box labels, most of the travel ads of the period — both those produced in the United States and in Cuba — are in a distinctly modern mode, abstracted and stylized, influenced by high art, first Art Nouveau and then Art Deco. They target a moneyed, cosmopolitan, leisure class, both men and women, in a style that reflects their self-image as adventurous and innovative.

While working-class Cubans came to Key West and later Tampa for jobs in the cigar industry, upper-class Cubans traveled for pleasure or business to Europe and New York. Prosperous Anglo-Americans traveled to Havana, the "Paris of the Caribbean," for night life, gambling, water sports, and old world charm. The travel advertisements both reflect and engender popular perceptions of Havana, picturing well-dressed travelers in tropical whites, sleek steamships, attentive waiters, elegant cocktails and food, picturesque peasants, and lively *latinas* in ruffled rumba costumes. Cuba is presented as exotic but at the same time comfortable and familiar, as piquantly foreign but also modern and convenient. A group of images that document travel between South Florida and Cuba demonstrates how the style, as well as the imagery, carries the message.

A pamphlet produced by a United States company to advertise overnight steamship service between Havana and Miami in 1929 projects the romance and glamour of travel with a strikingly simplified graphic design (fig. 12). An equally modish and modern Cuban travel image, signed by Enrique Riverón, graces the January 1932 cover of the Havana periodical *Bohemia* (fig. 13).

Bohemia, like another Cuban periodical, *Social*, appealed to a cosmopolitan and sophisticated readership (fig. 14). *Social*, whose director was the talented artist Conrado W. Massaguer (1889–1965), had a content similar to that of *The New Yorker* from the same period. It included articles on art, fashion, literature, and new ideas and regularly featured a roundup of cartoons from *Life*, *Punch*, *Le Journal Amusant*, and *The New Yorker*. Its close ties to New York and United States consumer society are documented by advertisements for the Hotel McAlpin and Great Northern Hotels in Manhattan and by ads for

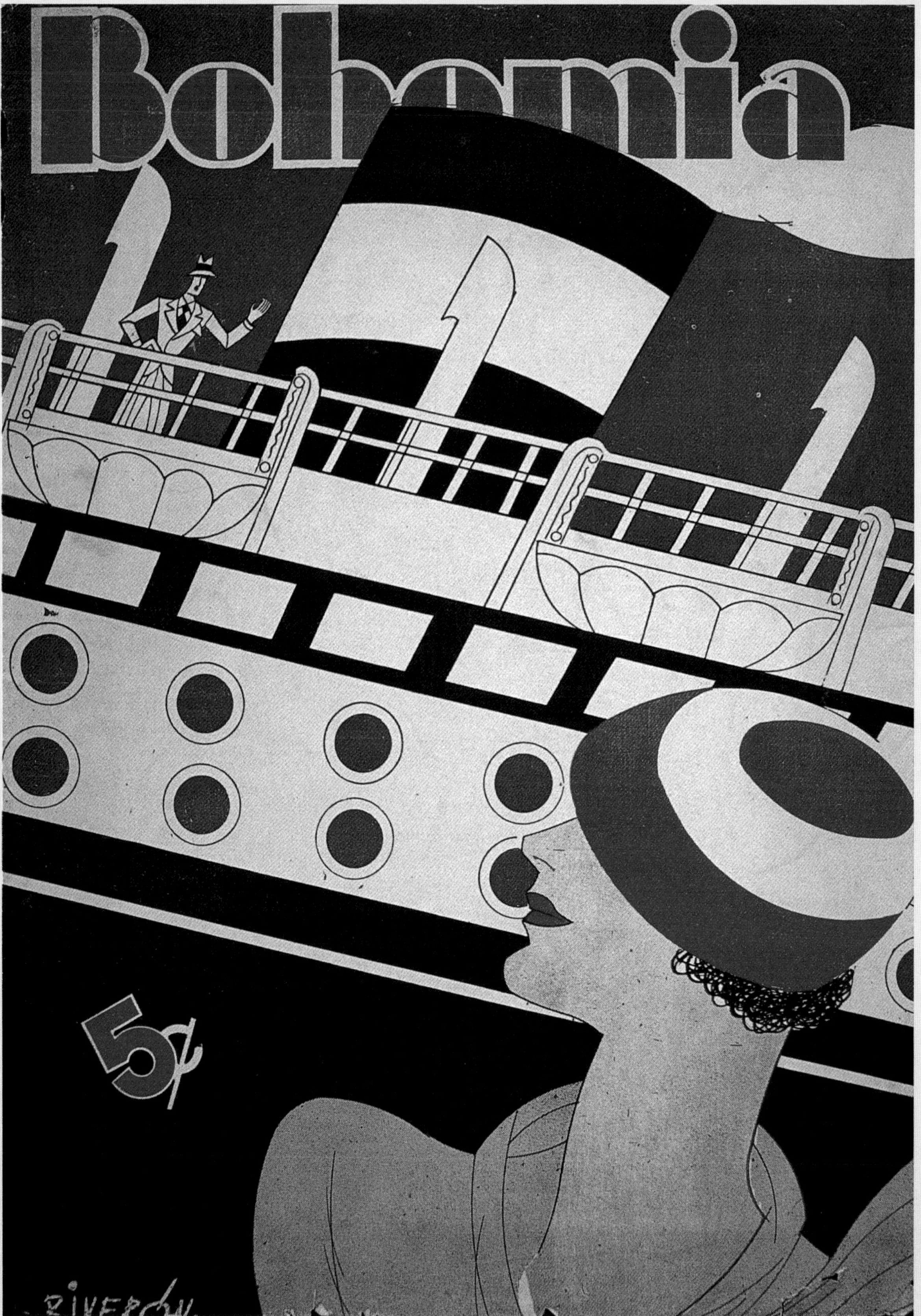
Bohemia
5¢
RIVERON

A. Sulka, Steinway, Victrola, Arrow, and Kotex. A 1938 travel ad in *Social* by Anuncios Kesevén, designed by Massaguer, encourages readers to "Take a little hop to Miami" in a lively, lighthearted image combined with Art Deco typography (fig. 15).

The cover of the pamphlet for the Cuban pavilion at the 1939 New York World's Fair is in a stodgier style, not modern but simple and even naive (fig. 16). It was drawn by Massaguer, certainly capable of far more elegance and innovation, so presumably he intended to target a broader and less sophisticated segment of the public. The imagery is similar to that of much travel advertising — sunshine, water sports, and picturesque natives — but the style sets an old-fashioned and folkloric tone. The text of the brochure also presents the Old World ways of Cuba as an asset, romanticizing the nostalgia of country life, the *campesinos*, the duennas, the feminine modesty of Cuban women, while at the same time pointing out Cuba's modern clubs, banks, and businesses.

Fig. 15. Conrado W. Massaguer, travel advertisement from *Social*, May–June 1938. The Mitchell Wolfson Jr. Collection, The Wolfsonian, Miami Beach, Florida, and Genoa, Italy.

Fig. 16. Conrado W. Massaguer, cover of pamphlet for the Cuban pavilion, New York World's Fair, 1939–1940. The Mitchell Wolfson Jr. Collection, The Wolfsonian, Miami Beach, Florida, and Genoa, Italy.

The beautiful *señorita* in rumba costume with *maracas*, one of the persistent stereotypes of travel advertising, appears in an image published by the Cuban Tourist Commission in the early 1940s (fig. 17). The artist is again Massaguer, but this time working in a stylish mode with a touch of self-reflective humor. Both the picture and the slogan, "Visit Cuba. So Near and Yet So Foreign," summarize popular perceptions and even comment on them with a buoyant irony, an approach that is thoroughly modernist.

It seems clear, even from a small selection of examples of the public architecture and advertising of the era, that both Cubans and South Floridians depend heavily on style to project self-images and reinforce popular perceptions. The styles chosen are sometimes significantly traditional, as in the San Carlos Institute, the Villa Paula, the workers' homes, and the Cuban Circle in Ybor City. These established forms of architecture emphasize continuity with the European past and connote stability and solidity. In advertising, the realistic, nineteenth-century style of the cigar box labels is intended to suggest the long history of quality cigars and the (perhaps unconscious) wish of gentlemen of substance

Fig. 17. Conrado W. Massaguer, "Visit Cuba. So Near and Yet So Foreign," postcard, early 1940s. Cuban Tourist Commission. Collection of Dina and Jeffrey Knapp, Miami Beach, Florida.

Fig. 17. Conrado W. Massaguer, "Visit Cuba. So Near and Yet So Foreign," postcard, early 1940s. Cuban Tourist Commission. Collection of Dina and Jeffrey Knapp, Miami Beach, Florida.

to follow the time-honored "ways of the fathers." For most of the designers of travel advertisments, this nineteenth-century echo was definitely not appropriate for their message of adventure, of "breaking the mold," and seeking new and exciting experiences. They chose an anti-traditional art as a metaphor for innovative lifestyles. But, as so often has happened in the history of the new, it was comforting to mix familiar images with avant-garde styles; to continue the tradition of selling old wine in fashionable new bottles. □

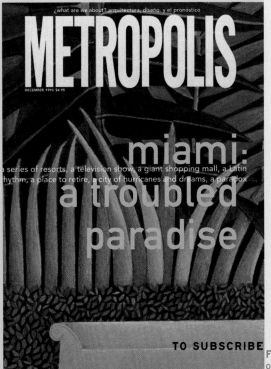

The Dacra Companies

230 Fifth Street Miami Beach FL 33139 Tel 305 531 8700 Fax 305 531 6102

Residential Commercial Brokerage

THE PRIVATE SMOKE

CUBA CLUB

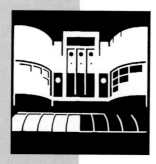

Charles Cowles Gallery

420 West Broadway
New York 10012
Tel (212) 925-3500
Fax (212) 925-3501

Charles Arnoldi	Terence La Noue
David Bates	Doug Martin
Howard Ben Tré	Jim Martin
Marsha Burns	Wilhelm Moser
Dale Chihuly	Manuel Neri
Gene Davis	Beverly Pepper
Elizabeth Enders	Ken Price
Vernon Fisher	Peter Schlesinger
Caio Fonseca	Daniel Senise
Tom Holland	Toshiko Takaezu
Patrick Ireland	Peter Voulkos
Harry Kramer	Darren Waterston

CUBAN ART AT SOTHEBY'S

Mario Carreño, *Arlequín,* signed and dated *Paris-39,*
oil on canvas, *31⁹⁄₁₆ by 23⅝ in.* Sold for a record
price for the artist, $310,500.

SOTHEBY'S

FOR INFORMATION ABOUT BUYING OR SELLING
Latin American Art at Sotheby's, call (212) 606-7290. To purchase a catalogue, call (800) 444-3709.
Sotheby's, 1334 York Avenue, New York, NY 10021.

CUBAN ART AT SOTHEBY'S

Cundo Bermúdez, *Mujer peinando a su amante*,
signed and dated *45*, oil on canvas *29¾ by 23¼ in.*
Sold for a record price for the artist, $343,500.

SOTHEBY'S

© Sotheby's, Inc. 1996 William F. Ruprecht, principal auctioneer, #0794917

CUBAN ART AT SOTHEBY'S

Mariano Rodríguez, *El gallo pintado,* signed and dated *41,*
oil on canvas, *25¼ by 21 in.* Sold for a record price
for the artist, $299,500.

SOTHEBY'S

CUBAN ART AT SOTHEBY'S

Wifredo Lam, *La mañana verde,* oil on paper
mounted on canvas, *73½ by 48¼ in.*
Executed in 1943. Sold for a record price
for the artist, $965,000.

SOTHEBY'S

The *Journal of Design History* plays an active role in the development of design history (including the history of crafts and applied arts), by publishing new research, by providing an international forum for dialogue and debate, and by addressing current issues of interest. The journal also seeks to promote links with other disciplines which explore visual and material culture. In addition, it is the editors' expressed wish to encourage contributions on design in preindustrial periods in nonEuropean societies, as well as on hitherto neglected or unfamiliar areas, periods or themes.

In addition to full-length articles, the *Journal of Design History* publishes shorter case studies, carries regular book reviews, and reports on new educational initiatives, and on resources for design history, including the application of new technology.

RECENT AND FORTHCOMING ARTICLES

Chris Bailey on the work of the Rural Industries Bureau

Gerry Beegan on nineteenth-century wood engraving and mechanization

Christine Boydell on women freelance textile designers in Britain in the 1930's

Barbara Burman on the Men's Dress Reform Party

Rafael Cardoso Denis on the rise of Victorian art and design education

Heather Hendershot on the shifting design of Betty Boop

John Hewitt on Tom Purvis's poster designs for the LNER

Guy Julier on recent initiatives in Spanish design

Richard Martin on Japanese fashion design

Lesley Miller on the eighteenth-century Lyonnais silk designer Jean Revel

Charles Saumarez Smith on architecture and museums

Claire Walsh on shop design and the display of goods in eighteenth-century London

Jonathan Woodham on the early years of the Council of Industrial Design

---

Journal of *Design* *History*

Volume 9   1996

Edited by
Jeremy Aynsley;
Christopher Bailey;
Charlotte Benton;
Anthony Coulson; Pat Kirkham;
Tag Gronberg; Tim Putnam;
Jonathan Woodham

OXFORD JOURNALS

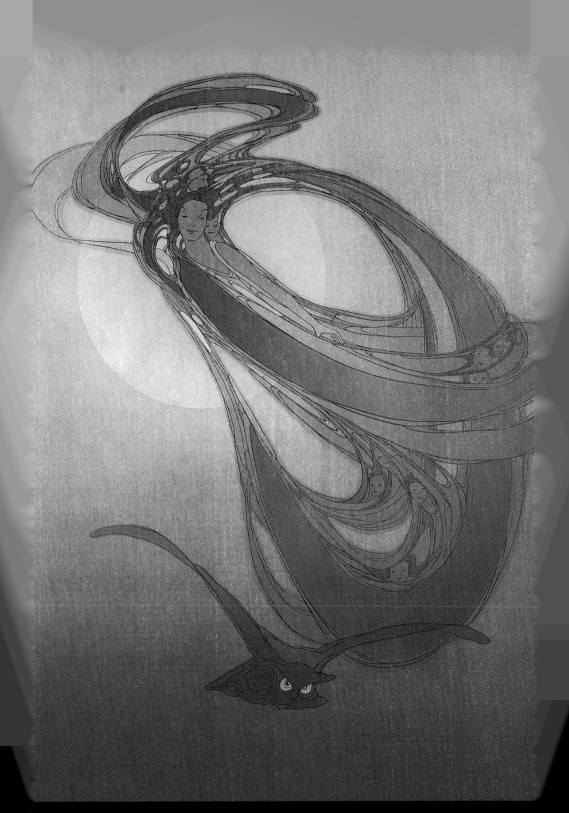

The Arts & Crafts Movement
Twentieth Century Design: 1870 to Present
Furnishings . Studio Ceramics . Latin American & American Modernist Paintings

Bryce Bannatyne Gallery

2439 Main Street . Santa Monica . CA 80495 . 310 396 8668

Some Investments Are Priceless.

We salute the

Wolfson Foundation of Decorative and Propaganda Arts

on the 10th Anniversary

of its founding of

The Journal of Decorative and Propaganda Arts.

THE CHASE MANHATTAN PRIVATE BANK

Cuba's Modern and Contemporary Artists

Rene Portocarrero   Graphite on Paper   17⅜ x 21½ inches   1940

Also exhibiting and brokering exceptional Latin American, European and American works by notable emerging, mid-career, and master artists since 1974.

Virginia Miller Galleries

169 Madeira Avenue, Coral Gables (Miami), Florida 33134 • (305) 444-4493 • Fax: (305) 444-9844

Featuring fine American Impressionist, Regionalist and Modern paintings, prints and sculpture.

New 80-p. catalogue, <u>Recent Acquisitions – 1996</u>, available for $18.00 postpaid.

ROBERT HENRY ADAMS FINE ART

715 N. FRANKLIN • CHICAGO, IL 60610 • 312/642-8700 • fax 312/642-8785

Miami Design Preservation League (MDPL) is a non-profit historic preservation group and arts organization founded in 1976 by the late Barbara Baer Capitman. It was the first of many Art Deco societies, and has led the worldwide movement to educate the public about early 20th Century architecture and design — and to protect it. MDPL has fostered appreciation of South Florida history, emphasizing the art, music, dance, fashion, photography and typography from the period between the two world wars. In 1996 the Society of American Travel Writers (SATW) awarded MDPL the prestigious PHOENIX AWARD in recognition of the role the League has played in reviving tourism in Miami Beach through the use of historic preservation.

MDPL's efforts have gained stature because of the unique "Art Deco District" of Miami Beach, which members identified, surveyed and nominated to the National Register of Historic Places. The District was listed in the National Register in 1979, becoming the first 20th Century historic district. Today, twenty years after its founding, MDPL continues to sponsor activities which educate the public about the District, promoting it throughout the world. Most successful among the many activities are the guided walking and bicycle tours conducted each weekend, the self-paced audio-cassette walking tour available daily throughout the week, and the world famous Art Deco Weekend® festival which takes place each January.

The twentieth annual Art Deco Weekend will take place January 17-20, 1997. "ART DECO AT SEA: A SALUTE TO THE GREAT OCEAN LINERS OF THE 1930s." will be the theme. MDPL is happy to announce that the Steamship Historical Society of America (SSHSA) has agreed to participate in Art Deco Weekend 1997 as a co-sponsor. The cooperation between the two organizations is a "natural fit" since the heyday of Ocean Liner travel took place during the Art Deco era. The SSHSA will lend its expertise in planning lectures, films, videos and other theme-related events during the January festival. Please contact MDPL for information about membership, Art Deco Weekend, or any of our activities:

Miami Design Preservation League
PO Box 190180
Miami Beach, Florida 33119
Phone: (305) 672-2014
Fax: (305) 672-4319

CHRISTIE'S
IS PROUD TO CELEBRATE
15 YEARS OF LATIN AMERICAN ART
THROUGHOUT 1996

Established by Lisa Palmer, Senior Director, in 1981 and now under the direction of Silvia Coxe, Christie's Latin American Department has been a leader in this field, set countless world records and brought Latin American art to the forefront of the international art market.

Christie's Fall auction will include an exceptional selection of Latin American art, including masterworks by the most recognized and sought after Cuban artists. Christie's is proud of its long tradition in bringing Cuban art to the world through its auctions and paintings tours.

The Fall auction will take place on November 26 at 7 pm and November 27 at 10 am. Admission to the evening sale is by ticket only, to place an order please call Karen Christian at 212 546 1129. For further information please contact Lisa Palmer, Silvia Coxe or Vivian Pfeiffer at 212 546 1099.

To order catalogues, please call Christie's Publications at 1 800 395 5600; outside the USA at 1 718 784 1480.

Illustrated on the opposite page: Mario Carreño, *Desnudos con Mangos*, signed and dated "Carreño 43" lower right—oil on canvas 40 ⅝ x 31 in. (103.3 x 78.8cm.). Sold for $354,500 on May 15, 1995.

CHRISTIE'S

CESAR TRASOBARES
ARTISTA INDEPENDIENTE

e-mail: intralbl@ix.netcom.com

WORKS FROM FIRST CUBAN PERIOD:
Quinceañeras y Chaperonas, 1976-77 (destroyed)
cardboard, fabric, glue
Los Carritos and *Estaciones* drawings, 1972-73
solvents and transfer-type on paper

RARE BOOKS
ART REFERENCE
ILLUSTRATED BOOKS
CATALOGUES ISSUED

WILLIAM + VICTORIA DAILEY

8216 MELROSE AVENUE, P.O. BOX 69160, LOS ANGELES CA 90069 ≋ 213 658-8515

The Journal of Decorative and Propaganda Arts

Founded in 1986 and published annually by the Wolfson Foundation of Decorative and Propaganda Arts, the Journal fosters scholarship in the period 1875–1945.

For further information on current and back issues, contact the Journal office:

2399 NE 2nd Avenue
Miami, FL 33137 USA
305.573.9170 Phone
305.573.0409 Fax

"Many excellent cooks are spoilt by going into the arts." Paul Gaugin (1838-1903)

ARS CULiNARiA

iT'S DiViNE

iNNOVATiVE CUBAN CUiSiNE

501 LiNCOLN ROAD
FOR RESERVATiONS AND iNFORMATiON
PLEASE CALL 305-532-YUCA

AMBROSINO GALLERY
3155 PONCE DE LEON BOULEVARD
CORAL GABLES, FLORIDA 33134-6825
TEL: 305.445.2211 FAX: 305.444.0101

ZADOK	BEN DAVID
RICARDO	BENAIM
STEVE	BOLLMAN
MARIA MAGDALENA	CAMPOS PONS
HUMBERTO	CASTRO
ANA ALBERTINA	DELGADO
STEFANO	DI STASIO
ARTURO	DUCLOS
ADONAY	DUQUE
ROBERT	FLYNN
REGINA	FRANK
JUAN CARLOS	GARCIA LAVIN
LEONEL	GONZALEZ
JOSE ANTONIO	GONZALEZ GUTIERREZ
LYLE ASHTON	HARRIS
ARTURO	HERRERA
HILLA LULU	LIN
DONALD	LIPSKI
LUIS	LIZARDO
MAURO	MACHADO
SARA	MANIERO
DEAN	MCNEIL
GLEXIS	NOVOA
JAIME	PALACIOS
CESAR	TRASOBARES
SANTIAGO	URIBE HOLGUIN
MIGUEL	VON DANGEL
CARLOS	ZERPA

XŪM BOXED SETS
limited signed edition

classically designed flatware, cutlery, and china

bissell & wilhite co.

8306 Wilshire Boulevard, Suite 39, Beverly Hills, California 213·380·2027

WILLIAM ASHBY McCLOY

American b. 1913

Two Philosophers   1937   tempera resin & oil on masonite   36" x 48"

MARTIN-ZAMBITO FINE ART

721 EAST PIKE
SEATTLE, WA 98122-3719
206 726-9509

19TH-20TH CENTURY AMERICAN ART

Selected by Library Journal as one of the ten best magazines of 1993 from 789 new publications.

STUDIES IN THE

Decorative Arts

Published semiannually by The Bard Graduate Center for Studies in the Decorative Arts

The journal is an international forum for new research and scholarly discussion providing fresh knowledge and insight on the decorative arts. The wide-ranging articles span all cultures and periods while emphasizing an interdisciplinary context.

Recent issues include stimulating articles on English silver, French lacquerwork, Piranesi's chimneypiece designs, Connecticut chests, design education in Russia, British Modernist design, Persian metalwork.

Subscriptions:
$30 US/ $35 Canada, Mexico/ $37 Overseas
Payment by American Express, Visa, MasterCard (provide cardholder's name), or by check in U.S. dollars drawn on a bank located in the U.S., payable to The Bard Graduate Center.

Send Payment to:
Journal Office, Dept. PA, The Bard Graduate Center,
18 West 86th Street, New York, NY 10024

The Cuban Art of Cigar Making

Caribbean Cigar Factory

is the largest hand-made cigar factory in the United States, offering nine brands of premium cigars: *Signature Collection by Santiago Cabana, Havana Classico, Calle Ocho, Free Cuba, Morro Castle* and *Domino Park*— in addition to our flavored cigars, *Island Amaretto, West*

Indies Vanilla and the famous *Rum Runner* cigar. Over 40 Cuban masters

construct cigars of perfection with tobaccos from Santo Domingo, Honduras, Nicaragua, Equador and Mexico. The unique blends are what have created Caribbean Cigar Factory's reputation as the maker of OUTSTANDING cigars.

CARIBBEAN CIGAR FACTORY

Visit Our Factory and Our Retail Stores

Caribbean Cigar Factory serves the Keys and South Florida with the most impressive collection of imported cigars and cigarettes and the largest selection of humidors, accessories and lighters. Cigar rollers are also at each location, so you can watch the art of cigar making! We Ship Worldwide.

South Beach	**Little Havana Factory**	**Key Largo**	**Key West**
760 Ocean Drive	6265 S.W. 8th St.	103400 Overseas	112 Fitzpartick
Miami Beach, FL 33139	Miami, FL 33144	Highway MM 103	Key West, FL 33040
305.538.6062	305.267.3911	Key Largo, FL 33037	305.292.9595
fax: 538.0779	fax: 267.6026	305.453.4014	fax: 292.3643
		fax: 453.0448	

FrēWil

FreWil, 605 N. La Brea Ave., Los Angeles, CA 90036
213/934-8474   Fax: 213/857-1916

1

French Bred

Bil Wilson admits a weakness—or shall we call it a fortitude—for browsing through antique shops in search of hidden treasures by great French designers such as Jean Michel Frank, Pierre Charreau, Jean Prouve, Rene Prou and Jean Royere. On his last trip to Europe, Wilson hit 25 galleries, took 20 rolls of film and found out-of-print catalogues for inspiration. Through his Los Angeles-based furniture company, FreWil, Wilson is offering some of his finds for wider consumption. Some are intended as reproductions; others are rescaled or retooled for today's consumer.

The Getty table (1), based on a model from the San Francisco mansion of the same name, was first designed by Jean Michel Frank in 1926. The original model's most recent sale reportedly had a price tag of $147,000. FreWil's version, chiseled only on the top surface rather than all around, and sandblasted on the sides, stands 18 in. high and has a net price of $1,600. The JMF round table (2), based on an original 24 in. in diameter, is being offered in various sizes and shapes. And from a series of Royere designs come the iron floor lamp (3) and lamp table (4).

Garth Alexander Oldershaw, an interior designer who, since FreWil's inception in 1990, has designed much of FreWil's collection, also pays homage to this French genre. The Virginia Lounge chair (5) represents one of Oldershaw's own designs.

2

4

3

5

rinted with permission from
rior Design Market *March 1996*
en by Andrea Loukin, Senior Market Editor

4th Annual

MIAMI Modernism

At Home in the Twentieth Century

JANUARY 24 - JANUARY 26, 1997
Gala Preview:
THURSDAY, JANUARY 23 6-10 P.M.

Sixty-five high quality exhibitors from across the country & Europe representing all major movements 1900 - 1970

NEW
LOCATION!

Ramada
Deauville Resort-
MIAMI BEACH
6701 Collins

TRAVEL ARRANGEMENTS:
ARTours International, Inc.
800-226-6972

DC AUSSIN PRODUCTIONS INC.   12150 E. Outer Drive • Detroit, MI 48224
(313) 886-3443

The most significant collection of Latin American Masters. Full color catalogues are available of individual artists, notable exhibitions, and auctions.

Gary Nader Editions is the exclusive distributor of the Wifredo Lam Catalogue Raisonne. The complete chronology and biography of the Cuban master: 1923-1960. This book includes 650 pages with 250 color illustrations and 1200 illustrations in black and white.

The updated edition of the *Latin American Art Price Guide* is available. This book contains all of the sales records from Sotheby's and Christie's auctions: May 1977 thru May 1996. There are 17,000 works by 1300 artists.

Gary Nader fine art

3306 Ponce de Leon Boulevard, Coral Gables/Miami, Florida 33134
Tel: (305)442-0256 / Fax: (305)443-9285

MODERNISM GALLERY
FINE AND DECORATIVE ART OF THE 20th CENTURY

Rug Fragment from Design by Ruth Reeves for Radio City Music Hall 1932.
Bookshelf by Donald Deskey for Widdicomb 1930's. Three Vases by Loetz 1920's.
Center Vase by Deque, France 1930's. Hunt Champagne Set by Bimini Werkstatte 1920's.

RIC EMMETT
305/442-8743   FAX: 305/443-3074
1622 PONCE DeLEON BOULEVARD / CORAL GABLES, FLORIDA 33134

THE CUBAN NATIONAL HERITAGE

**A NOT-FOR-PROFIT CORPORATION ESTABLISHED ON
JANUARY 22, 1994 TO PRESERVE THE CULTURAL ROOTS OF
THE CUBAN NATION**

INQUIRIES ON PROGRAMS AND MEMBERSHIP ARE WELCOMED AT:

**300 Aragon Avenue #260
Coral Gables, Florida 33134**

**(305) 443-1522 phone
(305) 443-3347 fax**

BOARD OF DIRECTORS

Gerardo Abascal II, Esq.
Alberto S. Bustamante, M.D.
David Cabarrocas, Arch.
Salomé Casanova-Agüero
Armando F. Cobelo, D.D.S.
María T. Fernández-Concheso
Tina Fanjul
Fernando García-Chacón, Esq.
Felipe García, M.D.
Raúl B. García, Arch.

Malvina Godoy
Rafael Gómez, M.D.
Celso González-Falla
Justo A. Martínez, CFP
Alicia Meyer-Tremols
Juan Portela
Sofía Powell-Cossio, Esq.
Pedro E. Prado
Gabriel Pratts, CPA
Nicolás Quintana, Arch.

MARCIO ROITER

20th century decorative arts

At the turn of the century, Rio de Janeiro was a town of cultural importance, and one of Émile Gallé's greatest retail outlets.

Gallé created a series of vases depicting Rio. The views include Sugarloaf Mountain, Guanabara Bay, Corcovado, Gavea Mountain, and São Conrado Beach.

We can say that these pieces date to the very beginning of the century because the Sugarloaf cable car, inaugurated in 1910, is not shown.

Rua Pacheco Leão, 110 / CEP 22460.030 / Rio de Janeiro / RJ / Brazil /

EUROPEAN POSTERS

RARE AMERICAN +

Stenberg Bros. *Man With a Movie Camera*, 1928

Lester Beall. *Farm Work*, 1937

Lorenzo Goñi. *Els Provocadors...*, c. 1937

Ib Andersen. *Bygge og Bolig Udstilling*, 1929

steve turner gallery

Joel Edelstein

arte contemporânea

NINA MORAES
Glass, Water and plastic
30,5 x 26 x 9 cm
1993

Rua Jangadeiros, 14 - B - Ipanema - Rio de Janeiro - Brasil - CEP 22410-010
Tel.: (55 21) 267-2549 Fax: (55 21) 267-1254

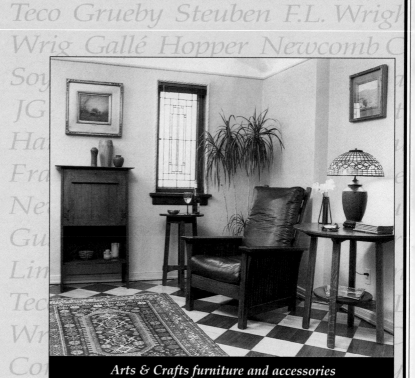

RICHARD
HIMMEL
ANTIQUE
and
DECORATIVE
FURNITURE

PHILIP MICHAEL WOLFSON

An American's American Debut • *Golden Distortions* is a collection of eight solid and veneered wood side tables, pedestals and cabinets composed of architectural forms based on the proportions of the Golden Section.

CHICAGO
1800 Merchandise Mart Plaza • Chicago, IL 60654 • 312.527.5700 Fax 312.527.2169

FLORIDA
Design Center of the Americas • 1855 Griffin Road • Suite B-386 • Dania, FL 33004 • 954.922.3880 Fax 954.922.8087
320 Royal Poinciana Plaza • Palm Beach, FL 33480 • 407.655.0009 Fax 407.655.0998

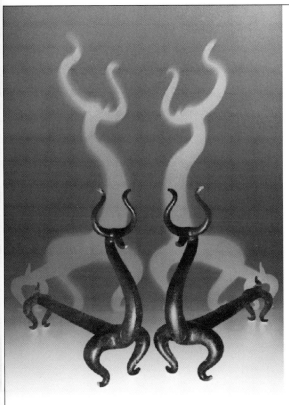

The Scandal of Pleasure ART IN AN AGE OF FUNDAMENTALISM

WENDY STEINER

"Sanity, sanity, sanity, as Steiner squarely addresses a number of contemporary cultural conflicts and teases out their subtler meanings. . . . Ranging from the S & M photos of Robert Mapplethorpe to the *fatwa* against Salman Rushdie to that discredited doyen of deconstructionism, Paul de Man, Steiner argues for a conception of art that cuts between aestheticism and literalism. . . . A welcome association of sense and sensibility."—*Kirkus Reviews*

Cloth $24.95 256 pages 30 halftones

Discovering Design EXPLORATIONS IN DESIGN STUDIES

EDITED BY RICHARD BUCHANAN AND VICTOR MARGOLIN

"Rarely has the subject of design been analyzed so fully and so perceptively. This is a collection of provocative, often contradictory opinions that never strays from the central task of exploring the forces that shape the everyday material world."—Jeffrey L. Meikle, University of Texas, Austin

Paper $14.95 283 pages Cloth edition available

Art & Money

MARC SHELL

"Quirky and fascinating. . . . The key to the relation between aesthetic and monetary realms, in Mr. Shell's view, is that both are symbols of something else."
—Charles Hagen, *The New York Times*

Cloth $35.00 230 pages color frontispiece, 8 color plates, 114 halftones

Artists, Advertising, and the Borders of Art

MICHELE H. BOGART

"A sparkling, highly illuminating account of some key issues in twentieth-century American cultural history. Bogart's fascinating book is widely and deeply researched, impressively resistant to formula, and extraordinarily sensitive to the varieties of artistic experience."—Jackson Lears

Cloth $40.00 488 pages 85 halftones

Now in Paper

Mies van der Rohe A CRITICAL BIOGRAPHY

FRANZ SCHULZE

"Schulze's excellent book . . . is absolutely worthy of its subject. Soundly researched, vividly detailed, and hard to fault critically, it is the most complete survey ever written of Mies' life and works. . . . No one else has approached Schulze's achievement in telling the whole story over eight decades."—Allan Temko, *San Francisco Chronicle Review*

Paper $24.95 380 pages 220 halftones and line drawings

The University of Chicago Press 5801 South Ellis Avenue, Chicago, Illinois 60637

T H E   W O L F S O N I A N

1001 WASHINGTON AVENUE   MIAMI BEACH   FLORIDA   33139

The Wolfsonian is a museum and research center in the Art Deco district of Miami Beach, Florida. Founded in 1986, the Wolfsonian oversees a collection of more than 70,000 objects from the late-nineteenth to mid-twentieth centuries, including furniture, decorative arts, sculpture, works on paper, and archives relating to the period. The Wolfsonian Research Center was established in 1993 to promote interdisciplinary research through fellowships, publications, and special events.

In addition to its ongoing calendar of exhibitions, the Wolfsonian offers a wide range of educational public programs. Contact the Wolfsonian for more information about forthcoming group tours, films, lectures, symposia, and student and family workshops.

The Wolfsonian's inaugural exhibition, *The Arts of Reform and Persuasion, 1885–1945*, kicked off its worldwide tour at the Los Angeles County Museum of Art (summer 1996), and continues:

Seattle Art Museum	**October 24, 1996 — January 12, 1997**
Carnegie Museum of Art, Pittsburgh	**February 22, 1997 — May 18, 1997**
Indianapolis Museum of Art	**November 15, 1997 — February 1, 1998**
Japan	**June 1998 — December 1998**
Australia	**February 1999 — October 1999**
New Zealand	**December 1999 — March 2000**

For membership or general information, please call the Wolfsonian at (305) 535-2631.

To purchase Wolfsonian products or a copy of *Designing Modernity* — the award-winning book that accompanies the museum's inaugural exhibition — contact the Wolfsonian Museum Shop at (305) 535-2680.